CAMEL TRAILS, SPICE MARKETS

Andrew Coffey is of Anglo-Irish background, born in Spital Wirral in 1938. He studied under prominent artist Jehan Daly at St Martin's School of Art, London, in 1960–62, and has spent much of his working life as a freelance artist, photographer and writer who especially enjoys travelogue writing. The globe-trotting artist is passionate about the great outdoors and environmental issues.

Most of his summers are spent drawing portraits at holiday resorts in the UK. He is a regular contributor to such journals as *Eagle Times* (a magazine devoted to the memory of the famous 1950s boys' Christian-based paper started by the Rev. Marcus Morris).

As with his earlier travel book *Welsh Adventures* Mr Coffey takes the reader with him on his travels, and invites readers to join him in these present jaunts. The present volume differs markedly though, in that the author stops meditatively in many locations connected with the Bible. Mr Coffey has done many journeys to the Middle East since the 1970s but has based his book on that period simply because he finds that set of journeys particularly interesting. However the Bible references dwelt upon give the book a timeless appeal.

Married to Anne Coffey, with a grown-up daughter Katherine, the author resides in Great Yarmouth, Norfolk.

Camel Trails, Spice Markets

Journeys through the lands of the Bible

with illustrations and photographs by the author

ANDREW COFFEY

ARAXA BOOKS
Great Yarmouth

First published 2003

Published by Araxa Books
11 Camden Place, Great Yarmouth, Norfolk NR30 3HX

ISBN 0 9546100 0 8

Printed in Great Britain.
Book design and production for the publisher by
Bookprint Creative Services, P.O. Box 827, BN21 3YJ, England.

CONTENTS

INTRODUCTION

For as long as I can remember, those mysterious and mystic lands of the Middle East, Turkey and North Africa have fired my imagination. Stirring heroic tales and exotic images were imprinted on my mind – both sacred and profane. Here Bible stories jostled with images from *The Arabian Nights*. I could see old Baghdad with images of people with baggy trousers and turbans amid tall jars and even taller minarets. A plethora of films, stories and paintings on the subject added to the process. We have all found even Christmas cards evocative with their images of kings on camels following the star to the Christ child. From Victorian times onwards heroes like Gordon, Doughty and T.E. Lawrence played their part in popularising the Bible lands. The craze for tourist travel took off in the eighteenth and nineteenth centuries. To indulge my own Middle East travels was something I had long contemplated. In the 1970s I was able to realise the dream, and so many of the traditional Eastern images came to life before my gaze.

Medieval adventurers with their trading and colonisation, of course, had a hand in bringing Europeans into contact with the Orient. However even they would be surprised at the extent of tourism and travel from the eighteenth century through to today. For, despite this wider context, like those enterprising men of yesteryear we too travel the globe. Like our forbears we have our brand of romanticism. The delectation of the wealthy classes always has to be catered for. The horrors of the times have always to be offset. Today the modern world is upon us with innovations that the Victorians would scarcely have dreamed possible beyond the fantasies of Jules Verne. We are no longer at the zenith of the British Empire. The world has changed dramatically and radically in so many ways, and we view everything, including the Middle East, from a modern perspective.

Central to today's Middle East situation is the modern state of Israel and Saudi Arabia, the world's major oil producer. Modernisation has influenced but not entirely eradicated the colour and time-honoured Eastern imagery. Even from our modern standpoint we often refer back to our Victorian friends. For example, archaeology is very popular today, but as a serious science it began with the Victorians. We remember the greats of Victorian archaeology like Flinders Petrie and Jean François Champollion whose pioneering spirit brought biblical treasures to light before an incredulous public. Even if archaeology began as a single discipline, it was soon to divide into several. One expert dealt with shards of pottery whilst another was called on to decipher strange unknown texts. Today I often wander the galleries of the British Museum to study and enjoy the fruits of their labours. We can admire Assyrian reliefs, and those huge human-headed winged bulls that once stood sentinel at a gateway to Saragon's Palace at Korsabad thousands of years ago. The Egyptian and Hittite galleries are equally fascinating. The Victorian contribution was immeasurable and we owe them a great deal. Even a passing glimpse at our local town halls with their mock Corinthian columns, or a perusal of Victorian novels and paintings, keeps them in view. The subject of Victorian creativity in both art and science is a considerable one and cannot be dealt with fully here.

Whilst thinking of our modern world from Victorian times to the present we should remember that much of it had its origins in the Bible lands – like the wheels we see everywhere, to say nothing of our widespread use of metal. Metallurgy was discovered in the Middle East, farming first began there, as did the alphabet and writing, and a system of coinage and government, amongst other things. Cradles of civilisation indeed!

But now for my personal journeys in these lands.

CHAPTER ONE

INITIATION

At the outset of these journeys, the strange allure and fascination beckoned and led me on as never before. My curiosity and wanderlust stirred within me. The fact that the Middle East was, like today, always the focus of world attention was another influential factor, and added to the interest even more.

My first encounter with the Near East was a cruise to Tangier in what was formerly French North Africa. I relished seeing those streets of Tangier animated with djellabah-clad figures. Through narrow little streets of the casbah donkeys struggled with burdening loads of sticks. Veiled women glided gracefully past. Scenes such as this were straight from the pages of holy writ. It was a foretaste of many more exciting trips to come – almost like the hors d'oeuvre of an exotic menu.

After much deliberation I decided to make Jordan my first main port of call. The capital Amman gave me my initial Jordanian experience. Flags and bunting fluttered in the streets for King Hussein's birthday celebrations. On my first day I rose at the crack of dawn, as the sun was coming up, and came upon the Al-Hussein Mosque. On the outskirts of the town a tired-looking horse dragged its cart and driver. Everything was permeated by a yellow-ochre colour.

I daresay that characters from Amman's distant past would be hard-pressed to recognise the place today. The reason for today's dramatic growth of Amman from mud village to modern town of many thousands soon becomes clear. World War I brought to an end Ottoman rule in the Middle East. However the turmoil that redistribution of land brought about was scarcely anticipated. Apart from the activities of King Abdullah and Glubb Pasha, the years between the two world wars saw the League of Nations creating the British and French Protectorates. Transjordan and Palestine came under British rule. The British Mandate led to the setting up of a Jewish homeland in Palestine. This meant that Jerusalem was divided. Decentralisation of the city made Jordanians gravitate towards Amman as their capital and administrative centre. Amman was free from the conflict that gripped Jerusalem. As for biblical and historical connections, Amman is as bountiful as many other Middle Eastern locations. It was in Amman that the huge iron bedstead of Og, King of Bashan, was placed and Uriah was killed, and it had its share of attacks. The town was captured by Joab, then by the Amorites. The Romans named the place Philadelphia.

The Hashemite Kingdom of Jordan is a truly spellbinding place situated in a sensitive part of the Middle East today, as it was in the past. It has treasures and riches in abundance. I don't mean rubies, diamonds or much in the way of mineral wealth besides. Unlike its neighbouring Gulf States, Jordan is unable to enjoy vast oil revenues – although Saudi Arabian pipelines do cross its territory. Jordan's riches are of a different order – to which I will abundantly refer as my story proceeds. The Jordanians, like their Israeli neighbours, have reclaimed land in the grand biblical tradition for agriculture, carefully utilising any water that is found. Fresh discoveries of water pockets below ground are greeted with delight in this parched and barren land.

So it was Jordan that became the scene of my initiation into all things Middle Eastern – something I had previously admired from afar. After a short connecting flight, I stepped off the plane at Akaba, my base for the next week or two. What captivated me at once was the surrounding landscape, haunting, stark and primeval. I was to discover many such places in the lands of the Bible.

This region alone soon revealed to this enraptured visitor many more dramatic and spellbinding landscapes. The vast tracts of desert found here tend to be dusty rather than sandy. 'Mile after mile of useless dust', as Edwin Muir the poet once wrote about another time and place altogether. I mentioned the country's programme of land reclamation. Lush vine-yards have sprung up here, quite recalling Old Testament days.

Amidst all this revelling in the wonderful attractions Jordan has to offer, I was very soon made aware of the fact that here was a country at war. A strong military presence was everywhere in Akaba. After all, the border with Israel is very close and there was tension in the air.

At the time of my visit, the border was permanently closed on the shoreline. However I was soon based at the Coral Beach Hotel. Here I was introduced to a genial middle-aged man from Sevenoaks called Ronald Brownlow, who reminded me of a retired professor. He helped me a good deal in my 'Initiation' into Middle Eastern culture.

'You touch your forehead like this' he said, demonstrating the move, 'and say Salaam Alaykum.'

Then I tried it out for myself. 'Salaam Alaykum', I

repeated. 'Salaam Alaykum', I said to the nearest Arab. 'Alaykum Salaam,' he replied.

From the hotel's beach the cast of the Lawrence of Arabia film used to swim after a busy day filming. A vast range of rugged hills formed a superb backdrop to the locale. Indeed everything was a vision of delight. There was a clear and peerless blue sky, a local Venus emerged from the sea, a desert hawk flew overhead whilst having an altercation with a wagtail, and a Palestinian sunbird drank nectar from flowers in the hotel garden. As for that range of hills, I not only saw them in bright sunlight but towards sundown as well. Then I saw the stark primeval glory take on a riot of reds and purples that has to be seen to be believed. Well this is said to be a mysterious jinn-haunted land.

Akaba is renowned as a haunt of scuba-divers and water-skiers as well as fishermen and sailing enthusiasts. The divers in our party were soon fitted out with wetsuits, flippers, and aqualungs. Instead of scuba-diving I was content to view exotic brightly-coloured fish from the comfort of a glass-bottomed boat. The fish swam in and out of coral reefs as I watched – surgeon-fish, angel-fish, and many others besides – making the crystal-clear waters a riot of colour. It was officially wintertime, but the heat of the day was still considerable. Summers in the Hashemite Kingdom are sweltering, with temperatures soaring and mosquitoes biting. I appeared to have picked the best time to visit the country. Flights of helicopters in formation droned back and forth across the town and gunboats patrolled the sea in an impressive show of force. King Hussein was in residence at his Aquaba Palace, thus security was tight and sensitivity prevailed. Sea and air patrols continued at regular intervals. Sometimes visitors would discuss the complexities of the Arab–Israeli situation, though many thought that the subject was best avoided. So tense was the feeling in the air that a soldier had to accompany the diving team.

Ronald suggested a walk to town. I followed his advice and found it smaller than expected. Mostly it consisted of small squat typically Middle Eastern buildings. Typical, too, was the pungent spicy aroma which filled the air in a street of shops and stores. They appeared to sell everything – fruit and vegetables, as well as flowing robes, keffiehs, coffee pots with curved spouts, curved wicked-looking daggers, camel saddles, sheepskins, and a whole range of exotic merchandise besides. Prices were fixed. This was contrary to all I had been given to understand about Eastern haggling. Outside another store hung wickerwork cages containing canaries and goldfinches. Arabs love to own songbirds in cages so that their sweet songs can be always available.

I sat down at a pavement café to eat Arabic pastries and drink thick sweet Turkish coffee, which always comes in very tiny cups. I conversed for a while with a naval commander and his wife from the hotel, who had just arrived on the scene. Past the main shopping concourse I entered an area which could best be described as a shanty town, where I was nearly stoned by local boys demanding money. The timely intervention of an adult saved the day, much to my relief. Later I found myself back at the beach watching the water-skiing. I understand the King himself was very keen on the sport. Sometimes he could be seen hurtling past on his water-skis. Mr Brownlow also gained some distinction as a water-skier during his stay at the resort. His prowess at the sport and noted style, which included a characteristic wave at the start of his skiing sessions, became legendary.

Being a complete novice at both skiing and diving, all I could do for the moment was to watch from the sidelines. Camel riding was something I did get involved in, though, and this Jordan trip gave me my first genuine experience in riding these extraordinary beasts. As a preliminary to riding in the Wadi Rhumm I decided to try the beach camel. On this beach you don't have long to wait before a beach camel complete with rider comes trotting into view. There seemed to be a supercilious look on the face of the camel that appeared complete with rider. Both seemed to be saying, 'Here's a likely customer.' The splendid bull camel knelt, roaring and bellowing as it did so. The agile young rider swiftly dismounted and invited me to take his place in the saddle. By this time I had adopted the local white keffieh headdress with thick black egal cord. I was soon in the saddle. The camel reared up and we were soon on the move – in the direction of the crowded beach next to the Coral Beach Hotel. Suddenly umpteen holidaymakers leapt into action with their cameras, taking photographs of this real live Lawrence of Arabia act. People were even filming me from the hotel verandah. Had I just ridden with the Howautats, Beni Sakhr or Sirhan tribes that still inhabit the Jordan wastes? It must surely have seemed so.

I rode the beach camel several times before tackling longer rides out in the Wadi Rhumm. This is a scenically striking area, and its great cliffscapes were used to great effect in the Lawrence film. Well-known are these tales about the Wadi being a tribal battleground where blood-feuds and battles have raged for centuries. I also got to learn about the jinn, ghostly ghoulish beings, not always benevolent by any means, who weave mysterious spells on the populace. The jinn are supposed to dwell beneath every man's threshold. Also, they are supposed to live in fires. Thus the proper salutations must be given before quenching a fire – or else!

I had to decide on transportation to the Wadi Rhumm, and got in touch with a storekeeper in the town, who offered to

drive me and a couple from the Hotel out there for five dinars. We arrived at the appointed place after breakfast one morning. When I produced the five dinars the truck suddenly appeared as if from nowhere. We climbed into the truck and were driven off along a road which wound its way through the rocky pass. The stark ethereal rock formations continued to fascinate me. Presently the jeep turned off the tarmac road, bouncing and swaying over the sandy track until we reached the spellbinding Wadi Rhumm itself. In the strong sunlight the cliffs became a riot of colour in their own right. Very soon these great cliffs began to embrace us. We soon stopped outside the rest house of the Jordanian Desert Police, or the Camel Corps as they are also called. The uniforms of the Jordanian Desert Police, are very distinctive. They wear long khaki garments down to their feet, lashed down with bandoliers and Sam Browne and topped by red-flecked keffieh and egal headdress. I wandered over to a black tent, many of which dot the stark landscape, and doubtless have done so since the days of Abraham. There were a number of Bedouin inside, men and their womenfolk. I duly gave my salaams and entered the tent when invited to do so by one of the men. He looked elderly, but may have looked older than his calendar years. In these parts people can appear emaciated at an earlier age due to the climate and constant weathering. Some of the faces that I saw inside the tent were very wizened indeed. Desert etiquette must always be properly observed, so I sat cross-legged, my feet tucked well out of sight. I was offered weak tea which had been poured into a tiny cup. After I had drunk my fill I rocked the cup in my fingers to signify the fact. They studied me eagerly as I sketched a group of them. Even a routine matter like sharpening my pencil came under their close scrutiny. With a shout the headman ordered his womenfolk into the adjoining compartment of the tent. The men warbled softly amongst themselves.

Just beyond the tent-opening I caught sight of a young camel crouching. I indicated a desire to ride him. The camel was a beautiful animal, I thought, with a strong furry coat. It was smaller than the beach camel but still capable of carrying me. I watched fascinated as one of the men saddled the beast. The saddle he used was a half-wooden construction which I had noticed earlier. Did I detect an insolent look on the man's face as we set off across the Wadi towards one of the precipitous cliffs? It was not long before he crouched the camel and screamed for more money. Reluctantly I obliged with a second small payment, telling him to continue as far as the cliff towards which we were headed. The whole ride lasted for about half-an-hour. In such situations you can in your imagination identify with all the great cameleers of history. The camel was crouched once more immediately below the magnificent towering cliff. Now came a spell of rest for both men and camel. My companion unrolled his prayer mat in the sand and bowed towards Mecca. No doubt he was thanking Allah for this fresh windfall from yours truly. Presently I remounted and was led back to the Jordanian Desert Police Rest House.

Before climbing back into the Land-Rover with the couple from the hotel, I was again confronted by the camel man – again screaming for money. Apparently I should have paid him for posing for photographs as well. The man even contrived to have a Desert Policeman stand over me with a rifle. Under such circumstances how could I not give him another, albeit small, amount of cash? We were soon heading back towards Akaba. I'm sure the fellow had a till inside his tent somewhere. Back at the hotel, I related the day's adventures to Mr Brownlow over dinner.

My second visit to the Wadi Rhumm a day or two later was in the company of Jens, a young German traveller. Jens was keen to visit the Wadi Rhumm. I sketched his portrait, he gave me a lift out to the Wadi in his van – fair exchange! On this occasion the weather was overcast to begin with. The rocky cliffs were now cast in sombre shades. Jens and I were able to ascend the Rest House tower looking out over the terrain from a high vantage point. Soon my companion produced a small portable stove and brewed tea for all present. Half the Camel Corps must have received free tea courtesy of Jens. When you travel round and live in your van as Jens was doing, practical things like owning a portable stove become second nature. About half-a-dozen camels were being loaded up with waterbags, which were being filled with the aid of a hosepipe. I noticed oil-drums (containing water?) and a few chickens which probably helped poor Bedouin eke out a bare living in the Wadi.

My third visit to the Wadi Rhumm followed very soon after the second. This time half the party from the hotel came along for the ride, including Mr Brownlow. Various members of the party watched as I prepared to do my camel-riding act again. News of my exploits had got around, and seeing my efforts was surely a must for my spectators. This new camel I had mounted let out a bellowing commotion of protest. The more the animal protested thus, the more the Arabs present burst out laughing. Happily I, too, could see the funny side. I was wearing a white keffieh which caused one Arab onlooker to shout 'Sheik'. 'Sheik,' I called back, emphasising that last guttural syllable. The laughter continued and frankly did not subside until I dismounted the unwilling beast. Clearly I had presented my hosts with a priceless comic vignette which they would remember for some time to come.

Now, however, I was looking for an alternative camel. 'Maybe you can find me something better,' I suggested. No sooner said than done. A lad appeared leading a huge bull camel by the nose! 'This is more like it,' I mused. I soon mounted my new charge, and set off with the boy leading. Not only was I allowed to ride to the opposite cliff but was able to continue riding for some distance down the Wadi. By now cloud had descended over the clifftops, and I could see huge ribbons of waterfall cascading down cliff walls. All of a sudden the clouds burst in earnest. It rained heavily and I was soon soaked to the skin. This was totally unexpected. When the storm became too severe, the boy made my steed crouch. I dismounted, and we took shelter behind a huge boulder. My young companion then took a sheepskin from the camel's back and wrapped it round himself.

When the storm abated, we resumed the ride and I took in more of this truly fascinating landscape. When we decided to turn back and return to the Rest House I felt that the boy couldn't possibly walk all that way again. I suggested that he should ride with me back to where the Jordanian Police would be waiting for us. I leaned down from the saddle and took the boy's hand. Thus assisted he leaped up into the saddle behind me in one swift nimble movement. The beast broke into a canter as we approached the Rest House. The rest of my party, whom I had forgotten about during the storm, broke out into spontaneous applause. My riding must have looked good. The Commander, his wife and Mr Brownlow all seemed suitably impressed, judging by their remarks.

Mr Brownlow had politely declined the offer of joining me for tea in a Bedouin tent. Obviously he preferred the tea served at the hotel. That evening I was walking through the spacious lounge when the manager spoke up.

'How was the Wadi Rhumm today?' he asked.

'Fine,' I replied, 'just fine.'

The next day I looked for the beach camel and his master. Neither man nor beast were anywhere to be seen. I decided to search for them. During a walk round the town, I happened to observe a little group of locals seated at a table playing backgammon whilst drinking tea from tiny glasses. One of them was smoking a hubble-bubble water pipe. It was my sketching of this typically Arabic scene that brought about a first arrest. A little crowd of Arab boys had gathered. A hand fell on my shoulder. 'Come with us,' said a thin Arab in a brown suit. I was duly steered to the police station and questioned about places that I had visited. I was driven off to another police building. There I was allowed to sit on a bench to await their verdict.

At length I was told that I was free to go. My antics were a trifle outlandish, and this must have aroused the suspicions of the Jordanians. However I was certain that I had not photographed or sketched any military installations. The confiscated sketchbook and passport were returned to me and I left.

By now camel riding was becoming a keen interest, almost a passion. I was disappointed when next day the beach camel was nowhere to be seen and I decided to go and look for it. This search landed me in trouble again. Unintentionally I found myself trespassing. There I was heading straight for the Army camp, unaware of doing anything amiss. As I approached a clump of trees, an Arab youth leapt towards me. He ordered me to stand exactly where I was. Placing his fingers in his mouth he let out a loud whistle. Armed soldiers appeared scurrying towards me. I was too rooted to the spot even to think of running for it. Two soldiers came up to me and ordered me to accompany them. I was their prisoner. Nobody was laughing now, least of all me.

CHAPTER TWO

THE LOVELY ROSE-RED PETRA

More soldiers arrived on the scene and I was literally surrounded by them. No chance of escape then. 'Sleep,' ordered an NCO (meaning rest, I think). Words close in meaning can be confusing to a foreigner. My fears were rather more immediate. What would happen to me now? Many a prisoner has similarly pondered his fate. After a brief rest in the sentry box I was ordered to my feet and taken further into the military complex. We stopped before a typical Army building. I was shown inside, then led into a tiny office. A sergeant-major, if ever I saw one, stood over me. I waited there for some time before being sent for by the Commandant. I was soon ushered into the presence of a friendly and charming officer who was to interview me. He was not unlike King Hussein in appearance. The thought occurred to me – was I being interviewed by His Majesty the King? Or was it a look-alike? Either way it was a daunting experience. But my interviewer soon put me at ease with his pleasant manner. He quickly dispelled my fears. I blurted out my apologies for trespassing and assured the Commandant – or was he the King? – that I entertained no ulterior motives. I was just looking for the beach camel and I had not taken any photographs of military significance. We conversed on all manner of topics thereafter. I was invited to stay and have lunch with the officers in their mess. Afterwards I was free to go. The Commandant politely excused himself, saying that he had business elsewhere. I spent an interesting hour or so dining with the officers. After the dinner we rose as one man and retired from the table.

As usual I told Mr Brownlow of the day's adventures over an evening meal, and added, 'Come to think of it, the Commandant *did* look very much like the King.'

Mr Brownlow suggested the judicious use of caution in future forays. 'They're sweet people but remember they are at war and they are naturally curious about visitors who wander off the beaten track.'

I agreed wholeheartedly, and vowed to be more circumspect in future.

'Now let's turn to something else – we are planning a visit to Petra. Several of us have put our names down. Are you interested in joining us?'

'I'd be delighted,' I said unequivocally. Certainly I had heard about this fabled ancient city hidden in the mountains of Edom. Now I was about to go there. A fleet of taxis with our party aboard was soon heading along the desert highway towards the fabled city. I quoted one of Petra's popular titles. Mr Brownlow was evidently unaware of it. 'What did you say it was called?' he asked.

'The Rose-Red City half as old as time,' I repeated.

'The Rose-Red City,' he intoned softly. 'What a fantastic description.'

'Yes, and don't forget that until recent times it was very remote and inaccessable. This modern desert highway enables us to visit the place in comfort.'

Someone else chipped into the conversation at this point. 'This is the Wilderness of Zin: Zin with a Z not an S.'

'Wasn't this the home of the Amalakites?' I asked.

It was possibly their descendants we saw tending their flocks of black goats. They were amusing animals, these goats, with their long ears hanging down so. Bedouin tents were visible, too, in the arid waste, along with little shanty towns. Probably these belonged to Palestinian refugees. Women dressed in black were there with veiled faces.

We reached the Wadi Musa, where Moses struck the rock and found water. The abundance of greenery in the area seemed to bear this out. Indeed, it is the only substantial patch for miles around. Horses and guides were ready for us at the appointed time and place. Each one of us mounted a horse and soon we started the ride which would bring us to Petra. Gradually stony barren areas gave way to mounds and dramatic rock shapes. The rock formations became more dramatic still, and soon the rocky walls enveloped us. Passages were now narrower. The course twisted. The increasingly fantastic enclaves took on strange forms. The deep reddish sandstone seemed to glow with an esoteric quality all its own. On we rode with the corridor growing higher and higher. As we rode through the Siq (the main approach to the Treasury facade) any light overhead was almost completely blocked out. The end of the gorge opens abruptly into an open space. Just as abruptly the sight of El Khazneh, the Treasury, breaks upon the visitor. We all dismounted before the Treasury facade. I was pleased to be in a wider open space but we were still enclosed by formidable rocky walls. The Treasury was built by Aretus, a Nabataean king, who was Herod Antipas' father-in-law. Although this facade is clearly of Roman times, its origins are of earlier times. Tombs carved from the rock were everywhere. We continued to come across them when

Bedouin encampment as seen today. Much of the traditional flavour remains, but modern nomads rely more on modern amenities like trucks to supply food. One Arab in this illustration wears a djellebah whilst the other is seen wearing a western-style jacket below his keffieh.

we emerged into wide open spaces beyond the Treasury. Arab merchants with trays of trinkets harassed us constantly. Even when you are transported to a wonderland such problems can arise. I climbed to the top of the Roman Amphitheatre to further view the scene.

One of our guides suggested doing away with the horses as a means of transportation through the gorge, and installing a miniature railway instead. The suggestion drew gasps of horror from most of us. Much of the wonderful atmosphere in what someone has called the 'perpetual twilight' would be irreparably damaged. The time-honoured way of riding through the gorge on horseback must, we felt, be adhered to. Substantial damming work had now been completed to prevent an undesirable repetition of the 1963 flooding in which a number of people were drowned. We continued along the road leading away from the Treasury, ruined triumphal arch and amphitheatre towards the Petra Rest House. A young girl in peasant dress rode past on a donkey, like a vision from Petra's past. The road's surface had remained virtually the same as when the legions of Ancient Rome marched along them. In the Petra Rest House we sat down to well-earned refreshments. Our chief guide was a tall dignified Arab named Mohammed Easa Falahat, who had an excellent command of English.

The history of Petra is a long and fascinating one. The first settlers were probably the Horites. Genesis 14:6 refers to their habitation in Mount Seir, meaning the Petra region. The Edomites occupied Petra later on. Biblical references to them and their rule of Petra are numerous.

And Jacob sent messengers before him to Esau his brother unto the land of Seir, the country of Edom . . . and these are the generations of Esau the father of the Edomites. (Genesis 32:3, 36:9)

The prophet Obadiah gives us a graphic description of Petra in his short book of only twenty-one verses:

> Thus saith the Lord God concerning Edom . . . The pride of thine heart hath deceived thee, thou that dwellest in the clefts of the rock, whose habitation is high. (Obadiah v.3)

King Saul and King David had their battles with the Edomites and defeated them, as did King Amaziah. So there was little love lost between the Israelites and the Edomites. Territorial disputes apart, the prosperity the Edomites gained through far-flung trade with India, Asia Minor, Greece, Tyre and Sidon, North Africa and other places besides inevitably attracted covetous attention. In fulfilment of Obadiah's prophecy Petra was overwhelmed in 586 BC.

Perhaps the best-known inhabitants of Petra were the Nabataeans, who also ruled over a vast area as far as Damascus. At the zenith of their power, the Nabataeans controlled the incense trade routes from Arabia to Damascus. This was helped in no small measure by the Pax Romana – the Roman Peace – when trade routes by land and sea were cleared of marauding brigands and pirates. The Nabataeans were great builders, influenced strongly by the Assyrians and Romans, as we can see today. They invented a system of coinage, were highly-skilled potters (shards of fine distinctive Nabataean pottery are still to be found here) and were ingenious at channelling water into public baths and cisterns. The demand for water was always great in Petra. Their rule in Damascus was brief, and Trajan conquered them in AD 106. After the Roman occupation, Christians took over for a time (4th–5th centuries AD), when crosses carved on tombs mingled with pagan deities.

The great periods of Petra's history were soon over. The

once-busy overland trade routes declined, as seagoing trade routes became easier and more popular. It is still possible to see the Christian quarter of Petra known locally as Haret el Nasara. Another Arab period in the city was followed by the Crusaders who came this way, building a fortress close to the Roman tombs. Then Petra was closed to the gaze of men for many centuries. It was rediscovered by the famous nineteenth-century Swiss explorer Johann Ludwig Burckhardt. Lawrence of Arabia used the Siq in his campaign against the Turks. On October 21st, 1917 Lawrence and his band of Arab warriors were engaging their Turkish enemies, hemming them in within the narrow walls of the gorge. Rocks rained down and bullets flew in all directions, and panic set in amongst the Turks at this point.

This hemming-in strategy has been used a number of times since King David's battle here. Even Alexander the Great was held at bay in like manner by the Nabataeans. My mind was in an almost surreal kaleidoscopic whirl with all these red sandstone shapes, with their gaping tomb holes and wonderful ornamentation left by Nabataean masons, as seen, for example, in the step carvings. Likewise the Romans left their mark on Petra. There was Hadrian's triumphal arch, market places once alive with the sights and sounds of ancient commerce, the inevitable Roman baths, the temple, numerous niches with statues, and so much more. For some reason the Romans avoided any interference with the Nabataeans' High Place. Perhaps they were strangely haunted by it, with feelings of superstition even. The king's throne, tables of sacrifice still with their blood runnels intact, and altar spoke to the Romans of something best left alone. Our guide had, of course, pointed out the High Place to us earlier.

My enchantment with Petra could have lasted for ages, but it was soon time to leave. I took a last lingering look at the stunning monuments to past ages amid the oleander bushes. We remounted our horses by the Treasury facade and began the ride back up the Siq. Back we sped across the bleak and forbidding Wilderness of Zin, with the Rose-Red City still resonating in my mind.

Back at the beach close to our hotel, I joined a glass-bottomed boat sail. This, too, provides the visitor with a breathtaking spectacle. I needed no excuse for joining another of these excursions. Indeed most visitors cannot get enough of them. This time half the guests at the hotel were joining the sail. Two rows of us sat, one on either side of the glass panel on the bottom of the boat, having beaten the price down. One of the guests made a spontaneous leap over the side, making a huge splash in the crystal-clear water. Small jellyfish swam immediately below the surface. Long thin pipefish could be seen, and a number of angel-fish. There were red fish, yellow fish, and fish of all colours.

Further out in the Gulf we looked down into the water again and saw the wreck of a Turkish ship, and also the wreck of a Turkish plane complete with its propellers still recognisable – both relics of World War I, when Akaba was wrenched from the Turks by Lawrence of Arabia. I was amazed that ship and aircraft alike were still in reasonably good condition after all that time in the water. Slowly the boat cruised away from the wrecks. A short distance away we caught sight of a turtle swimming on the surface. It dived out of view, though, as we tried to edge in closer to it. Well, they are considered a delicacy as turtle soup. Then came the spectacle of masses of tiny fish leaping out of the water, as though someone had sprinkled stardust across the surface of the sea. Illuminated by sunlight it is indeed made another irresistible sight to behold.

It was from here, at the head of the Gulf of Akaba, that

King Solomon launched his navy and traded with Tarshish, Somalia, Ophir and Egypt. Those ships would have returned here laden with fabulous cargoes of silver, gold, spices, silks, apes and peacocks, to say nothing of ivories and other valuable goods as well. At the potash works on the Arabian side of the Gulf, ships are still moored.

There was a café in Akaba to which several of us from the hotel used to retreat. Rafik the café owner was a hospitable and friendly man. He told us that he doubled for Omar Sharif in the Lawrence film, something he was very proud of. Clearly this accounts for the impressive legend on his card, *Kafeteria Hydepark-Cocktail Omar Al-Sharif*. Rafik gladly demonstrated his part in the film by donning a black robe and headdress and striding across the café floor. He invited me to try doing the same. I tried! A portrait sketch I did of Rafik soon had pride of place before the counter with numerous legends scrawled on it. On the way back to the hotel little bands of Arab boys would waylay us and try to teach us some Arabic. I made some headway in this but more often than not I have to fall back on a mixture of English, French and sign-language in my travels in the Arab lands.

In the shopping centre, I purchased a sheepskin – not long off the back of a sheep. It had a fine thick pile. It was a delight to run a hand through it. Tales of my bravado had circulated. These tales, together with my adopted Arab garb, had given rise to the nickname of 'Lawrence of Arabia'. In some ways my visit here had developed into a shocking parody of that desert warrior's exploits. After all, I had experienced camel rides, captures, and dressing up in Arab robes.

Mr Brownlow saw what appeared to be an Arab in full traditional dress entering the main foyer of the Coral Beach Hotel. The parody and pantomime of the whole thing was continuing. Imagine the man's surprise when I turned my keffieh-swathed head – and he saw that it was me. After this charade, I went for another ride on the beach camel and was still amusing all present. My camel wandered into the sea with me in the saddle, and the beast took considerable coaxing before it waded back to the shore. I chanced to meet people from southern England who were connected with railway construction in the Middle East. They remembered the old Hejaz Railway which transported truckloads of pilgrims from Damascus to Medina. One engineer spoke of the secrecy of their work.

'You couldn't discuss business openly in a restaurant in front of a waiter like this.'

Looking at Akaba today with its generally peaceful aspect, it is difficult to picture the scene during World War I when Lawrence and his men took the town from the Turks. The British had been planning to attack the Turks in Medina and Akaba. The attack on Medina was cancelled, but the attack on Akaba went ahead. Covered by the guns of the British Navy, the Marines attempted the first assault. They forced the Turks into a temporary withdrawal, but could not hold Akaba for long. When the enemy seized positions in the hills behind the town they forced the Marines to withdraw. Clearly the Turks were a wily enemy to engage in battle, and were quick to make use of any advantageous strategy. Lawrence and his men broke through the Turkish lines after the desert crossing. Out in the mountain pass of Wadi Ithm Lawrence overcame the last Turkish obstacles. In the mêlée, Lawrence shot his own camel. Auda Abu Tighe narrowly missed death when bullets shattered his field glasses and tore his robes. No amount of well-poisoning or gunfire could finally prevent the capture of Akaba. The town was important as a supply port for guns, ammunition and food via the Suez Canal.

Contemporary with all this, a Hashemite descendant of the Prophet Mohammed, Sherif Hussein, led a revolt against the Ottoman Turks and their German allies in 1916. The only tangible reminder of World War I battles hereabouts was the sunken Turkish boat and plane to which I have already alluded, casualties of that conflict for sure.

After World War I the great share-out of Middle Eastern and North African territories took place under Britain and France. In 1921 Emir Abdullah, son of Sherif Hussein, became Emir of Transjordan on the East Bank and in 1946 the Emir became monarch. Thus began the days of King Abdullah and the Hashemite Kingdom free from British and French control, as the former Transjordan had been.

At the time of the armistice agreement of 1948 the West Bank was taken by Glubb Pasha's Arab Legion. The area has since been taken by Israel and much of it is now a buffer zone. (The present day finds King Abdullah's great-grandson and namesake on the throne of Jordan.) We shall certainly be returning to these subjects elsewhere in this book.

I turned from my reverie and reluctantly prepared to leave this fabled land. Weeks later I was to return.

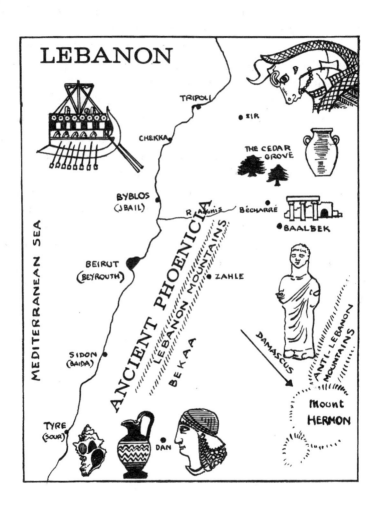

LEBANON

MEDITERRANEAN SEA

TRIPOLI

CHEKKA

KIR

THE CEDAR GROVE

BYBLOS
(JBAIL)

R. ADONIS   BÉCHARRÉ

BAALBEK

BEIRUT
(BEYROUTH)

ZAHLE

ANCIENT PHOENICIA

LEBANON MOUNTAINS

BEKAA

SIDON
(SAIDA)

DAMASCUS

ANTI-LEBANON MOUNTAINS

Mount
HERMON

TYRE
(SOUR)

DAN

CHAPTER THREE

THE ROAD TO DAMASCUS

I arrived at Beirut airport in pitch darkness. After disembark-
ing and going through customs formalities, I met up with
new companions, for I had joined a tour organised through
the Interchurch Organisation. The group consisted of five
other British and one genial American. Our arrival clearly
had coincided with the hour of prayer. A host of devout
Moslems were bowing low towards Mecca in the airport
lounge. Our guide appeared, and pointed out to us a spark-
ling 'Mountain of Lights' – a view of Beirut from the city's
airport at night. It had a compelling beauty all its own. We
were ushered to a waiting minibus and quickly transported
to our hotel.

Beirut, the capital of Lebanon, I found to be big, sprawling, noisy and bustling. In common with other Middle
Eastern countries, Lebanon has a history that goes back
across millennia. Invading armies have included
Phoenicians, Hittites, Egyptians, Assyrians, Ionians and
Dorians. In post-biblical times the stream of invaders has
continued in the shape of Byzantines, Turks, Crusaders and
modern Allied Armies. Since the introduction of French rule

after World War I, Beirut has enjoyed its status as the great cultural centre of the Middle East. Its art, theatre and concerts have vied with Paris for sophistication. Cedar festivals, flower festivals, harvest festivals, and grape festivals are held. The Civil War, and the vast upheaval that it caused, curtailed cultural activity. The War began after my visit in 1975. It was a terrible irony to see the busy building programmes in progress. From my hotel room balcony I could see hordes of Arab workmen working on huge multi-storey buildings. They were going up all around the hotel. So many buildings in Beirut were razed to the ground during the conflict.

At the time of my stay the War had not yet happened, however. 1970s Beirut, as I experienced it in the spring of 1975, was a stylish cosmopolitan city in a land that prided itself in true democracy. So much of it was very Parisian in feeling, as I saw in the shopping areas with their suave shops and pavement cafés. In this connection, I was intrigued by the remarks of a Victorian traveller* in Beirut. The city can scarcely have been as sprawling then, but the French influence was nevertheless strong: 'The pedestrian . . . finds himself in the midst of cafés that might almost have been transplanted – waiters, fare, and company – from the Bois de Boulogne or L'Île de Rousseau.' To think that this preceded French rule following World War I! What, I wonder, would our Victorian traveller have made of the modern chic French-influenced scene that I saw during my stay? We can only conjecture. I spent many happy hours exploring the busy streets. Traffic control seemed to be almost totally lacking. The loud honking of car horns echoed in my ears all the time. Actually

---

* Samuel G. Green D.D. (ed), *Pictures from the Bible Lands*, London: circa 1800s.

it seemed that the locals loved the sound of their car horns, as in the Champs-Elysées.

Other aspects of Beirut that fascinated me were the museums and bazaars. The latter consisted of a series of narrow winding passages in the old quarter of the city. Typically there was a cheerful, chaotic collection of stalls, all very oriental and colourful. Turbaned men stopped to talk in little groups, chickens were being decapitated in the narrowest of passages. In one area the Bazaar opened out into a clearing where awnings hung overhead. Here boys scurried about, carrying baskets on their backs to move goods about, in the bustling crowded place. The burden-bearer is another traditional part of the Middle Eastern scene. In the streets here I noticed several men carrying colossal loads of boxes on their backs with apparent ease.

We decided upon a visit to Baalbeck and Damascus and hired a minibus for the trip. Through the outskirts of Beirut we were driven before heading out into open country. The snow-splashed Hermon Mountains formed a perpetual backdrop to our journey, which took us across the immense Bekaa Plain. This lies between the Lebanon mountain range, which forms the backbone of the country, and the Anti-Lebanon range, which borders on Syria. The Plain was always renowned for its great fertility. The Romans were quick to realise its potential, for it formed a substantial part of the granary of Rome. I saw an abundance of fruit trees and vineyards. Farmers ploughed with animal-drawn wooden ploughs, taking us back to the time of the Patriarchs. Our vehicle was forced to stop in order to allow a farmer and his animals to pass on a narrow stretch of road. Horses and cows jostled with long-eared goats and sheep. At a wayside café we pulled up. I alighted dressed in Arab garb, and saw a figure similarly garbed. Once again the humorous side of life asserted itself. He came towards me. Here we were, two Europeans salaaming each other in mock-salutations. Along a modern highway, across a lovely cultivated landscape, we travelled for what seemed like ages.

The ruins of Baalbeck are impressive even from a distance. They are superb ruins – enough to keep archaeologists happy for years. Indeed I noticed several such pith-helmeted archaeologists busily studying the ruins as soon as I arrived. Even as a ruin Baalbeck displays some of the most beautiful and ornate carvings ever to have survived from antiquity. The Temple of Jupiter's huge blocks of stone impress the visitor with their sheer size. It was a feat of ancient engineering. Today there are only six of the original fifty-four columns still standing. Nearby stands the Temple of Bacchus, god of wine, seen in one carving as having a cluster of grapes and about his head. The court that separates the two temples is used for the annual Baalbeck International Festival. The year of my visit was its twentieth anniversary. The Festival follows a 2000-year-old tradition, for the Romans held festivals and competitions here which included music and theatre.

The victors of these competitions returned to their native cities to be afforded a triumphal welcome. Various niches had representations of Anthony and Cleopatra, with the lady clasping her asp. The ruins of the Temple of Venus we saw towards the centre of the complex. According to an old legend, Solomon erected a pagan temple here to gratify one of his foreign wives. We know that the King did have links with Baalbeck.

One of Baalbeck's finest architects, Callinius, was said to have discovered the legendary Greek wild fire. Abraham supposedly came here, and it is said to be the scene of Abel's murder by Cain. The city's Temple of the Sun was probably the most lavishly wrought, sumptuous temple in the entire Roman world at the time of the Emperor Nero. An eighteenth-century earthquake destroyed much of Baalbeck, and the visitor today is fortunate to see so much still intact. I came upon the famous lion's head waterspout. Originally it was one of a whole series which decorated the cornice of the Temple of Jupiter. Other wonderful ornate carvings include fruit garlands and leaves. A hundred bulls a day used to be sacrificed on an altar here. A mosaic portrays Socrates with the Seven Wise Men of Greece surrounding Calliope. Carvings of nymphs and cupids may also be seen.

A *son et lumière* held in Baalbeck depicts aspects of its history. I wandered off on my own for a while to explore the richness of these fantastic ruins. Whilst the early Canaanite founders named the city after their sun-god, the Greeks perpetuated the idea with the name Heliopolis – the City of the Sun. A camel and his master stood close to the ruins, hoping to do business with us Occidentals. Swifts screamed through the air, hordes of them, skimming past the crumbling stonework. Trinket-sellers harassed us with their Damascene junk. We pressed on with our journey to Damascus, passing through some very biblical countryside. There was an abundance of olive trees everywhere.

At length we reached the Syrian border. We had to stop here to arrange temporary visas. At the huge shed-like constructions, uniformed officials dealt with them for us. Inside Syria the landscape continued to be biblical, with stony hills, lime-trees and an abundance of arid rock formations. As we were getting very close to Damascus, I thought it appropriate for one of us to read aloud from Acts the story of Paul's conversion. I handed my Bible to one of the women, who read out the famous words:

'And as he journeyed, he came near Damascus: and suddenly
there shined round about him a light from heaven: and he fell to
the earth, and heard a voice saying unto him, Saul, Saul, why
persecutest thou me?' (Acts 9:3)

We were probably close to the spot where the dramatic
vision and turning-point in Paul's life took place.

Back in the present we were confronted with bilingual
signs in Arabic and English welcoming us to Damascus, the
focus of so much ancient history and famed craftsmanship –
more of which later. Passing a narrow part of the Orontes
River and the city's outskirts, we arrived in the city proper.
There were large old buildings and minarets. Was it anything
like the Damascus of the Bible, we might be tempted to ask?
Very unlikely, I thought. The city was conquered many times,
being held by both Turks and Arabs amongst others, so it
would have changed dramatically since ancient times.
Authentic-looking leads alluding to the world of St Paul
could be found. The Street called Straight is still there. The
bazaars with their colourful traders, a turbaned old man
riding a stubborn donkey across a busy street, and people
with crushing loads all helped to reinforce the impression. It
didn't seem to matter that such scenes were typical of the
Middle East. There were cinemas with garish posters adver-
tising films in Arabic, and honking cars all around. Our
vehicle threaded its way down a canopied, gaily animated
street where traders were going about their everyday business. 'This is the Street called Straight,' announced our guide.
Very soon we came to the Hanania Chapel, or the Chapel of
Ananias, where the house of Ananias was located.

And the Lord said unto him, Arise and go into the street which
is called Straight, and enquire in the house of Judas for one called
Saul, of Tarsus: for, behold, he prayeth. (Acts 9:11)

The story of Paul's conversion is well-known. After the dramatic encounter on the Road to Damascus he was brought here to receive his sight again by Ananias' laying-on of hands. Apparently the tiny house where this took place lies underground, and is today the Chapel of Ananias, which has an altar, burning candles, and rows of pews. It certainly felt authentic. The mile-long Street called Straight of today is surely one and the same with that of Paul's day. Then as now it links both halves of the city. At one end of the Street stands a Roman triple-arch. It has a main central arch with two smaller ones flanking it. These arches date from Roman times, but our guide was of the opinion that the arches were of later date.

I surmised that, even supposing these arches to be of later date, the archway was probably a replica of one that was here when Paul was brought to the house. It was sufficiently close in time to the events mentioned in Acts to lend a flavour of authentication to the scene. We left the little Chapel of Ananias, emerging into the light of day and modern street-level once more. Through one of the arches, we followed the old Roman wall to the site of the window from which Paul was lowered. Here we had to make do with a modern replica. The original wall and window had long gone. As for that Roman wall a degree of caution is need here also. It was almost certainly added to after those times. It did not detain us for long.

We paid a visit to St John the Baptist's Mosque – once destroyed by fire but now restored. In the huge courtyard I saw a tall minaret. This was the Madinet Isa, or Minaret of Jesus. Here, it is claimed, the Messiah will descend from heaven to judge the world on the last day. There are two other minarets attached to the Mosque: the Western Minaret, which dates from the fifteenth century, and the

oldest of the three, the Bride Minaret, dating from the twelfth century. After the customary removal of our shoes, we entered the Mosque. Inside we noted two rows of Corinthian columns which supported fine arches. Devout Moslems prayed towards Mecca on richly-embroidered carpets. Within the decorative central portion lies the head of John the Baptist, it is claimed. Many Westerners are surprised to learn that John the Baptist is revered by Moslems also. The head concealed beneath a huge slab of stone was untouched during a fire which once raged here.

A pagan temple stood on the site prior to this Omayyad Mosque. This temple was razed to the ground by Theodosius, who built the church dedicated to John the Baptist. Following a battle in AD 635 and a meeting of generals here, the grand building became a mosque and a Christian cathedral at the same time. This became an intolerable situation. Today Moslems are very much in control, even if Christians still visit the place.

I spent some time wandering through the covered bazaars, taking in the heady Eastern flavour of this wonderful old city that was established long before Thebes, Troy or Baalbeck. The Street called Straight was effectively one long bazaar. In New Testament times it probably had much more of a classical feel to it, with rows of columns flanking it on either side. The triple archway doubtless indicated the Street's original width. In one of the crowded bazaars I met a blind man with a stick, and he reminded me of Paul in his blinded state being led to that house to meet Ananias.

Swifts screamed through the air here as in Baalbeck. Minarets were circled by them. As non-Moslems we were not allowed to visit the Tomb of Saladin, which is close by the Omayyad Mosque. There is so much to ponder in this the oldest continually-inhabited city in the world. Long before the time of Paul, a great procession of historic figures had passed this way. The Old Testament contains a number of references to Damascus. Genesis 14 tells how Abram chased the King of Sodom's army as far as Hobah, north of the city. King David conquered Damascus (II Samuel 8:6 and I Chronicles 18:6). The reign of King Rezon is mentioned in I Kings 11:24. He developed a position of great power and often made things difficult for Israel. Ahab's treaty with Damascus is recorded (I Kings 20:34), while Elisha's visit here to deliver a terrible prophecy (II Kings 8:7) resulted in the murder of King Ben Hadad by Hazael, who became king and committed terrible atrocities. The Assyrian King Tiglath Pileser took the city (II Kings 16:9). The allied forces of Pekah of Israel and Rezin of Damascus fought against Tiglath Pileser and Ahaz of Judah. Chaldeans, Persians, Macedonians and Romans can be added to the list of conquerers who prevailed against the ancient city.

Closer to our own day, Lawrence of Arabia came here after the defeat of the Ottoman Turks in World War I. We may usefully recall that final ride of his into Damascus. Lawrence found himself the wildly-acclaimed deliverer of the Arabs. He rode through the city in his 'Blue Mist' Rolls-Royce while the dancing, shooting of bullets into the air and other celebrations took place. There were unpleasant aspects, however. Terrible squalor was found at a Turkish hospital. The dead were everywhere – some still dressed in their uniforms, some naked and some in underclothing, some in an advanced state of decay. Wounded men in filthy conditions were there, too weak to fend for themselves. Lawrence organised a clean-up, and some semblance of order was restored. Usurpers who had seized the throne were ousted, and the organisation of civil administration went ahead. An Arab Military Governor was appointed to control

Damascus, subject to Faisal's command. After this Lawrence's desert adventures were over. He felt that his task was done, now that Faisal was in charge.

It is usually recognised that the greatest flowering of the city's architectural glory took place during the Omayyad period. This dynasty was founded by Prince Mu'awiyah in the seventh century AD. Damascus became his capital city, as might be expected. Like ancient biblical kings before them, the Omayyads were prolific and accomplished builders. The Omayyad Mosque, which we had not long before visited, is a fine example of their work, and is rightly regarded as something of a classic and showpiece of their work. Time permitted us a brief look at the sixteenth-century El Tekkieh Mosque, built by Suleyman in AD 1750. Opposite the Mosque stands the National Museum.

The craftsmen of Damascus have justly gained a fine reputation. They are great metalworkers. Damascus swords are famous, as is their glassblowing. Most people have heard of Damascus silk – called damask, naturally. Then there is their cotton. English manufacturers have long imitated Damascus cloth. Foodstuffs such as grain and damsons originated here.

We stopped at a café beside the main Central Square. A portly Arab in a crumpled brown suit served with us with wine poured from an old beer bottle. Afterwards I stood looking at that busy Central Square with its endless comings and goings. Presently we were back in our van, threading through busy main streets. Neon lights and garish cinema hoardings flashed past in a strange kind of blur, contrasting somewhat with those exquisite mosques and their gardens. Islamic architecture has always presented Westerners with a vision of great ostentation. Damascus has preserved much of its oriental and Islamic atmosphere in a way that would have been impossible in big bustling Beirut. In the courtyard of the

Azem Palace we lingered awhile, admiring the beautiful sym-
metry of its rows of arches and striped stonework. This was
by way of a lasting parting glance at this wonderful old city.
The sun was setting as we journeyed the one hundred and ten
kilometres back to Beirut. The sky was filled with a reddish
glow, as if to set a seal on what had been a fantastic trip.

Back in big bustling Beirut, the next item on our itinerary
was a complete guided tour. Our first stop was the Beirut
Museum, where a superb collection of ancient Lebanese
artefacts awaited our perusal, and that reflected Lebanon's
biblical past. There were mosaics taken from Roman villas
where today's suburbs lie. One huge wall-mounted mosaic
was a birds and animals design with each creature beautifully portrayed. Space problems forbid me to describe other
lovely mosaics here, like those from Byblos. I saw a stone
from Herod the Great's Temple which he had built here in
order to win the favour of the Emperor Augustus. It records
the beautification of that Temple by Herod's grandchildren
Agrippa and Berendice. Columns from the Temple are now
to be found in front of this National Museum. We visited
the Alphabet Gallery, which has original old inscriptions –
very apt, for Lebanon is ancient Phoenicia, where every
alphabet originated. Other exhibits – too many to be
described here – included stylised bulls' heads in metal, a fertility goddess, a huge statue from Byblos, also the Obelisks
from the Obelisks Temple, Babylon. I could have stayed all
day in the Museum but it was time to go, for there was still
much to see hereabouts.

A huge warehouse was our next stopping point, along
with a host of other European visitors. We were looking at
a vast collection of lovely silk carpets. An Arab salesman
turned over carpet after exquisite carpet before our gaze.
Many visitors were buying and having carpets of their

choice parcelled ready for posting. Breaking free from the others I returned to the old souk, and wandered for hours through the life-throbbing passageways. This time it seemed as though half of Beirut was streaming through them. A vast array of goods was illuminated by naked light-bulbs hanging in makeshift fashion. The Central Square was likewise alive with activity. Here palms towered skywards. I was near a parking place for charabancs and taxis. The oppressive heat made me splash my face with water from a container at one market stall. I was even asked to pose for a local photographer (I was wearing Arab garb). More cars honked. I observed more wizened faces, full of character, of people seated at little café tables. One ageing man wore a fez and sported a full military moustache like some vaguely-remembered cartoon image. Indeed, there were several mustachioed men present. They were Druse Moslems. Women with babies, policemen and soldiers added to the colour of the scene.

Later that afternoon, I was down on the coast, looking out towards the Pigeon Rocks. Nearby, I came across a mobile refreshment van bearing signs in Arabic. After my coastal walk the heat made me retire to the hotel. The following Wednesday we visited two famous coastal towns, Tyre and Sidon, over which the penetrating vision and lament of the prophet Ezekiel soared:

> Behold, I am against thee, O Tyrus, and will cause many nations to . . . destroy the walls of Tyrus, and break down her towers. (Ezekiel 26:3–4)

There are whole passages dealing with divine retribution towards Tyre and Sidon in Ezekiel's book. Graphic descriptions of life and ancient trade abound there. These mighty seafaring coastal towns of antiquity were famous for their trading with many parts of the world. Ships had masts of cedarwood. There was trading in ivory, embroidered work and ebony. Trade with Damascus, the merchant city, and Arabia and Greece was carried out from here. The Phoenicians even sailed as far as Britain to obtain tin and other metals.

Persons of rank and esteem here wore robes of gorgeous purple. One day a local dignitary, Hercules, was out walking his dog when the dog picked up a murex snail in its mouth, which became reddish-purple. The wife of Hercules decided to use the dye for the robes of important people, and a great tradition was born. Thus the Phoenicians became known to the Greeks as *Phoinikos* or purple men. From this was derived 'Phoenician' and 'Phoenicia'. Sidon was eclipsed by its famous neighbour, although it was used by the Greeks, Persians and Romans later on. Tyre's age-old trading ended when Phoenicia became a vassal state. Later times saw a continuation of this process as Persians and Macedonians were conquered by Alexander the Great in 333 BC and the Romans by Pompey the Great in 64 BC. It was a tale of sad decline and eventual switching of trade to Beirut.

We drove along the coastal road until the shape of a Crusader castle loomed ahead – virtually all that was left of Sidon. A few scattered chunks of the old biblical city still project above the sea's surface. I greeted an enormous portly Arab who was to be our guide. He led us inside the shell of the Crusader castle. At least it was cool and refreshing within these enormously thick walls, with their long narrow slits. Outside locals lazed in the sun, looking very bronzed. Here we were very close to the Israeli border, and I reminded myself that Christ himself came to the coasts of Tyre and Sidon. 'And from thence he arose, and went into the borders of Tyre and Sidon' (Mark 7:24). The Gospel story relates how Christ healed the daughter of a Syrophoenician woman. Not far away lies the Grotto of the Awaiting where, tradition has it, Mary waited for Jesus whilst he visited the cities. Actually the Grotto predates Christianity by centuries, and was a shrine to the pagan goddess Astarte.

The Crusader fortress has a colourful history also. To begin with, the Crusaders of 1099 did not attempt to take Sidon. Instead they took a payment of gold from the inhabitants. However King Baldwin of Jerusalem did attack and take over the fortress in 1111. Later it was taken by Saladin after the defeat of the Crusaders at Hattim. Sidon was rebuilt at a later date by King Louis IX. Although the Templars arrived on the scene and took over, they soon left it to the elements. Most of the architectural finds – those of any value – from here now stand in various museums. Before leaving the fortress I thought about those brave Crusader knights of long ago. Their courage and sense of adventure is legendary. On the debit side, though, they certainly had their faults, one of them being the dreadful state of their medical knowledge. Sometimes Crusaders entrusted the curing of their loved ones to an Arab physician. (The Crusaders indulged in such crude practices as cutting crosses into the skulls of patients.) We shall meet the Crusaders again later in this book.

The name Sidon comes from the Arabic 'Saida', which means fishing town and describes how the town was first established. In time it grew in importance as a seaport, but playing second fiddle to Tyre, as we have seen. There was a god of Sidon known as Eshmoun – the god of health and medicine. This makes my comments on Christ's healing visit here, and my comments on the Arab physicians, very apt. Like its sister port, Sidon was, of course, overrun by those invading armies over the millennia. One very interesting find

near Sidon was the sarcophagus of Echmounazar the King of
Sidon who helped the Persians against the Egyptians in 538
BC. It was here at Sidon that Paul was allowed to visit friends
whilst a prisoner of Rome.

After admiring an ancient-looking mosque, only to discover that it was modern, we decided to have a closer look
at the Roman remains of Tyre. We saw the splendid triumphal arch, with various columns and sarcophagi, not to
mention a splendid road and its own version of the Circus
Maximus. I noticed a number of men in broad-brimmed hats
of straw (some would say hats in the Chicago style) working
on the excavations. Workers in the fields were similarly
dressed.

History-drenched places such as this can detain the visitor
for ages, at least in thought if not in reality. It was founded
2730 years before Christ. Herodotus learned that Tyre had
been founded 2300 years before his visit. This gives some idea
of the antiquity of the place. Undoubtedly one of the most significant periods in the city's history was King Hiram's building programme here when Hiram built his embankment.
Joining two little islands to the mainland, he created ideal
conditions for the city to flourish. The building of harbours
and a breakwater further consolidated the situation of Tyre.
It was all a very accomplished piece of engineering. Hiram's
men even dug a canal to add to Tyre's efficiency. Then they
had a Temple dedicated to Baal on the small island. On the
large island stood the Main City and Royal Palace plus a
lavish Temple to Astarte. It is known that it had a gold pillar
and an emerald one. Multi-storey dwellings were erected to
accommodate the populace. The market place was no doubt
very like that of modern Beirut in its bustling activity, and the
Forum likewise. As we would expect, a factory for dyeing
was to be found here as well. Several shades of purple were

obtained. Only very exalted persons were allowed to wear garments of the deepest purple. These were strictly for kings and queens and probably princes as well. In the production of these dyes, the unpleasant smell the molluscs made was always something of a problem. Stacks of empty shells were placed well clear of human habitation.

These things apart, the Phoenicians were superb in many fields of human endeavour. They were fine sailors, mathematicians, philosophers, farmers and wine-producers. One way and another the Middle East has spread its influence far and wide. The term 'Wisdom of the East' is no empty one. So many aspects of Western culture can be traced back to Middle Eastern, Greek and Roman roots. As regards the former, Crusaders took home with them foodstuffs such as rhubarb, spices and artichokes. The windmill and the compass originated with the Phoenicians, permeating to the West via the Crusaders. We have already mentioned the Phoenician alphabet, which meant that communications were greatly improved. Hitherto writing had largely been the province of scribes but the creation of an alphabet meant that writing was available to businessmen and indeed people everywhere. The colonisation of parts of North Africa, together with Tarnia and Sicily, made the Phoenicians undisputed masters of the Mediterranean world. Their prowess as astronomers soon enabled them to navigate by the stars, steering by the constellation of the Little Bear. The Greeks were later to name this the Phoenician star in recognition of the skills of the Phoenicians who preceded them.

After the death of Hiram came upstart monarchs like Ethbaal. The notorious Jezebel was his daughter who married King Ahab of Israel. Her infamy became a byword for evil even centuries later. Later in the history of Tyre Princess Elissa left the city with her entourage and treasures.

Eventually she founded the illustrious Carthage, which the Romans later built up into one of their most fabulous cities. Princess Elissa is identified with Dido in Virgil's *Aeneid*. Six miles from Tyre there is a tomb of very great age which is recognised as the tomb of Hiram. In places you can see use of pseudo-sections of walling (very modern), which was designed to imitate ancient cladding work. It helps the visitor to gain an impression of what it must have been like. It lends credence to the ruins.

CHAPTER FOUR

CEDARS TO JERUSALEM

We set off for the cedar groves, Lebanon, which supplied the wood for the building of the Temple in Jerusalem. It was, of course, spring and a springtime journey up into these snow-capped Hermon mountains can prove instructive as well as invigorating. Blossom was on the trees and a sense of well-being prevailed. Was Mount Hermon really the scene of Christ's transfiguration? I wondered. Alternatively it happened on Mount Tabor in Galilee, says another tradition.

On the way to the cedar groves is Bechare, a winter playground of the rich, an Eastern St Moritz. Here Gulf sheiks and rich businessmen come to ski and stay at luxurious hotels. I was delighted that we had stopped here. The beauty of this village is quite unlike anything I had experienced thus far in the Bible lands. The altitude seemed to convey to us fantastic peace and tranquillity. There is a superb panoramic view from the window of the Hotel Chebat where we took refreshments. I was transfixed by the snow-studded ridges of the mountains (now very close-to), all delicately framed by pretty pink blossoms spangling the fruit-trees outside.

Close by was a museum dedicated to the village's most

famous son, the internationally famous poet Gibran Khalil Gibran. Alas the museum was closed on this day of our visit. A man emerged from a nearby dwelling, climbed onto the back of a donkey and rode off at a jaunty pace. Soon we had to leave this charming place with its fruit tree gardens, springs and lovely views and head off like the man on the donkey. The long winding mountain road gave us continually splendid views down terraced slopes to the valley below.

Later we arrived at the old cedar groves where all those centuries ago the Phoenicians cut trees for King Solomon. The oldest and largest of the trees may have dated from Solomon's time. They can be seen from a distance, and are a joy to behold with their mighty spreading limbs. Much denuded now, the groves would have covered the whole mountainside in antiquity. It was interesting to see young cedars springing up beside their ancient fellows. It seemed strange to think of snow here in the Bible lands. Usually it is the image of sandy desert that springs more readily to mind.

It is not difficult to see how the configuration of things placed the Phoenicians in the enviable position of being the greatest traders and exporters of cedarwood in the ancient world. The scarcity of serviceable wood in Egypt and Palestine and the abundance of it in Lebanon was a spur for reaching out towards other lands by sea. The Phoenicians seem to have had their beginnings in the Late Bronze Age, when the saga of human creativity, exploration and adventure was well underway. There was a population explosion and their agriculture was unable to sustain the general populace. So everything pointed towards expansion and intercourse with other people. This led to Phoenician towns being studded all along the Levant coast, and further expansion, of course, followed.

From the Old Testament we learn of the contact the

Phoenicians had with the kings of Israel. King David's meeting with Hiram is recorded thus:

'And Hiram king of Tyre sent messengers to David, and cedar trees, and carpenters, and masons; and they built David an house.' (II Samuel 5:11).

Solomon, the son of David, likewise enlisted the aid of the Phoenicians. The building that they erected for Solomon was the sumptuous Temple. We feel immediately from reading the account given in the First Book of Kings that a bond of friendship developed between Hiram and Solomon that was not there in the contacts between Hiram and David. The conviviality that the later alliance knew fostered a whole series of exchanges that were to greatly benefit both peoples.

And Hiram sent to Solomon, saying, I have considered the things which thou sentest to me for: and I will do all thy desire concerning timber of cedar, and concerning timber of fir. My servants shall bring them down from Lebanon unto the sea: and I will convey them by sea in floats unto the place that thou shalt appoint me . . . and thou shalt accomplish my desire, in giving food for my household. (I Kings 5:8–9)

Later on it was King Solomon's turn to reciprocate:

And Solomon gave Hiram twenty thousand measures of wheat . . . and twenty measures of pure oil: thus gave Solomon to Hiram year by year . . . and there was peace between Hiram and Solomon; and they two made a league together. (I Kings 5:11–12)

The story goes on to relate how Solomon pressed thirty-thousand Israelites into service for the labour necessary in the obtaining of raw materials for the Temple.

King Solomon of ancient Israel was a monarch whose opulence, power, wit, and wisdom are proverbial. It was the Lebanon room of the King's sumptuous Palace that contained 200 large gold shields and 300 smaller shields. The fabulous riches that the King enjoyed also included his daily delivery. Imagine having a consignment each day of thirty measures of flour, sixty measures of meal, thirty oxen. As for the animals delivered there were a hundred sheep, harts, roebuck, deer and numerous fowl.

The Bible tells us of other contacts between Israel and Phoenicia. In the book of Ezra we learn that the people of Tyre and Sidon helped Jewish captives returning from exile:

> They gave money also unto the masons, and to the carpenters; and meat, and drink, and oil, unto them of Zidon, and to them of Tyre, to bring cedar trees from Lebanon to the sea of Joppa, according to the grant that they had of Cyrus king of Persia. (Ezra 3:7)

On occasion, however, the prophets of old railed against Tyre and Sidon, as we have seen. Centuries later Jesus was to refer to Tyre and Sidon when he said:

> Woe unto thee, Chorazin! woe unto thee, Bethsaida! for if the mighty works, which were done in you, had been done in Tyre and Sidon, they would have repented long ago in sackcloth and ashes. (Matthew 11:21)

It would seem that Jesus did not consider the old Phoenicians as bad as some.

I continued wandering among the cedar trees. Understandably, the cedar is the national symbol of Lebanon. Visitors are even offered young Cedar saplings to take away. Thus the distinctive cedar shape is distributed far and wide. It was something of a unique sensation treading snow beneath the spreading limbs of these huge trees, with the hot sun caressing my back. Deep within the grove stood a tiny church. Standing outside was another of those characters with a bristling military moustache. He had a white keffieh about his head – a Druse Moslem. He showed me a little round metal object. I was puzzled as to what it was. I couldn't decide whether it was some sort of lucky charm, or religious symbol. Other Moslems in Lebanon are Sunnites and Shiites. Catholic Christians are represented by Maronites and Greeks. Also there are Greek Orthodox and Armenian, Georgian and Protestant Sects. Politically, the president is traditionally a Maronite Catholic. The prime minister is a Sunnite Moslem, the president of the House of Representatives a Shiite Moslem. The vice-president of the House of Representatives is a Greek Orthodox.

Before parting from the cedar grove I purchased a single cone from one of those famous trees as a fitting souvenir.

I was most interested to come across facsimile drawings of ancient relief carvings left by the Assyrians, and from Greek vases. These showed images of Phoenician ships. Firstly there were long ships with a two-tier arrangement of oars and rowers. Generally they were used as vessels of war; the round ships were used for commercial purposes. Further developments occurred over the years. In the seventh century BC a ship with a three-tier system came into being. Later the Greeks were to follow the Phoenician example, but with modifications of their own. It is possible that certain distinguishing features indicate ship designs of other races. For example, a sharply-pointed ramming device on one ship is thought to be Mycenaean in design rather than Phoenician. (The Mycenaeans and Minoans had dominated the seaways before the Phoenicians.) Later generations favoured a new system. Doing away with the old two- and three-tier arrangements, they adopted a single-decker plan, using long oars pulled by many rowers. This was called the quadrireme, with four sets of oars. The quinquereme, with five sets of oars, later became the standard type of vessel used throughout the Mediterranean world. What a dominant influence the Phoenicians were! How proudly those horse-headed, swan-necked fish-tailed Phoenician vessels must have breasted the waves of long ago!

Another coastal city of old in the region is Byblos – a name which has given us our word Bible. This is said to be the world's oldest city (as opposed to Damascus, the world's oldest inhabited city). It was a gloriously sunny day when we visited Byblos. I looked out over the ruins towards a beautiful shimmering blue sea. The structure immediately before me was a Crusader castle, the first of its kind to be built on the Levant coast. Earlier structures had clearly been drastically altered or destroyed to accommodate this castle built by the Knights of the Cross.

Back in Phoenician times, each town and city was careful to designate their own particular gods and goddesses as protectors. Byblos favoured Astarte, the mother goddess (other names include Selene and Diana). The long history of pagan religions would fill books, hence the limited treatment of the subject in this present work. Astarte's husband was called Adonis, and we find a living link with him in the nearby Adonis river. There's a link perhaps with the god El and his wife Asherat. Their son Baal was a god of the mountains – a horned god who held a club and thunderbolts. Temples to Baal and Dagon were built in the vicinity. Motifs and ideas in Eastern pagan religions were freely passed between races. Thus a goddess like Astarte with her husband and means of fecundation, Adonis, readily find parallels in the deities of other pagan races.

The principal commodity landed at Byblos was papyrus

from Egypt. It took the form of paper rolls and ropes for the Phoenician ships. It was here in Byblos that the Greeks first set eyes on this new writing material of the Phoenicians. By Greek times the words Byblos and papyrus became inextricably linked. The Greeks brought in the name Byblos, whilst the city's original name was Gebail or Jebail – still used by the Arabs. The Franks also used the word Jebail, no doubt after the Lords of Gibelet. Today we find the two names being used interchangeably – Jebail and Byblos. The latter is in any case a corruption of the word papyrus. The Scriptures came to be written in Greek on papyrus, in the form of scrolls called *biblia*. From this came our word Bible. Apart from a few inscriptions on stone and metal nothing of Phoenician literature survives. What staggering irony! Eventually events took a turn for the worse. Hordes of warlike Assyrians swept across Israel and Phoenicia. It was the end of Phoenician independence. They were now merely a vassal state. When Alexander the Great overran them it was the start of a process which was to Hellenise the Phoenicians. This in turn caused a further evolution of the alphabet. The Phoenicians soon became absorbed into Graeco-Roman civilisation.

There is an obelisk temple here of unknown purpose, where a number of miniature obelisks are grouped together. Some are arranged in definite patterns whilst others are more isolated. The sarcophagus of Ahiram, King of Byblos (thirteenth century BC), found here can now be seen in the National Museum. Costly alabaster vases were found in the tomb. King Ahiram lived at the time of Ramases II. This may have meant that he was alive at the time of the Exodus. Five-thousand-year-old funerary urns containing bodies in the foetal position from Byblos are also to be found in the Nation Museum. In the Roman ruins here there is a pleasant garden where a few columns have been re-erected and a little amphitheatre restored in part. Close by stands a Crusader church still in use – the Church of St John the Baptist. It is a Byzantine-style building with patterned arabesque arches. Granite from Aswan in Egypt that had been traded for Lebanese timber may still be seen in Byblos and elsewhere in the Lebanon. This stone is solid granite but colourwise it resembles the exquisite red colouring of Petra.

Some distance away from Byblos our driver pulled up by the Dog River, where we could examine the many many inscriptions that military leaders had for centuries placed on the rock walls. The tradition began in early biblical times, and continued long after, persisting up until modern times. I stared in wonderment at that rock-face, thinking about the vast sweep of history contained therein. My gaze finally came to rest on two stelae that were erected in recent times. One of them was a rather ornate piece of work with raised outer borders, a lip of stonework on top, and a repeated pattern below. In the centre, topped by a cedar tree symbol and a pointed arch motif, was an inscription in Arabic. Close by in the rock-face was a plain unadorned slab of stone down which streaks of weathering stains had run. It com-memorated the capture of Damascus by Hussein in 1918. Even though the stone was badly weathered, I was able to make out the following legend:

> The desert mounted corps composed of British, Australian, New Zealand and Indian Cavalry with a French Regiment of Spahis and Chasseurs D'Afrique and the Arab forces of King Hussein captured Damascus, Homse and Aleppo October 1918.

But for the blatant vandalism of Napoleon, I might have viewed an authentic inscription left by Ramases. The latter's inscription was obliterated by the French despot who placed his own on top of the Pharaoh's. This rock-face is an interesting study in itself, but we must move on. A modern road, probably replacing a much older one, is contained within the cliff-face and a low wall which zig-zags in places. I returned to where our van was parked near a ramshackle Arab café which displayed brash signs, some in English, certainly belonging to our day and age.

There was one outstanding example of nineteenth-century Lebanese architecture on our route that I simply couldn't miss. It was the mountain palace built by the Emir Bechir, known as Beit Eddine. Ostentatious elegance and delicacy of Eastern style met my delighted gaze. I noted the clever work of mosaic and inlaid marble, and fountains which flowed with cooling waters. I wandered across the courtyard, and looked over the flower-decked terraces through cleanly-pointed arches. My gaze continued over to the terraced hills beyond. There is a huge main archway and a series of smaller arches. I loved the use of simple geometric pattern in the facade above the main doorway.

The Emir Bechir was a formidable and impressive figure by all accounts, and a wily individual when the occasion demanded it. Contemporary portraits of the Emir show a striking countenance complete with huge black beard. Contained within the palace was all that was essential for the needs of the Emir and his family. This seems to be reflected in the abundance of poplar, cypress and fruit-trees in the terraces. After the death of the Emir's first wife he sent for another from Constantinople. Three were sent and the Emir chose the prettiest. He persuaded her to renounce her faith by offering her the option of marriage to him or long hours of drudgery of kitchen slavery. She chose the former. In other matters, too, the Emir was resourceful. He provided himself and his family with a grooved handrail to facilitate the running of water down a staircase, preventing them from suffering discomfort in hot weather. The marble tomb of the Emir and his wife stands in the gardens among the cypress trees.

Thanks to the Department of Antiquities restoration was carried out to ensure that the palace's original glory was maintained. Sometimes functions are held here – a delightful setting for them indeed!

Before leaving Lebanon there was one more town I decided to visit – Tripoli! The name by which we know the town today comes from the Greek word for it, Tripolis, and the name Triple given by the Crusaders. Both names remind us that the town was the ninth-century BC confederation of three peoples – from Tyre, Sidon and Arwad. All of them built walled defences against the Hittites. The town's great Mosque was once the Crusader Cathedral of St Mary. Practically all the time we spent in Tripoli was on the castle – the highest elevation in the entire town. From these heights we had an excellent view of the town, looking out over hundreds of rooftops and hundreds of square dwellings seemingly stacked in one enormous mound against the hilly slopes opposite. At first a Crusader castle stood on the site, with later destruction and rebuilding by the Mameluke Turks. Inside the castle there are splendid banqueting halls, staircases, and old archways.

We left the old castle with all its imposing splendour, and wandered into a tiny bazaar close by. Here I purchased a tiny abstract brass camel with Arabic lettering on it – probably quotations from the Koran. Nearby were old Arab watchtowers built as part of Tripoli's defence system in days gone by. There used to be several – now only two are still standing. First we have the Lion Tower, so named because of its lion relief carvings. This is the best preserved of the two towers. The second, on the Abu river, is not nearly as good.

Back in busy bustling Beirut we had a day in hand before

the flight to Amman. I wandered those streets close to the bazaar and watched as men struggled with enormous loads on their backs again. One man, I noted, was humping twenty sizeable wooden boxes in one lift. In the bazaar merchants carried on their business as usual. Sunlight filtered through gaps in the overhead awnings. Old men were busy sweeping up the debris that so often collects on the ground near stalls like these. Large colourful umbrella sunshades were up in some parts of the bazaar, lending an all-too expected Parisian look to that area. Old colonial buildings stood close to the bazaar in its more open areas. These sported little balconies, in some cases hanging immediately over the sunshades. Certain of these buildings had shuttered windows, more balconies and elegant wrought-iron rails through which plants hung – a whole series of hanging gardens. Here and there windows with arabesque arches could be seen. All this was in complete contrast to the modern buildings that overlook the sea. In the market area something else was evident. I saw a fair number of well-dressed Arabs and their families, clearly from an elite affluent class.

Beirut flourished greatly in Roman times. It was able to boast the finest academy, apparently superior to other places of learning in the Roman Empire. For example, the Law School in Beirut was said to have outshone others in the classical world, such as Athens or Alexandria. Beirut enjoyed this reputation for three hundred years and was called Nutrix Legum, or literally Mother of Law. The Crusaders built the Church of St John, which under later Moslem rule became the Omar Mosque. Saladin took over the city in 1187 and was followed by certain emirs. The Ottoman Turk was driven out of Beirut, as from elsewhere in the Middle East, in 1918. I was intrigued to discover that the legend of St George and the Dragon has links with Beirut. The dragon-slaying incident for which the saint is renowned supposedly took place hereabouts.

A war memorial comprised of bronze statues of martyrs who were killed in the conflict that took place before the Turks were driven out stands in the aptly-named Martyrs Square. People I met at the hotel talked enthusiastically about the Jeita caves not far from Beirut, which contained fantastic natural rock formations. I was forced to omit the caves from my itinerary. We had to press on to Jordan for the second half of the tour and time was precious. We had, of course, seen the Dog river that flows from its source in those caves. The discovery of the caves was completely accidental by a tourist climbing in the area. The tourist stumbled into an opening and found himself in this wonderland. Firing a shot into the void, he heard it echo through the caverns. There was the sound of running water. Thus the grotto was discovered for the delight of hordes of visitors who were to follow in his steps. Today visitors can move about the grotto by boat, viewing wonderfully illuminated stalactites. The grotto's discoverer might be thought of as a male counterpart of Alice in Wonderland.

The next day we flew on to Amman for the second half of our trip. Our base was now the Caravan Hotel on the outskirts of the town. It seemed like no time at all since I was last there. Here I was on this occasion with a group less amicable than that encountered on my first visit here. The rest of the group took off for Petra for a couple of days whilst I continued on my own. I wandered round Amman looking at pottery and other exhibits in the museum. Crowds filled the streets and lined the pavements. An important head of state was visiting Jordan and presently drove past in a plush car with King Hussein, father of Jordan's present king. I never found out which head of state it was who visited on that occasion. The event seemed nevertheless to provide the locals with a pleasant diversion.

Hiring a taxi for the day, I got the driver to head for Jerash. Its ruins are the best-preserved of all the Decapolis cities from the time of Jesus. The Decapolis was a confederation of Graeco-Roman gentile cities scattered over a wide area in first-century Palestine. I joined a guide who showed me round the forum with its columns. As we walked down the Street of Columns a Greek Orthodox priest walked towards us from the opposite direction. He was accompanied by an elderly couple. The old priest, white-bearded, robes fluttering, staff in hand, looking very patriarchal, for all the world like Abraham himself, breezed past nodding a greeting as he did so.

The splendid Street of Columns runs the city's length – all the way from the Forum to the North Gate. Jerash was one of ten Decapolis cities, and it was important for many reasons. Columns stood gracefully above cheerfully littered chunks of fallen masonry from New Testament times. I could make out old Corinthian capitals on the columns. As we explored and wandered the site, a guide drew my attention to one standing column in particular, which was inclined to rock slightly. It is nicknamed 'the Whispering Column', probably on account of sounds produced when wind pierces the gaps. I observed the tell-tale ruts left in the road by chariot wheels of long ago. By now strong shadows had fallen across the ancient streets from pillars and walls. In the amphitheatre boys were scrambling over the old tiers of seating. I saw one boy atop a standing pillar. How he got there is a mystery. Visiting all three theatres, the temples, baths, hippodrome and all the rest can easily occupy half a day or longer, especially if you are a student of ancient history. I saw one superb example of mosaic flooring (wonderful pictures made with tiny stones set in mortar). This entire Graeco-Roman town lay undisturbed and buried beneath the soil of this Gilead mountain valley for nearly two millennia. Twentieth-century archaeologists observed a number of columns projecting above ground. Soon spade and pick began to unearth one of the finest Roman ruins to be seen. The Pompeii of the Middle East it is called today! Old caravan routes crossed here and the city was the scene of much lively and bustling trade and exchange. Travelling merchants traded in silks, spices, ivory and all manner of merchandise – including precious stones. Jerash was blessed with an abundance of water. Springs are here in plenty – always welcome in a hot, dry and thirsty land such as this. I wondered just how many mean and insignificant-looking Arab villages concealed fantastic archaeological treasures beneath their soil or sand.

The second century AD is regarded as the zenith of the city's glory. During this period old buildings were replaced with new – and they were exquisite replacements. The Triumphal Arch of Hadrian is still very impressive indeed, as is the Forum with its semi-circular curve of columns, and the massive Temple of Artemis, where I had seen the Whispering Column. It was wintertime in AD 129–30 when Hadrian visited Jerash and the fine Triple Gateway built to commemorate his visit can still be seen. Both Corinthian and Ionic capitals appear on columns in the city and could reflect changes of rulers. The West Bath was as exclusive as any London club today, for a bath in those times was as much a social gathering place as it was a place to perform your ablutions. We have seen Jerash was well-supplied with water. It had an elaborate system of plumbing and piping of water to all parts of the complex. Other Graeco-Roman cities were, of course, similarly supplied.

Here, as in Petra and other places, Christian churches stood in close proximity to pagan temples dedicated to Zeus

and Artemis. Later periods of history were not so kind to Jerash. In Byzantine times it fared reasonably well as a Christian centre, but extensive damage took place due to an earthquake in the eighth century AD. Baldwin II treated Jerash sacrilegiously, using the place as a fortification and tearing down some of the best artefacts that had been left by those that had gone before, which included some of the best second-century work. How those Roman generals would have winced at such crass vandalism!

Today restoration work goes on and experts are inclined to think that Jerash was even larger and more extensive than was originally thought to be the case. After a picnic lunch with my driver, his family and friend we drove on. Perhaps it was nicer to have picnicked in this pleasant spot than, say, in the vicinity of a busy town or city.

As far as I could make out, the Arabs encountered in Jordan fall into different racial categories. My driver, for example, was of the stocky round-faced variety, whereas his friend obviously belonged to the lean long-headed variety that we think of as being indigenous to the area. Swarthy of face and silent of manner, they could come straight from the pages of the Bible. Not being particularly well-versed in the sciences of ethonology or anthropology, I tend to rely more or less on straightforward observation, whether of people or the evidence provided by archaeology. The round-faced Arab, or brachycephalic type, we think of as originating from elsewhere in the Orient, his dolichocephalic or long-headed neighbour possibly being the more typical son of Ishmael. Experts in this field would probably insist on more precise terms of reference. Things like cranial measurement and the maxillary angle would be taken into consideration – but enough of this! Let's continue with the drive and the next stop was Madaba.

At first glance Madaba seems a stark sort of place. Make enquiries, however, and you will realise that here the most fascinating collection of antique mosaics is to be found. Many residents have discovered that their modern houses were built over ancient mosaic floors. We drove straight up to the most famous of these. I entered the St George's Greek Orthodox Church and my companions rolled up a carpet on the church floor to reveal to my gaze the famed sixth-century Byzantine mosaic map of Palestine (part of Egypt is shown, too). The stylised picture of Jerusalem that the map contains gives us, in all probability, a contemporary view of Jerusalem of those times. A city wall is seen with towers at intervals. Colonnaded streets and buildings are seen within the walls. The Church of the Holy Sepulchre is there, and gates are seen piercing the city walls. The old city of Jerusalem cannot have changed greatly since those days, as I was soon to discover for myself. The mosaic is made up of an exquisite balance of black-and-white pieces set against pastel colours like yellow and pink. Roofs are coloured pink, church walls are done in pale yellow, roads being in black-and-white, and so on.

The museum at Madaba has a collection of other fine mosaics found in the area. Mythological subjects, such as Achilles and his fatal heel, and the goat-footed god Pan, are depicted. Other interesting exhibits are there too. The history of Madaba goes back to the Moabites, Ammonites and Nabataeans, before Alexander the Great turned it into a provincial town which flourished under trade. It became a prominent town in the Middle East. Fortunately the Byzantine mosaics survived later sacking by Persians and occupation by Arabs. Also Madaba lived through other vicissitudes such as an earthquake in AD 747, amongst other things. It was the Christian community that moved in during the nineteenth century that excavated there and uncovered the mosaics. Sleepy Madaba is certainly a town with a history.

Mount Nebo was the next port of call. I spotted two donkeys pulling an age-old type of plough and asked the driver to stop for me. The yoke that bound the two animals was a simple rounded piece of timber. Presently we pulled beside a huge hangar-like construction which covered ruins of a church and monastery. Rows of old columns belonging to an ancient basilica were found by Franciscan monks. This place is known as Syagha. It was the place where the wicked King Balak of the Moabites attempted to curse the Israelites by enlisting the aid of another wicked man – Balaam. It was an evil enterprise that did not succeed. Undoubtedly the best-known Old Testament incident was the viewing of the Promised Land by Moses, which view I was about to enjoy myself. Across desert and through rugged mountain passes the nomads had struggled. The years of weary toil were almost over. They were encamped somewhere below the mountain, whilst Moses struggled to the peak to see the breathtaking view of the land of Canaan. Moses died soon afterwards. The location of his tomb is not authenticated, but it must be close by – perhaps at Madaba. I found the view of the Promised Land as breathtaking as Moses must have done. That line from the famous hymn came readily to mind: 'If we could stand where Moses stood and view the land-scape o'er.' Well, here I was doing exactly that. It was a strange sensation. I looked out over the vast stretching plain, arid and at the same time beautiful and stirring. A gentle breeze blew over me as I stood looking out at the view over the tops of bushes. 'Over there,' said my guide pointing, 'you can see a whitish tower.' I looked and could just make out a tiny speck of a tower in the far distance. 'That is Jerusalem.'

Below it slightly to one side was a blob of greenery which was Jericho and I could make out a bluish thread, no doubt caught by the light, which was the River Jordan. This was the land 'flowing with milk and honey' which was presented to the Children of Israel after two hundred and fifteen years in Egypt as slaves under the whips of Pharaoh's taskmasters, followed by all those years of nomadic existence in the wild-erness. We were joined by an old Arab, swathed from head to foot in dark brown robes, who conversed with the driver and his friend.

Back down the mountain we drove and some time later I was back in Amman. There I wandered the streets stopping to talk to some of the locals. A boy of perhaps twelve years held up a little black goat for me to stroke. A Jordanian soldier taking a rest from the heat also stopped to talk. I then decided it was time for some food again – even after two meals with the taxi-driver and his family, both outside Jerash and in their home. I took my place in a restaurant, and took care to remember the Arabic word for yoghurt and asked for 'laban'.

'Oh, you mean yoghurt?' responded the waiter.

My former companions were back from Petra, and I was busily arranging a trip to Jerusalem with a local tour organiser. The necessary formalities were soon completed. Now it was just a matter of waiting until the following morning for transport to the Allenby Bridge – the first stage of the journey and the border between Jordan and Israel. One tour operator in Amman thought that I would 'see nothing' in the short space of time that I was to spend over in Israel. Certainly you need time to do justice to any historic place. Next morning a car arrived for me well behind schedule. Then I was speeding across the bleak desolate Jordan valley until the Allenby Bridge came into view. It is here that the traveller must disembark for entry into Israel. The Allenby Bridge itself is disappointingly tiny. I rather expected something more elaborate to commemorate the famous war leader. The Jordan River is little more than a dyke at this point in its course. After crossing the bridge I underwent Israeli customs formalities. A soldier surveyed my person with a metal detector. What little luggage I was carrying was checked also. Formalities over, I received a beaming 'Welcome to our country' from a Yemenite Jew. Soon I was driven on towards my destination. We stopped in Jericho on the way. My exploration of this little town – which I saw as a little green blob from Mount Nebo – would have to wait until later that year. Close to I had a view of tall palm trees with hills a splendid backdrop. Onward we drove towards our goal through typically rocky terrain, picking up two Spanish ladies.

At last we arrived at our grand destination. Jerusalem!

what feelings of sublime majesty the very name distils! This was the first time I had visited the city and I was greatly impressed and felt a tingle of excitement. Wasting little time I plunged down the warren of passageways via the Damascus Gate or 'Gate of the Pillar' – so named because Hadrian's pillar once stood here. These labyrinthine passageways inside Old Jerusalem were almost one continuous souk. The two streets running off the Damascus Gate were colonnaded in Roman and Byzantine times. Today's Old Jerusalem gives an impression of what the biblical version of it must have looked like. The words of Psalm 122:2 came to mind: 'Our feet shall stand within thy gates, O Jerusalem.' It is important to understand the topography of the area. Jerusalem stands on four hills with some deep valleys. One such – now filled in – is within the present city walls, namely the Tyropean Valley, close to the old Temple area. The hilly nature of the terrain explains why the Bible speaks of going up to Jerusalem. There was expectancy and excitement as I proceeded through the ancient souks. In a sense the very air seems laden with the sanctity and devotion of the ages, despite the inevitable high-pressure Arab salesmen in the souks. Prophets wept over the city during the dreadful periods of its dissolution. Two such prophets were Jeremiah and Nehemiah, and, of course, Jesus wept over Jerusalem from the Mount of Olives. Bases of columns may still be seen, reminding us of the days when Roman temples and statues adorned the city. Today Classical splendour has given way to a more oriental feel, even if it is made up of encrustations of the ages.

Eventually I emerged into the open once more through St Stephen's Gate, location of the Pool of Bethesda ruins and sheep market and where the first Christian martyr was stoned to death. I happened to ask an Arab sitting against a wall the way to the Mount of Olives. He directed me but screamed for backsheesh. The only way to get rid of him was to give him a coin. I continued down the slope towards the Church of All Nations. In the grounds of this church stands the Garden of Gethsemane. Whether or not its size is the same as in the time of Jesus it is difficult to say. Apparently there was a continuation of the garden on the other side of the road which ascends the mount. Close by stands the Tomb of the Virgin Mary down a long flight of steps. Jesus prayed in great anguish on that solemn night before his crucifixion hereabouts under a full moon. Inside the church I met Father Tom O'Hanlon, from County Kerry in Ireland, who offered to show me round some holy sites and I gladly took up his offer.

There was a tinkling of bells as a flock of sheep were led across a slope by a traditionally robed shepherd. What vivid biblical imagery! Shades of Psalm 23: 'The Lord is my shepherd' and John 10: 'I am the good shepherd: the good shepherd giveth his life for the sheep.' Sheep, of course, feature strongly in the Bible and in the history of both Jew and Arab. Many an Arab has gorged himself on the tail of a Holy Land sheep and it is something of a speciality to them. The ancient patriarchs owned sheep by the thousand. Sheep were sacrificial animals to the ancient Jews, as indeed they still are to people of Samaria and the Arabs. Religious ritual and symbolism apart, sheep are always valuable for their meat and fleece, the latter being woven for garments. They are a different strain from European sheep.

Father O'Hanlon and I walked up the steep road on the Mount of Olives, passing the Russian Orthodox Church with its gold domes, which I had first seen on emerging from St Stephen's Gate. We stopped at an old Jewish cemetery, where for centuries Jews have been buried in readiness for the Messiah's entry through Jerusalem's Golden Gate. The view from the top of the Mount of Olives is rather splendid, taking in as it does the entire length of the Old City of Jerusalem with its terraces of little walls leading down into the Valley of Hinnon. Whilst on Olivet, I haggled with a lean cantankerous Arab for the hire of his camel. At length the bargain was struck and I enjoyed a camel ride across the top of the Mount. Another Arab went by leading a thin camel caked in dung. We looked towards the Pillar of Absolom – a monument said to mark the grave of David's wayward son. As we walked I told Father Tom about my past fortnight's tour. By the end of the day I had visited many holy places – the Church of the Holy Sepulchre and Gordon's Calvary among them. It is left until later – my second Jerusalem visit – to consider these places in more detail. However this chapter contains exploration of the Convent of the Flagellation and the Church of the Nativity in Bethlehem.

In the Via Dolorosa I saw copies of nineteenth-century woodcuts, camelskin drums, and camel saddles fabulously woven by Arab women. Leaving this narrow souk I closely followed a storekeeper's directions and came out by the Dome of the Rock. I was soon captivated by its vibrant blue tilework. A Swiss pastor and his wife whom I had accompanied from Amman appeared again suddenly. They were staying at the Ecce Homo Hotel. I walked beneath the arches adjacent to the Dome of the Rock. It is here, according to some, that the scales of Judgement will hang on the last day. After my visit to the Mosque I continued on my way to Jerusalem's famous Wailing Wall or better known now as the Western Wall, where Jews in black prayed in a row facing those huge stone slabs of Herodian and later times. Mostly, it represented a section of the perimeter wall that surrounded Herod's Temple. I talked with some Jews at the wall and inserted a prayer of my own into the gaps there – as anyone, Jew or Gentile, may do.

Close by the wall archaeological excavations were under-way – though there were no sunhatted professors and their helpers present at the time of my visit. Recent activities in the realm of archaeology have often brought the distant biblical past into the light of day. When people ask if there is any-thing to see from Bible times the answer is usually in the affir-mative. Then there is the Bible's reflection in the living present, apart from the sheep already mentioned. Some things have survived like living fossils, and a fossilisation that can give insight into many biblical subjects. For example, there are both beasts and men of burden, animals yoked together, chaff being blown away by a winnower.

I re-entered the City some time later with Father Tom via St Stephen's Gate to visit the Convent of the Flagellation, whether Father Tom was to officiate at the Mass. Once there he quickly donned his robes of office. The little service pro-ceeded with Father Tom, myself and an American woman. As a Protestant, I was not allowed to participate in the Mass itself, but enjoyed the service just the same. Afterwards we went down into the lowest section of the Convent – and cer-tainly the oldest parts of it. Authentic slabs of Roman paving form the old courtyard, known as the Lithostros, where Jesus was scourged. On one flag of paving we can see scratches from a Roman dice game, recalling the gambling of the soldiers for the cloak of Christ. Here, in all probability, that mock-coronation was carried out and the scourging. Grooves were cut – and can still be seen – to prevent the horses' hooves from slipping.

Soon we left for the Casa Nova Hotel, where Father Tom was staying along with a host of other Catholic clergymen. I was invited to join a dinner that evening with that host of clergymen in attendance. We all sat at very long tables like those seen in Leonardo Da Vinci's painting of the Last Supper. Everyone enjoyed good food and wine and good conversation. There were generous helpings of food and big flagons of red wine, which I was cordially offered. Sitting opposite to me was an Australian priest to whom I was introduced. In the gentle hum of general conversation I could make out heavy French accents, perhaps from the fields of Provence. It was a splendid and happy gathering at which I stayed for some time before taking my leave of these gentlemen and thanking them for their kind hospitality. Before long I returned to the Pilgrim Hotel, where I had booked in for the night.

I reflected on the warmth and sincerity of Father Tom at the service when he shook my hand. He had allowed me to read the lesson – the first time I had done so near the holy sites of Jerusalem. I remembered, too, the beautiful sky there had been at dusk. I was up at 5.30 the next morning, having a very tight schedule to keep that day. The dining room of the hotel was full of breakfasting Americans, and it was not yet six o'clock. Possibly they are early risers by nature or maybe, like me, they needed to make an early start. Would I be mithered at different sites today, I wondered, or would mitherers allow a decent interval before accosting me? I proceeded to the New Gate and made my way back to the Casa Nova Hotel. Realising that I had half-an-hour or so before my rendezvous with Father Tom, I made my way to the Jaffa Gate and stopped to look at the Citadel, sometimes called 'David's Tower'. The present tower is of much later date, though. An old Armenian told me about Hezekiah's pool nearby. I was directed up a flight of steps inside a hotel within the Jaffa Gate. It was a seedy establishment. Looking through a dining-room window I could make out a courtyard – a narrow one, as I recall. Traditionally this was where David set eyes on Bathsheba. It was almost next door to the shop where I had purchased woodcut prints.

At 7.30 I met Father Tom as arranged and we headed for a place outside the walls where communal taxis known as cheroots were parked. We were going to make a fleeting visit to Bethlehem, principally to see the Church of the Nativity. In one of the cheroots we were speeding towards Bethlehem. The ride lasted about fifteen minutes. Bethlehem is a far less hectic place than Jerusalem. The dominant shape of the Church of the Nativity in Manger Square is very soon evident to the visitor. We had to lower our heads to enter the basilica, like many another visitor to this hallowed place. Apparently the smallness of the door was to prevent the entry of men on horseback in times gone by. The huge interior of the basilica was spread out before us with rows of ancient columns from the time of Justinian. There is a huge decorative screen at the far end of the building, hung with icons and silver lamps, too, in some places. The atmosphere reminded me of an Old Master painting. A mysterious Rembrandt gloom? Yes – and pierced through with a brilliant shaft of light from high clearstory windows, caressing the ancient stonework, like the Light of Christ shining in the darkness. Parts of the basilica were built by the Emperor Justinian and other parts by Constantine. Some of Constantine's work was destroyed by the Samaritans in AD 529. The beautiful Constantinian floor is covered in order to protect it. When I was there we were able to see a smallish portion of it which was uncovered at the time. You can sense the devotion of centuries as you stand there in the stillness. It was about an hour before we could enter the crypt, as a service was in progress at the time of our arrival. One Greek Orthodox priest, in his black clerical garb, was in no doubt about the authenticity of the sacred site. When we were eventually able to enter the Grotto we had the shrine to ourselves for a while before a woman entered, prostrated herself before the altar and buried her face in the niche with the silver star said to mark the exact spot where Jesus was born. She was weeping loudly. Amazing to think of the thousands that must have knelt or prostrated themselves in like manner. This would, of course, have included famous figures from history like Crusaders Simon de Montfort and Richard Cœur de Lion straight from encounters with Saladin.

Outside again we visited the Shepherds' Fields. My gaze followed Father Tom's indicated direction, looking out towards the timeless Judean hills. The names of various establishments in Bethlehem reflect its famous biblical associations, such as the King David Cinema, the Good Shepherd Store, the Herodian Store, and the Holy Manger Store. The British occupation is seen in a Boy Scout Troop there. When for the moment I took my leave of Bethlehem one of my most endearing memories was the striking dark-eyed Bethlehemite people themselves.

Back in Jerusalem I bade farewell to Father Tom, promising to write to him at his parents' home in County Kerry. I was left with visions of venerated sacred places and seemingly incongruous sights of soldiers, newspaper vendors and tourist offices. You cannot help but see the Holy Land as a place of contrasts. As arranged I caught the transport back across into Jordanian territory, again stopping at the Allenby Bridge before re-entering. The bridge opens and closes at appointed times – my main reason for the day's tight schedule, as the bridge was soon to close and we crossed in the nick of time. Then the hard and bumpy ride to Amman again by jeep followed. During the ride we had taken aboard a Jordanian soldier.

ISRAEL & JORDAN

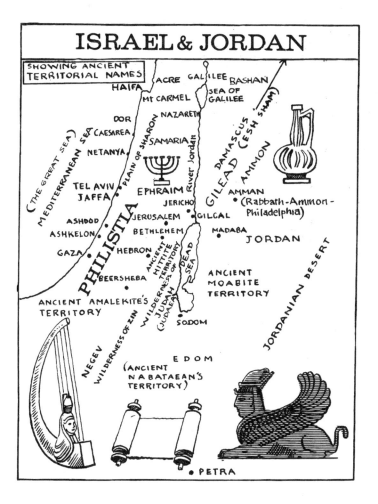

SHOWING ANCIENT
TERRITORIAL NAMES

ACRE GALILEE BASHAN
HAIFA
Mt CARMEL SEA OF
GALILEE
NAZARETH
DOR
CAESAREA
NETANYA
SAMARIA
DAMASCUS (ESH SHAM)
(THE GREAT SEA)
MEDITERRANEAN SEA
PLAIN OF SHARON
River Jordan
GILEAD
AMMON
TEL AVIV
JAFFA
EPHRAIM
AMMAN
• (Rabbath-Ammon-
Philadelphia)
PHILISTIA
JERICHO
JERUSALEM • GILGAL
ASHDOD BETHLEHEM
MADABA
•
ASHKELON
JORDAN
GAZA HEBRON
ANCIENT
HITTITE
TERRITORY
DEAD
SEA
BEERSHEBA
ANCIENT
MOABITE
TERRITORY
ANCIENT AMALEKITE'S
TERRITORY
WILDERNESS OF
JUDAH
(JUDAEA)
• SODOM
JORDANIAN DESERT
NEGEV
WILDERNESS OF ZIN
E D O M
(ANCIENT
NABATAEAN'S
TERRITORY)

• PETRA

CHAPTER FIVE

ISRAEL

The late summer of that year found me back in Israel. On leaving Ben Gurion Airport the first place I headed for was Tel Aviv, the modern Israeli capital. After spending the night in a small hotel run by a German Jew, I emerged the following morning into the brilliant Tel Aviv sunshine, exploring the city for myself. Old city and new merge somewhat and one may be thought of as part of the other. Jaffa, or Joppa as it used to be called, is the Old City and is the ancient port of Israel with numerous biblical associations. Indeed, figures from profane and biblical history. Here Solomon's men took delivery of cedar wood from Lebanon, and Jonah set out for Tarshish, later to be swallowed by that whale or big fish, only to be coughed up on a beach near Ninevah. The Assyrians landed here to attack ancient Israel. Alexander the Great took the city centuries afterwards, as did Judas Maccabee and his brothers in the second century BC, when they won Jaffa for the Seleucids. The Jaffa of New Testament times is well-known to us from the book of Acts. Dorcas (whose name means gazelle) was raised from the dead here (Acts 9:36). Then Acts 10 relates how the angel tells

Cornelius, the roman centurion, to seek Peter at the house of Simon the tanner and Peter has his vision of the sheet full of living things. Jaffa was even owned by Cleopatra, for Anthony gave it to her. Tel Aviv, the new city, is an out-and-out modern place, somewhat in contrast to its other half.

I wandered through the maze of much-restored streets near the house of Simon the tanner and watched a photographic shoot involving a model girl, typical of the upbeat and forward-looking attitude of modern Israel. Coming out into the open seafront area, I noticed the intense azure blue of sea and sky. The bright sunlight cast strong oblique shadows across white sea walls. Palms bowed gently between me and the shoreline. Visitors gathered in little cafés. The local authorities have constructed a stylised artificial version of Jonah's whale as part of a playground complex. I wondered how those first Zionists felt when they landed here in 1840. Could they have foreseen what the Jaffa–Tel Aviv complex was to become in our day and age? Little groups of Arabs, wizened, thin and shabbily dressed, gathered in tiny cafés there to smoke their hubble-bubble pipes, sip tea from little glasses, play board-games, or just sit and think, breaking out of their reveries every now and then to chatter quietly among themselves.

Baibars, the Mameluke Sultan at the time of the Crusades, sacked the city and destroyed it. Despite the ravages of time and war, however, the place is very much alive today and the modern rebuilding work is rather impressive. Presently I walked back towards Tel Aviv. The seafront was still gloriously sun-drenched.

I later boarded a bus bound for Jerusalem (marked in both Hebrew and English) at the Tel Aviv bus depot. For what seemed ages we rumbled through arid stony country until at last Jerusalem came into view. Soon we alighted there and it was great to be back in this most famous of biblical cities that I had left only weeks previously. It was a bustling animated scene at the Jerusalem bus depot and I soon made my way back to the Old City of Jerusalem's walls and the Pilgrim Hotel, where I stayed for the first two nights here. I had planned to base myself at Jerusalem for the first week, during which time I was to savour again the delights of this venerated place. I couldn't wait to start exploring again and resume where I had left off. Within the Damascus Gate I descended the steps of the Damascus Gate road. Here there were a number of little cafés in which Arabs sat contentedly with their water pipes bubbling. From a loudspeaker near a crescent symbol the Moslem call to prayer wailed. The faithful headed for their mosques, thumbing strings of prayer beads as they walked. (As each bead is thumbed, the name of Allah is intoned. There are forty beads on each string.)

I was back in the labyrinth of passageways. The pungent smell of spicy foodstuffs was evident. There were spices, peppers, nuts, and lentils laid out in little open sacks. There were all sorts of Aladdin's cave shops crammed with all kinds of exotic merchandise – sheepskin coats, camelhair blankets and huge Turkish coffee pots with long upcurved spout. Every Arab merchant was jockeying for my attention as usual. Donkeys and mules trotted past with impossibly heavy loads, soon vanishing down another narrow passageway. The man in charge of the beast nearly always yelled out in Arabic for people to make way. By now I was deep in the labyrinth where Greeks, Jews, Copts, Armenians are ever present. Overhanging garments brushed against my face. Mother-of-pearl goods from Bethlehem were on sale, as were Holy Land flower cards, rosaries, olivewood boxes, camel caravan sets. I was intrigued, too, by the oriental gold and silver goods, Holy Land slides, crosses, Nativity sets, and so forth. Aniseed and crushed fruit drinks were available, as were fresh vegetables. The Old City today is much as the Crusaders would have known it. No doubt they would have made excellent modern guides had they been here now.

In one tiny shop, well-hidden and close to the Jewish quarter, I was greeted in a dignified and courteous manner by an elderly Arab. His workshop bench displayed a cheerfully chaotic array of oddments. Another pungent aroma filled the air, as a wisp of smoke curled from a stick of incense on the bench. At the shopowner's invitation I received unmilked tea in a little glass, as on other occasions. Eventually I left the little shop and continued my exploration of the murky passageways of the Old City. Victorian travellers used to complain of squalor, filth, and sinking ankle-deep in mud. We can be thankful that today Old Jerusalem is kept clean, with modern water-sprinkling machines in some parts. I have seen one such machine sending little rivulets cascading down the huge steps of the Damascus Gate Road to collect in huge puddles at the lowest point.

I visited Uncle Moustache's restaurant just inside Herod's Gate. Uncle Moustache was a benevolent man, portly and, as his name suggests, he is adorned with a huge Turkish-style moustache. He provides good food at modest prices for poor people. After refreshments I resumed my wanderings through the ever-throbbing and colourful passageways.

Then I stopped at another of those little shops well-hidden in the souks. This was Uncle Kamel's shop. Uncle Kamel was another benign middle-aged Arab who asked me into his cramped space to drink more thick sweet Turkish coffee from a tiny cup. My host produced a crude musical instrument. He scraped a tune for me and the resulting sound was somehow distant and enigmatic. The square sound box was stretched over with deerskin. Other features included a simple handle and taut strings of hair strands. A curved stick with a string stretched from end to end served as a bow. It is known to the Arabs as a rababa. However, Uncle Kamel's speciality was his exotic perfume made of rose petals, jasmine, and musk from gazelles, dispensed in tiny unmarked bottles with plastic caps. He prided himself on producing the best perfume in the Middle East. I soon finished my glass of sage tea, which Uncle Kamel had prepared for me. 'Good for the stomach' was his comment. I haggled over colourful robes in the shop before leaving.

At another little niche of a shop I marvelled at thickly-woven camel saddles. They were lovely pieces of handiwork, woven by the women of the desert. I haggled playfully, as I had haggled for goods so often in the Middle East before. Moneychangers glared in my direction, ever eager to do business. In another shop I saw fine silverware embellished with bright green Eilat stone. Splendid copperwork abounds in these souks also, made out of copper straight out of King Solomon's mines. Then I came upon a shop displaying antiques. Among them I saw coins from Roman times bearing the profiles of long-dead Roman Emperors, and pottery from ancient Persia. In most of these antique shops Roman lamps abound, which can be purchased with a Government certificate of authentication. In another tiny recess a cobbler crouched, surrounded by the clutter of his trade. He was busy, as with each time I passed his little recess subsequently. As they say, there's a lesson in there somewhere! Other points of interest caught my eye – hangovers from the days of the Ottoman Empire, such as the dangling hand of Fatima, and the decorative eye symbol. An old Armenian explained to me that people generally read into these symbols whatever meaning takes their fancy. Moslems and Christians adapted these symbols to their respective faiths – a healing hand or all-seeing eye, and so on. The symbols are seen to decorate vehicles and little shops. There is even a brass-hand doorknocker on a convent here. The love of ornamentation in this part of the world has persisted for millennia. Like Rebecca of old, modern brides in these lands still wear plenty of jewellery.

Darkly-clad yashmak-veiled women of strict Moslem background glided silently past. Along the narrow passage-ways of the Via Dolorosa, with its famed Stations of the Cross, went a Greek Orthodox priest with hurried steps and bustling black cassock. He was distinctive, like most of the labyrinthine characters. Along part of its course the Via Dolorosa is strengthened by a series of picturesque arches, built to help stabilise the walls in the event of an earthquake. It was beneath these arches that I trod in the company of a host of pilgrims one Friday. I had joined the Friday proces-sion stopping at the various Stations of the Cross discussed elsewhere in this book. The rubble of centuries had, of course, raised the level of these narrow streets since the time of Jesus – it was rubble from the many dissolutions that Jerusalem had endured. Yet it is still possible to see artefacts from the time of our Lord which reflect the genuine world in which he lived. Most obviously there is the Wailing Wall in the Jewish Quarter with its huge Herodian blocks of stone.

During the 1800s the American scholar and archaeologist Edward Robinson and later Englishmen Captain Charles Warren and Colonel Sir Charles Wilson made significant dis-coveries. Digital remains of an arch in the Western Wall of the Haram were first noticed by Robinson, and today this digital arch is still named after him. Under the auspices of the Palestine Exploration Fund, Wilson, then a Captain, sunk shafts west of Robinson's Arch, discovering a series of piers. These had apparently supported other arches. Edward

Robinson had discovered a projection which, it is now believed, once supported a staircase leading up to the royal portico of the Temple complex. These and other flights of steps in the vicinity lend credence to the Bible's words going 'up to the Temple'. For his part, Colonel Sir Charles Wilson (later to become Major General Sir Charles Wilson), had found the remains of a viaduct built by the Hasmoneans which once spanned the Tyropean Valley, linking the Upper City with the Temple Mount. These and other features of Jerusalem at the time of the Second Temple are to be seen in a painstaking scale reconstruction of the Old City in the grounds of Jerusalem's Holy Land Hotel. With this in mind the enterprise and enthusiasm of the 1800s scholar adventurers bore abundant fruit for us today. It is reflected in their writings. Colonel Wilson produced delightful books under the title of *Picturesque Palestine* – reprints of which are on sale in Jerusalem. Incidentally, there's a lovely antique arch in Old Jerusalem named after him – Wilson's Arch. Also in the Western Wall Barclay's Gate can be found, though only the lintel is now above ground. Above it the Magrabi Gate gives access to the Temple Mount. Not so long ago Arab policemen with spiked helmets guarded the Wailing Wall, preventing all Jewry from being there. Somewhere nearby there was a ring of stonework where, it is said, Burak, the Prophet Mohammed's steed, was once tied.

In one little café within the Old City I tasted an exotic concoction of cornflour mixed with nuts, raisins, cinnamon, coconut and many other ingredients – just another of the city's delights. Presently a waterseller appeared, like an apparition from another age, with an exotic container on his back – a hangover from the Turkish occupation. Tourists were being shown a handprint in the stonework at one point in the Via Dolorosa's course, supposedly the handprint of Jesus as he stumbled whilst carrying his cross, but it was clearly of much later date! In an Armenian café I took a rest drinking tea from a little glass and amused myself with a water-pipe. Later I stood watching the tide of humanity spill from David Street into the open space of the Omar ibn el-Khattab Square. I saw Arabs carrying colossal burdens – one had two stools on his right shoulder.

Orthodox Jews in black appeared. Their hats were broad-rimmed, their faces framed in corkscrew curls. At the Wailing Wall I have seen Jews wearing *tefillin* – leather containers with portions of the Torah on their foreheads or left arms. Portions of the sacred Jewish writings are also placed in con-tainers at the city gates, which they touch as they go by. The characteristic black attire of these Jews is based on that worn in European ghettos. European Jews are called *Sephardim* (from Portugal and Spain) and *Ashkenazim* (from Germany and Eastern Europe). In the Jewish Quarter restoration of buildings was in progress, and buildings in suitably antique style were being built. At the Wailing Wall I saw a whirling, dancing burst of activity – a Jewish bar mitzvah with a thir-teen-year-old boy being initiated into manhood and the com-munity. He would now be eligible to wear the *tefillin* and also the prayer shawl or *tallith*. From now on he would observe the elaborate adult system of Orthodox Jewish life. There are official Jewish holidays such as *Succoth*, the Feast of Tabernacles; *Hanukkah*, the Feast of Lights; *Purim*, com-memorating Queen Esther; *Pesach* or Passover; *Yom Ha'atzmaut*, Independence Day; *Shavuot*, Pentecost. One interesting Jewish custom is the breaking of a glass at the con-clusion of a Jewish wedding in remembrance of the Temple's destruction.

I watched as the bar mitzvah people continued to dance arm-in-arm with much handclapping. Soon it would be sundown and the start of the Jewish Sabbath. Apart from legitimate duties everything would come to a standstill until the Sabbath was past. When the Jewish Quarter's rebuilding was complete there would be about six hundred dwellings, shops and other buildings. As would be expected many synagogues stand among them: the Karaite, the Ramban and the Habad synagogues. I passed through the Dung Gate, soon coming into the area of the old Jebusite City, which in turn became the City of David. The traditional tomb of David is to be found close by the site of the Last Supper, the Caenaculum.

Mention must be made of the Yad Vashem memorial, situated on Har Hazikaron (the Hill of Remembrance). The memorial is dedicated to the six million Jews murdered in the Holocaust of World War II. Close by is a building which houses an exhibition of photographs and various articles connected with the horrific events. Lest we forget . . .

Presently I came upon the striking church of St Peter in Gallicantu (St Peter of the Cockcrow). The site is a poignant one, said to mark the spot of Peter's denial, Christ's trial before Caiaphas and the Sanhedrin, and the prison where he was held before being delivered to Pilate. There I was in the crypt of this lovely church of gleaming white stone, thinking about its meaning. As I stood in the quiet of the church and its prison crypt, the prophetic words of Isaiah came to mind: 'He was taken from prison and from judgment' (Isaiah 53:8).

Likewise I could not help thinking of those haunting words from Luke's gospel "And the Lord turned and looked upon Peter. And Peter remembered the word of the Lord and how he had said unto him, Before the cock crow thou shalt deny me thrice. And Peter went out and wept bitterly" Luke 22 v61–62 see also Mark 14 v30 v66–72.

Later I stopped at the Pool of Siloam and the entrance to

Hezekiah's Tunnel, which is one of the few genuine artefacts from antiquity to survive intact – apart, that is, from the inscription from Hezekiah's time that was removed by the Turks and now resides in a museum in Istanbul, more of which later. Over the pool and tunnel entrance stands a tower with crescent symbol.

Then it was back to the Old City's labyrinth, where the fever of life continued unabated. A boy and his cart bounced down some steps towards me, oblivious, it seemed, of the mass of humanity threading its way through the narrow passageways. There was the tinkling of a donkey bell followed by a donkey vanishing down another passageway almost as soon as it appeared, carrying its boy passenger. A large gentleman wearing a pith helmet – possibly an archaeologist working in the area – came into view. For the umpteenth time I entered the Church of the Holy Sephulchre and lit a symbolic candle near the sephulchre itself. A priest sprinkled my hands with holy water from a little metal container. Outside, Arab labourers were busy preparing huge white blocks of stone for the repair of the building.

Resuming my explorations of the bazaar, I suddenly stopped at a place where a shaft of light penetrated the mêlée, edging the stalls with its radiance. Rather unexpectedly, I chanced to fall into conversation with another visitor, a girl whose appearance was one of petite delicately-dressed elegance. Her broad-brimmed hat crowned the dainty face, all wide wondering doe-eyes, and all the freshness of youth. In a little side-lane just a stone's throw from the bustling bazaar, I drew her portrait as Arab urchins looked on. Well, she was enough to inspire any artist. As we walked towards David's Tower she pointed out to me various oriental sweetmeats to be seen in some of the shops. She might have been Jewish and spoke with a charming Brooklyn accent. David's

Tower does not actually belong to the time of David – it's another Turkish construction. I left this vision of loveliness outside the Jaffa Gate and that was the last that I saw of her. Incidentally, it was through this very gate that the Kaiser made his dramatic entry into Jerusalem in 1898. The ornately-helmeted Kaiser, resplendent in white and silver cloak, rode into the Old City during his famed Eastern tour. He was involved in the inauguration of the Lutheran Church in Jerusalem but entertained dreams of widespread Eastern power, which was to have included India and Iraq.

On my previous visit to Jerusalem, I had briefly visited the Dome of the Rock. Now I was free to see it without hurrying. It is an exquisitely beautiful structure by any standard. We cannot help admiring the superb blue tilework, and the huge gold dome that surmounts the structure. There is a distinct Persian feel about the fantastic structure. This was clearly intentional. As with most of today's Old Jerusalem, the Mosque was built by Sultan Suleyman the Magnificent. The Caliph Omar merely established a place for a mosque. It was later that Caliph Abdul Malek Ibn Marwan built the Dome. The Crusaders soon converted the structure into a Christian church. However Saladin restored Moslem worship there when he took over. Passages from the Koran are lettered across the exterior. The overall design is Byzantine, octagonal in plan. In accord with Moslem tradition, as on other occasions I removed my shoes before entering. In the heart of the Mosque stands the rock on which Abraham offered Isaac, so we are told. This rock too bears a footmark said to have been left by the ascending Prophet Mohammed. They say the angel Gabriel held the rock down to stop it rising in the air with the Prophet. Remains of the biblical temples are indicated by grooves which carried the blood of the sacrifices. I wandered in the surrounding gardens of the Temple Mount. Many trees grow here, giving the visitor agreeable shade and greenery. David is supposed to have held judgement here at the Dome of the Chain. Also I visited at the El-Aksa Mosque built by the Caliph Al-Waked. Some of the original stonework survives, despite the ravages of time and earth-quakes. It was once used as an ammunition dump during the conflicts of the early twentieth century.

On the eastern wall facing the Mount of Olives we find St Stephen's Gate, close to the sheepmarket and the site of the Pool of Bethesda. Also there is that curious bricked-in opening known as the Golden Gate. Traditionally this was the one used for Jesus' triumphal entry into the city on that first Palm Sunday. According to some, it also fulfilled the Old Testament prophecy about the Golden Gate being shut. When Christ stood and wept over Jerusalem from the Mount of Olives, did he, I wonder, see in a flash as it were the entire pageant of history concerning the city pass before him? Very possibly, we might think. Christ's words echo down the centuries:

> O Jerusalem, Jerusalem, who kills the prophets and stones those who are sent to her! How often I wanted to gather your children together the way a hen gathers her chicks under her wings, and you were unwilling (Amplified Bible, Matthew 23:37. See also Luke 13:34; 19:41)

When we attempt our own *son et lumière*, visualising the vast procession of the centuries, it overwhelms the senses. There is certainly no shortage of intriguing characters in the Bible connected with Jerusalem. There are people such as Melchizedek, Abraham, Isaac and King David, shepherd and warrior king, who slayed thousands, and sweet singer of Psalms he wrote. He wrenched it from the Jebusites and established its Jewishness, but it was his son Solomon who created that magnificent Temple. Unstinting in terms of expense and energy, he plunged into the fantastic undertaking after his father David had been debarred by God from the work because he had spilled blood.

70,000 labourers worked on the Temple, along with 80,000 stonecutters and 3,600 foremen. Gold worth millions of pounds by today's standards was used. King Solomon was fabulously rich by any standards. He received millions of pounds from the kings of Arabia, with many other lands paying tribute to him also. His huge ivory throne was overlaid with gold. It had six steps of gold, a gold footstool and gold lions on each side of each step. Solomon's trading ships brought him cargoes of precious metals, apes and peacocks, sandalwood and spices. Solomon had a force of 1,400 chariots and recruited 12,000 cavalry to guard the chariot cities. The King's harem was very considerable. Even the Queen of Sheba was overwhelmed by the sights of Solomon's Jerusalem. Her train of camels loaded with riches must have looked poor by comparison. The Temple alone must have taken her breath away. Perhaps it was this unstinting excellence of ancient Jewish temples that inspired later Gothic builders of Medieval Europe to build their splendid cathedrals. Maharajahs and sheiks of later times have likewise enjoyed fabulous riches beyond the reach of most mortals, as we have already seen. In ancient Jerusalem ways were even devised to channel supplies of water from one place to another in the city. Tunnelling helped to facilitate matters considerably.

If ever there was a city that endured conflict over the centuries, and saw swords and spears and siege towers, it was here – Jerusalem. Jeremiah, 'the weeping Prophet', bears eloquent witness to the exile into Babylon under Nebuchadnezzar, as indeed does the writer of Psalm 137:

By the rivers of Babylon, there we sat down, yea, we wept, when we remembered Zion. We hanged our harps upon the willows . . . How shall we sing the Lord's song in a strange land?

It was something of an incredible irony that Abraham, Father of the Jews, came from Mesopotamia, the region to which the Jews were exiled. For seventy years the captives endured this sojourn, no doubt having flashbacks about the flying arrows of Nebuchadnezzar's archers and his army marching on Jerusalem with glinting spears and swords, not to mention the siege towers that enabled the city walls to be breached. Eventually the Jews returned from the other side of the Fertile Crescent that they had been forced to go. Cyrus the Great had issued a decree, as related by Nehemiah who tells of the sad state of Jerusalem after the return: 'the wall of Jerusalem also is broken down, and the gates thereof are burned' (Nehemiah 1:3. See also Jeremiah 52:12–15).

The Israelites, however, rebuilt the city and the Bible gives some graphic contemporary glimpses of Jerusalem in those days. Several gates are mentioned – the fountain gate, fish gate, old gate and sheep gate amongst others. How many of them correspond to those of today is perhaps difficult to determine. However, an eastern gate in biblical times was always important. Apart from security reasons, a gate was always a place where business was transacted, as their names indicate. Legal transactions were conducted there also. Thus the city gates became something of a convenient focal point for all. Traders, teachers, scribes, and even kings conducted business there. The Old Testament abounds in such references – Nehemiah 8:1–3; II Kings 7:1, Deuteronomy 16:18; Job 31:21.

Periodically war and bloodshed returned to Jerusalem. History repeated itself – Antiochus, Epiphanes, Crassius and others plundered. Capitulation on the part of the besieged Jews was often facilitated by them being starved into surrender. Two hundred years after the decree of Cyrus the Great and the rebuilding of Jerusalem by Nehemiah, the Greeks exerted a mighty influence and became leaders of the world. Alexander the Great appeared on the world stage, and the Persian Empire came under his sway. The Empire was however divided at Alexander's death. Palestine was controlled for a time by the Ptolemies of Egypt. The Seleucids of Syria took over after 198 BC. This Syrian period produced a most ruthless and evil ruler, Antiochus Epiphanes (175–164 BC), as already mentioned. Antiochus' imposition of Greek culture on the Jews was tyrannical in the extreme – to the extent of offering pig's flesh on the altar and leaving babies uncircumcised. Jews refusing to comply were executed. So terrible did the tyranny of Antiochus become that Judas Maccabee, one of four sons of the priest Mattathias, led a revolt against the oppressors. The Maccabean revolt of 167 BC is still celebrated by Jews everywhere as the *Hanukkah*, or Festival of Lights, which lasts for eight days, with eight lights – one for each day – and a pilot light.

The Maccabean victory meant independence for the Jews. When the Temple was consecrated the eternal flame continued burning for eight days even though the lamp had only one day's oil. The miraculous burning of the vessel is reflected in the hot oil used in the preparation of Hanukkah dishes. From 129 BC the country's government was taken over by the Hasmoneans. These were High Priests and descendants of the Maccabees. This independence was to end, however, with the Roman takeover in 63 BC. Civil war ensued with two brothers battling over who should serve in the High Priest's office. The eldest son won and the Roman General Pompey favoured him. Now Palestine was part of the Roman province of Syria, with Hyrcanus very much in charge. The Parthians invaded in 40 BC and Hyrcanus fell from power.

It was at this point in the story that Herod emerged. Herod was the son of the chief aide or adviser of Hyrcanus, and was a man of ambition, biding his time, awaiting the right moment which had now arrived. Herod travelled to Rome. Before long the Senate made him ruler of Judea. As we have seen Jerusalem had known many heavy-handed tyrannical rulers. Herod was another of these cruel and despotic men. The stage was being set for the arrival of Jesus Christ.

Strange to relate, Herod, who by all accounts was anything but religious, raised Jerusalem and its Temple to unparalleled heights of splendour. From the ancient Jewish historian Flavius Josephus we learn much of the background against which the New Testament scenes were enacted. Josephus' book *The Jewish War* is considered by far the best of his writings in this regard. The splendour of the Herodian Temple, now long vanished, is revealed to us. The dazzling temple was decorated with gold and other fine metals embellished with the finest classical craftsmanship. On it there was a great gold vine and massive gold grape clusters. The entire complex was surrounded by a great perimeter wall – a small portion of which still survives and is sacred still to Jewry worldwide – the Wailing Wall. As regards the Temple itself – within it there was a Gentile court, beyond which no non-Jewish person was allowed. In the central complex there was the Court of the Women. Here Joseph and Mary would have gone together to discharge their obligations at the birth of Jesus, buying some doves in the Temple arcades. The Priest's court lay beyond, and no women were permitted to enter there. This court had a flight of semi-circular steps leading up to it.

Seeing the Prussian eagle carving in Jerusalem's Muristan

area today, I was reminded of an incident in the city close to
the end of Herod's life, when his health was on the decline.
Certain prominent Jews decided on an uprising. The pagan
gold eagle that Herod had erected over the great gate of the
Temple in honour of Vipsanius Agrippa was targeted by
saboteurs. Josephus tells how a midday attack was carried
out, as masses wandered through the Temple courts. The
saboteurs lowered themselves down from the Temple roof
and proceeded to hack the Roman eagle down with axes.
Needless to say, retribution was swift and terrible, the cul-
prits being cruelly executed. Herod died soon afterwards and
was carried with all due pomp and ceremony to Herodium,
just outside Bethlehem, and there buried.

Soon Mary and Joseph along with the boy Jesus were to
return from Egypt. The Gospels say very little about Jesus'
early years, but he is mentioned as being found deep in conversation with the Temple elders when he was thirteen. I
wonder if he marvelled at those magnificent courts, porti-
coes, or massive lofty gold-plated gates that took twenty
men to move them – or was he concerned solely with the
deep spiritual significance of it all? I think undoubtedly the
latter was true! Remember how he drove out the money-
changers in the Temple colonnades. Today's Jerusalem
money-changers give you some shekels in exchange for your
ailing pound. In the time of Christ it was a case of changing money from foreign currency to the Jewish shekel
needed for the Temple. Something of Jesus' attitude might
be seen in his words concerning the Temple's dissolution:
'Do you see these things? Truly, I tell you, there will not be
left here one stone upon another that will not be thrown
down' (Amplified Bible Matthew 24:2. See also Mark 13:2;
Luke 21:6).

So it was soon to be razed to the ground, this magnificent

building. Jerusalem was to become the scene of great desolation again – and not for the last time either. The prevailing influence in the Herodian Temple's building had been Graeco-Roman, whereas King Solomon's Temple of Old Testament times had followed Egyptian lines. The destruction of Herod's Temple and the sacking of it is depicted on a well-known bas-relief on the Arch of Titus in Rome. Romans are shown carrying off the seven-branched candlestick. This destruction also brought down work done by Agrippa. This was a huge wall with ninety towers to the north of the city, raised to protect this vulnerable part of it. Scholars have hotly disputed the different areas which ancient walls enclosed at various times in Jerusalem's history. A clearer idea of its earlier periods is emerging due to the work of modern archaeologists.

The destruction of Jerusalem by Titus did not come without warning. Josephus clearly tells us of a series of ominous visions, harbingers of destruction to come. A star stood over the city, and a comet. The latter was suspended there for a year. Strange happenings persisted. A light shone round the Altar of the Sanctuary whilst the people gathered for the Feast of Unleavened Bread. It was not a good omen, although some believed it to be. A cow intended for sacrifice gave birth, not to a calf but to a lamb, in the Courts of the Temple. One night – at midnight – the east gate of the inner Sanctuary opened by itself (normally twenty men were required to move the solid bronze gate). On May 21st in the year preceding the destruction a terrifying vision filled the skies over Jerusalem. It was a vision of great armies with chariots and weapons of war. Even four years previously a man had appeared crying out woes to Jerusalem. In the face of all these dramatic warnings the populace were incredulous and nonchalant, like a people mesmerised.

Resentment had simmered in this land ever since the Roman occupation began. Jewish uprisings carried out by the Zealots were always breaking out, often triggered by oppressive Roman acts. The looting of the Temple treasures, for example, had caused the Jews to explode in fury. Eventually there was a fierce insurrection. When the news reached Rome, a vast army was dispatched to Judea, marching on Jerusalem to restore order, although it was not until Titus arrived on the scene from Egypt that Jerusalem was taken from the zealots, who had captured many parts of the city including the castle of Herod. After much conflict Titus raised a huge wall round the city as part of his strategy to trap and starve out its occupants. It was something of a gradual process involving battering rams and a great deal of bloody hand-to-hand fighting. Thus Christ's prophecy was fulfilled and not one stone remained standing of that splendid Temple. Jerusalem remained in ruins for a long time after Titus raised his commemorative arch in Rome to mark his victory.

In due course the walls of Jerusalem were raised yet again, but this rebuilding was nothing like the Jerusalem of former days when it reached its architectural zenith under kings like Solomon and Herod. Some time afterwards the Emperor Hadrian rebuilt the city as Aelia Capitolina (AD 135–330). The place seemed to have a new identity. Apart from the new name (named after the Emperor himself – his middle name was Aelius), it underwent an entirely new building programme. The new city had two public baths, a theatre and a fountain. What remained of the Second Temple was flattened and a Temple to Jupiter put in its place. Two triumphal arches were built, one of which survives. It's often pointed out as the place where Pilate brought Jesus Christ out to the crowds and said, 'Behold the man.' Today part of the arch is inside the Convent of the Sisters of Zion. Hadrian even had a personal statue raised within the city, facing eastwards. Possibly much of the Aelia Capitoline has persisted to the present day.

It was not until the time of the Emperor Constantine that pilgrimages could be resumed. A revival of interest in the Holy Places occurred. Under Constantine Christianity had become the State religion. The Emperor is said to have seen a great vision of the cross with the words 'By this conquer' and he was responsible for raising great Christian basilicas. His mother, Helena, apparently found the true cross in a pit – part of the pit may be viewed in the underground chambers of the Church of the Holy Sephulchre. A street close by the basilica bears the name of Helena.

Later on hospices and rest houses for pilgrims were erected by Pope Gregory and Emperor Justinian. After further conflicts Jerusalem fell into Moslem hands, from Arabs to Egyptians to Turks. Turkish governments extracted heavy tolls from pilgrims, even allowing robbers to frequent Holy Places to steal from pilgrims.

The Turkish persecution of Christian pilgrims continued unabated. It was a situation that became more brutal and intolerable as time went on. A substantial part of the Western world's response was to launch the Crusades. Pope Urban II addressed a venerable gathering of barons and Church dignitaries on November 27th, 1095. The Pope delivered a powerful speech denouncing this terrible treatment being visited upon pilgrims. Churches were desecrated. The atrocities being committed against Christians included the kidnapping of Christian women and children into slavery. In Spain Christians were already at war with Moslem oppressors. The Pope pointed out that Byzantium was under threat, and worst of all the Holy Land itself was in the grip of the Turks.

GODFREY DE BOUILLON led the first Crusade with Robert Duke of Normandy and Count Stephen of Blois.

In due course the first Crusade under Godfrey de Bouillon set out for the Holy Land, determined that it would be they who would hold the keys of the Holy Sepulchre and not the heathen Turk. Envoys, of course, were sent out to all the towns and villages of Europe to enlist the support of all Christendom. Medieval churches in Britain sometimes have old wooden chests that were used for Crusade collections. We can imagine the bold chivalrous knights of those days with the flashing steel of their armour, chain mail and weaponry. Emblazoned on their vestments was the blood-red emblem of the cross. Large contingents of European nobility travelled with the assembled force. Many of these nobles were themselves knights in many cases. Indeed, in places all over Europe princes were gathering armies. Places where this was happening, such as Lorraine and Normandy, were to become associated with warfare in the twentieth century. Between them the barons, town criers and wandering preachers did a splendid job of organising the armies. The rank and file of the peasantry showed willing, partly to escape the drudgery of the feudal system and partly to achieve higher things in the spiritual realm, they hoped.

The first Crusade attacked Jerusalem on 7th June, 1077 and was successful in overthrowing it. The Franks slew Moslem and Jew alike and the Latin Kingdom was established, at least for a time. Mosques were quickly converted into Christian churches. Raymond, Count of Toulouse, Bohemund of Otranto and Duke Robert of Normandy were among the nobles who raised great armies, persuading people to take the cross. Other nobles involved in the Crusades we shall meet soon.

Walter the Penniless and Peter the Hermit led the two Peasants' Crusades. Unfortunately they gave the Crusades rather a bad name because of all the looting and killing that they carried out. They quickly became an undisciplined rabble. In some places whole Jewish communities were wiped out. Across the Danube and on through Hungary the peasants continued in this barbaric fashion, but the Hungarians fought back. The ranks of the peasants were thinned considerably in the skirmish that ensued. Those that survived carried on with their evil deeds in Byzantium. When the Byzantine Emperor got to hear about the savage horde he arranged for them to be shipped off into Turkish territory, where the warlike Turks made short work of them. Whilst Peter returned to Constantinople, Walter the Penniless died along with the remaining peasants.

In complete contrast to the Peasants' Crusade, the well-organised and thoroughly disciplined Norman and Frankish knights launched their Crusade. This was the Knights' Crusade. When the knights reached Constantinople the Emperor Alexius demanded an oath of allegiance to him. After the disastrous chaos caused by the Peasants' Crusade, the Emperor had reason to be suspicious. The oath of allegiance meant the handing over of Byzantine territories occupied by the Turks once the Turks had been defeated. Emperor

Alexius gave the knights guides to take them across Asia Minor, along with money and fresh supplies. When the knights had defeated Asia Minor, a delighted Emperor Alexius moved in to reclaim the Byzantine territory.

The knights continued on their way, bedevilled by heat, thirst, hunger and bands of Turkish aggressors. By sleight of hand and further battles Crusader states were set up in places like Antioch and Edessa. Arguments and disputes broke out regarding the ultimate ownership of Antioch. Raymond of Tolouse insisted that the Emperor Alexis should be in control of it, whilst others claimed it was theirs. The leaders continued to argue until the rank and file of soldiers and pilgrims seized the initiative and ordered the march to Jerusalem to continue immediately or they would set fire to Antioch. Jerusalem was finally reached. After bitter fighting the Crusaders took the Holy City. The bloodshed was dreadful and the slaughter lasted three days. Afterwards the knights assembled in the Church of the Resurrection to give thanks for their victory. The Christian Kingdom based at Jerusalem was born. When Godfrey died Baldwin was created King of Jerusalem. His coronation took place on Christmas Day in 1101 and a few years later, in 1110, Bethlehem became an episcopal see. Very aptly Baldwin's coronation took place in the Church of the Nativity.

Whilst introducing law courts and a European feudal system, the Crusaders adopted many oriental customs. Like some European visitors of today, they wore Eastern robes and developed a taste for exotic Eastern dishes – and also exotic dancers. So with all those dancing girls, sherbert drinks, fruits (and medical services that were far superior to anything known in Europe at that time) the Crusaders enjoyed themselves and improved their lot considerably. In this two-way cultural exchange the Moslems adopted falconry and board games that the Crusaders had brought with them. In such a cross-current it is hardly surprising that in time friendships and marriages occurred between the two peoples. Travellers were flabbergasted at the way of life that had ultimately enveloped them. It was observed in the words of James Vitry that they had become 'Soft and effeminite, more used to baths than battles'. The Crusaders' womenfolk were also arrayed in robes, veiling their faces like Moslem women, but solely for the purpose of protecting their skins from the Eastern sun. Further, the European women used sweet-smelling perfume and make-up like their Moslem counterparts.

Whilst the Crusaders were languishing in luxury and indolence, the Moslem armies were gathering for war – the *Jihad* or Holy War under Saladin, who was awaiting his chance to strike. Saladin saw to it that supplies for the Christian Kingdom were undermined. All the time the Christian Kingdom's position was weakening. There were internal conflicts and disputes within the Crusader ranks. The Moslems made a well-timed attack, overrunning Jerusalem, and Christian states fell to the Moslems. Desecration of Christian symbols, like the cross outside the Church of the Holy Sephulchre, and widespread humiliation in general set off a wave of anger and anguish throughout Europe.

The second Crusade had failed but a third was soon launched. One of its leaders was King Richard I of England – Richard, Cœur de Lion, or Richard the Lionheart – renowned for his great courage and valour. He was a brilliant leader with a first-class mind for organisation. He was able to levy taxes, raise money and organise a mighty fleet of ships. In 1190 Richard set sail for the Holy Land. This third Crusade had two other leaders, Philip II of France, and Frederick I of Germany. The latter was drowned somewhere near Antioch, which led to the break-up of the German army, many of the

soldiers retiring from the Crusade altogether. Richard conquered Cyprus, making it into another Crusader state. Soon
both he and Philip had landed at Acre. This coastal town was
captured when these reinforcements arrived, which, of
course, strengthened the Crusaders' position.

Prior to the arrival of Richard and Philip at Acre the
position had been one of complete stalemate between the
forces of Saladin and those of Guy, the Christian King of
Jerusalem. After fierce conflict Saladin was forced to give
orders for a truce. Moslem and Christian leaders agreed on
a deal which meant the resident Moslems in Acre should pay
a huge ransom to the Christians, and that 2,500 Crusader
prisoners should go free. All Moslems who had not been ran-
somed were put to death on Richard's orders. Richard and
his army pressed on towards Jerusalem after Philip and King
Leopold had left for Europe. Most of the coastal towns were
taken, and Richard tore into Saladin's forces, ever driving
them back.

After all his forays in the Holy Land, Richard did not in
the end take Jerusalem. He did reach an agreement with
Saladin after the two men had gained a healthy respect for
each other. The coastal strip between Tyre and Jaffa was to
remain Christian. Indeed it became a Christian Kingdom of
Jerusalem. It was agreed to allow Christian access to
Jerusalem and the Holy Places, unmolested. All hostilities
between Christians and Moslems were to cease – at least for
a few years. There were eight Crusades in all, not all of them
being noble, valiant affairs by any means.

The fourth Crusade (1201–1204) set out with the con-
quest of Egypt in mind. This was seen as crucial to forcing
an eventual surrender of Jerusalem. However this Crusade
ended up by looting and pillaging Constantinople. Most historians seem to agree that this was arguably the most repre-

hensible of all the Crusades. The disgraceful scenes that occurred were far from the lofty aims and motives that were originally envisaged. This fourth Crusade was led by Philip of Swabia, Baldwin of Flanders, and Theobald III of Champagne.

The saddest Crusade of all was the Children's Crusade of 1212. Twenty thousand children set out for Palestine from Germany and France, led by a Cologne boy and a shepherd boy respectively. Needless to relate, it ended in disaster, not even getting beyond the bounds of Europe. Those children who did not die of malnutrition and disease were taken prisoner and sent into slavery.

Another attempt to take Egypt was made by Andrew of Hungary and Leopold VI of Austria in the fifth Crusade. Alas this attempt on Egypt failed also. Had they been able to hold the Egyptian town of Damietta they could have held it hostage, and demanded the handing over of Jerusalem. Although the Crusaders did take Damietta for a while, they were eventually forced to hand it back to the Egyptians – so nothing was really gained by this venture.

In the sixth Crusade Frederick II who was Emperor and King of Germany and Sicily retrieved Jerusalem with very little fighting, the actual handover of Jerusalem being done by negotiation. Frederick was an atheist, and at times a very cruel man. It is difficult to understand why he was allowed to lead a Crusade at all. Whatever the methods and motives of Frederick, he did sign a treaty on February 8th, 1229 which restored the places of pilgrimage to Christians. The Pope, however, did not like his methods and forbade all pilgrims to enter Jerusalem for the time being. Frederick marched into Jerusalem and had himself proclaimed King, but in 1266 Jerusalem fell to Baibars, who was to become a Mamelukian Sultan in Egypt in later years.

In 1248 the seventh Crusade, which was led by Louis IX of France, sailed for Egypt. The attempt to take Egypt was again routed, but Louis fortified the Levant coast, remaining there for some years. Almost all of the Crusader strongholds were defeated by Baibars in 1263.

The eighth Crusade and the last of the Crusades, also led by Louis, and accompanied by Edward of England, set out with the intention of capturing Tunis, but did not do so. Louis died at Carthage of the Bubonic plague, faintly whispering the name of the Holy City just before he died. Prince Edward made an attempt on Acre without success. In time Baibars took over all the Crusader castles along the Levant coast. He had declared another *Jihad* or Holy War but mostly with the Mongols on this occasion. Nevertheless it was not long before the Christian Kingdom – Outremer – was at an end. The Holy Land continued to pass from one ruler to another, and the Moslems held sway long after the Teutonic Knights and Templars had vanished from the scene, along with the rest of the Crusaders. After Saladin came the Mamelukes (1187–1517).

Some of the most beautiful ornamental architecture still to be seen within the Old City belongs to the Mameluke period. One notable example, and one which I particularly liked, was the Madrasa Ashrafiyya's wonderful gateway on the Temple Mount. It was the Mamelukes who brought back Moslem rule over the whole of Palestine.

Other Moslems had their sights on Jerusalem also. In time the Turks under Selim I took over from the Mamelukes. For four hundred years until our own times the Turks ruled the Holy Land. The defeat of the Turks in Palestine and the sequence of events which led to the rebirth of the state of Israel in the twentieth century are discussed more fully elsewhere in this book.

Adjacent to the quadrangle of the Church of the Holy Sepulchre lies the Muristan area of the Old City. Today it is comprised of handsomely-built streets and shops enclosed within the stylish portals. Most of the complex dates from Victorian times. It is a Greek market area built of traditional yellow stone. At the centre of the complex stands an ornate fountain. In the adjoining Muristan Street we find the German Lutheran Church which Kaiser Wilhelm II inaugurated. Over its main entrance we can see a Prussian eagle on the left, a cross on the right. In the middle space there is a cross and banner. At that time the Sultan gave part of the Muristan territory over to Prussia. The Church of St Mary Latin occupied the site previously. Its old cloister may still be seen inside. North of it there's an old doorway from the twelfth century on which the signs of the zodiac may be seen. A Benedictine monastery supposedly founded by Charlemagne, and the Church of St Mary Minor, stood where the Muristan fountain now stands. Later the merchants of Amalfi rebuilt the church. Close by the Church of St Mary Minor stood the Hospice and Chapel of St John Eleemon, built when the church became inadequate for housing the nuns.

Muristan is the medieval Arabic for hospital in particular the hospital of the Knights of St John, the order of the Hospitallers. As these Knights extended their activities in politics and the struggle against the enemy in general, they took possession of huge estates. 1130 to 1140 was their main period of hospice building. Their main hospice was a grandiose affair with 124 columns. Interestingly, the visitor may still see pointed arcades in David Street, which skirts the Muristan area. All that is left of the hospice is there.

In 1970 archaeologists were afforded an opportunity to carry out excavations in Jerusalem's Muristan area when extensive restorations were undertaken in the Lutheran

Church of the Redeemer. Their findings seemed to confirm the view that a quarry existed here where the church now stands. A wall under the church, once thought to be the second wall of Jerusalem, is now thought to be a Roman or Byzantine terrace. These excavations were carried out by the German Evangelical Institute of Archaeology in Jerusalem. Their work continued through much of the 1970s, and it led to doubts as to the accuracy of many maps of first-century Jerusalem.

The little Church of St John lies on the opposite side of the Muristan area. It is said to be the oldest church to be found within the Old City. It has three levels: street level, residence of the priest and then the church below. Underneath that lies the crypt. This three-apsed church became the model for many others that were to follow. A stone records the service that the Order of St John held here in 1926. Today the Muristan area is much connected with the Greeks who are now well-established in the Holy Land. An inscription I saw close by the Muristan seems to sum up much of its history: 'Saint Benedictos Polyclinic of the Greek Orthodox Patriarchate of Jerusalem with the participation of the Greek Orthodox Society of Myrrh Bearers for the relief of the destitute and sick'.

Whatever alterations and extensions people of bygone ages made to Jerusalem they were nothing in terms of sheer size compared with the modern Jewish extension north of the city. This belongs decidedly to our modern day and age. Whilst it does not please everybody, the energy and enthusiasm with which the Jewish people have built this modern extension is remarkable. Some would say almost miraculous, considering the relatively short space of time in which it was built. It consists of a whole vast complex of streets and buildings. There are museums, the Hebrew University, the Knesset or Jewish Parliament building, a YMCA and youth hostels. Other developments include a Biblical Zoo, war memorials, a modern bus station, a huge Stadium and Concert Hall, and a great deal besides. Development was proceeding rapidly in the modern Jerusalem of the late twentieth century and is doubtless developing still.

One day I stopped to look at a vast new shopping precinct. Constructions such as this could not have contrasted more with the sights of the Old City. I was able to watch a display of Israeli folk dancing at the Concert Hall. Performances like this take place somewhere in the area every week. At a café in the New City area a Russian Jew engaged me in conversation. We discussed the Jewish situation in general. It was explained to me how the real impetus for the creation of modern Israel came about. One great spur happened in the 1930s when the persecution of the Jews under Fascism created in the minds of dispersed Jewish people a longing for a national homeland. Fervour grew as increasing numbers of Jews landed on Palestinian soil. Modern Israel is a subject we must return to and discuss more fully in this book, and see also how the Zionist expansion has been viewed with disfavour by some.

The Israeli Government has given a great deal of freedom as regards religious observance. There are three Sabbaths in a row for one thing. The Old City is divided into Christian, Armenian, Jewish and Moslem Quarters. The Moslems are looked at in some detail elsewhere in the book. But what about the Christian denominations? Here we may usefully say a few words on the subject. Most of the Christian denominations in the Holy Land belong to the Eastern Churches: the Greek, Eastern Orthodox, Coptic, Armenian, Abyssinian. One of the languages used is akin to the Aramaic that Christ himself would have spoken. These Eastern sects often quarrel bitterly among themselves about sharing spaces with each other in the Church of the Holy Sepulchre and the Church of the Nativity. Indeed deep divisions have regrettably entered into many branches of the Christian Church. This applies not only in the old traditional Churches, but in the more modern breakaway branches also. Charismatics are in conflict with non-Charismatics, Catholics cannot agree with Protestants, and so on.

Holy Land schools, missions, hospitals and other charitable institutions are nearly all of European origin. Jewish institutions exist along these lines here also.

There must be few who cannot be moved by the long torturous history of this land as they traverse these narrow streets of Old Jerusalem. If only the very stones could cry out! Hereabouts we may think many things. From Jerusalem with its long memories of war, cruelty, suffering and triumph, I was to journey to some of the towns and villages that lie round about, scattered over the parched miles.

CHAPTER SIX

JERUSALEM'S NEIGHBOURING TOWNS

There can be few fields of enquiry embracing more conflicting ideas and uncertain traditions than the siting of holy places. The authentication of this site or that has frequently been challenged. Victorian thought on the subject often ran ridiculously amok. Our Victorian forefathers made meticulous studies and voiced heated arguments in support of their respective views.

Sometimes there are downright misnomers, a glaring example being David's Tower by the Jaffa Gate. The base of the structure is solidly Herodian. The relatively modern Turkish tower that stands atop it replaces the long-vanished towers that Herod placed there: Hippacus, Mariamne and Phasael towers. The visitor may well wonder how many of these traditions rest on old monkish tales, rumour or heresay. In the Church of the Holy Sepulchre we are confronted with a multiplicity of memorials under one roof. Pilgrims often kneel at prayer before the presumed holy places such as the Stone of Unction where, they say, the body of Christ was anointed for burial, its stones worn and smoothed by centuries of devotional tears and kisses. I wondered, too, about other traditional

111

sites like the Tomb of David on Mount Zion, skirted by part of what was once no man's land. I looked at many of the walls hereabouts, and saw the bullet-scars of twentieth-century conflicts and wondered just how many truly authentic holy sites have been destroyed in Jerusalem's past conflicts.

The study of holy relics is perhaps more the province of antiquarians and orientalists than of theologians and Bible scholars. The encrustations of centuries has also helped to confuse matters considerably. Of all the famed biblical towns able to boast layers of ancient history, surely Jericho deserves attention. I devoted a day to its exploration. Although not readily visible from the modern town, the traditional Mount of Temptation dominates the area of Tell Jericho. Whilst very little of Joshua's wall appears to have survived the passage of time, the Tell was not without abundant evidence of early civilisation. Very considerable excavations have taken place revealing thousands of years of human habitation – at least ten thousand years of it according to some estimates.

Successive layers of old civilisations were laid bare to my gaze in chronological order, as it were, with the oldest naturally lying at the deepest layer. I saw the famous Natufian's Tower in one area. The guide pointed out a few blocks of stone reputedly belonging to Joshua's wall. Very difficult now to visualise that story, with the drama of Rahab hiding Joshua's spies under bales of flax, and the felling of the walls of Jericho as Joshua's men marched round the walls blowing their shofar horns.

We meet both ancient and no so ancient in today's Jericho. It seemed to me that now there are four Jerichos to consider. Firstly there is the contemporary town, mostly Arab-occupied, with its tree-shaded streets. Then there is the 'ghost town' – row upon row of empty silent houses left by Palestinian refugees. Thirdly, there is a vast area containing the ruins of eighteenth-century Jericho, which includes the ruins of the Palace of Hisham Khirbet el Nafjar. Lastly there is the biblical Jericho already mentioned.

The next stop on this tour of Jericho was at Hisham's Palace. The Omayyad Caliph erected buildings over a large area. I found the old mosaics from this period particularly interesting, and studied pieces of old stonework. There was the head of a column or some such bearing beautiful curling patterns based on plant motifs. Along with other visitors I wandered in a shaded garden hung with vines on trelliswork. In the garden stood an old synagogue, complete with inscriptions in ancient Hebrew. It was deliciously cool in these gardens, a respite from the heat which was very oppressive indeed, even though it was late in the year. Beneath towering date palms in this town noted for its greenery I bought a drink of refreshing orange, crushed on the spot by a friendly vendor. Soon the Mount of Temptation came into view again. It is also called the Mount of Quarantine. Halfway up the mount stands an 1895 Greek Orthodox Convent. The reputed site of Christ's baptism is not far away. That doyen of Victorian Bible site enthusiasts, General Gordon, spent much time in locating such places.

Later I reflected on the words of the men of Jericho to Elisha about the pleasant aspects of Jericho and its situation. I could readily understand why, if the modern town in its general aspect was similar to that of Elisha's day. No wonder that Elisha tarried at Jericho. However the greenery of the town today is due in no small measure to the irrigation work of the Israelis. The fertility of the area called to mind the prophet's words:

> Thus says the Lord, I have healed these waters, there shall not be any more death, miscarriage or bareness because of it. (Amplified Bible, II Kings 2:21)

The water found in Jericho today is sweet water and this would seem to conflict Elisha's promise.

After this I revisited Bethlehem, the town where Christianity began. This time I was able to stay longer and make many more observations. I was back at the Church of the Nativity, the huge basilica that straddles the cave where Christ was born. Again I lowered my head to enter through that little doorway. At one time the basilica's entrance had conformed to the classical triple arch design. Again I crossed great slabs of ancient stone, worn in places by the feet of thousands of devoted pilgrims. That this is a long-established site seems certain. Chinham, King David's adopted son, was given land here. He probably became the local sheik, and David was anointed here (see I Sam 16:13; 20:6). Jeremiah mentioned Chinham's sojourn here, thus indicating the continuity of the site. Chinham's residence might even have stood on the site of the inn or caravanserai and its stable where in the fulness of time Jesus was born. The site was venerated from the time of the Apostles by early Christians. Later Hadrian profaned the site in AD 135 when he erected a statue of Adonis. St Jerome in his day was able to redress matters when he produced his famous Vulgate – an early translation of the Bible. The Vulgate is dated AD 348.

Like nearby Jerusalem, the little town of Bethlehem has a history of warfare and bloodshed. The Persians attacked Bethlehem. So did the Arabs and a host of other invaders besides. As regards the basilica, it seems probable that substantial portions of Constantine's structure remain. These were added to by Justinian at a later stage. The superb mosaic floor that I saw on my first visit certainly belongs to the Constantinian period. Another feature is the marble and mosaic work from the time of Baldwin I's coronation. Still another interesting feature is the ancient font with Crusader carvings on it. During the Middle Ages various countries contributed materials for the repair of the basilica. Edward IV of England sent lead, while the merchants of Venice sent timber. Medieval Bethlehem was described by the Venerable Bede when he quoted an earlier historian as saying that the town was 'A thousand paces from east to west in length, and it has a wall low without towers built round the circumference of the plateau.'

I was delighted to be back within this oldest church in Christendom. The rows of columns were genuine Roman ones, bearing the marks of ages. At the far end of the basilica there is a much-embellished altar. Here worshippers come regularly to kiss the icons. Soon I was joined by an Anglican priest and his party whom I had met an hour or so earlier in Jerusalem. After an exchange of greetings we entered the Grotto together. There followed a short service of Holy Communion conducted by a black priest. Visitors took a wafer whilst the priest drank the wine. In the Grotto as elsewhere in the area there is a sense of over-embellishment in the old churches. I briefly took in the details of the Grotto. The focal point is clearly the apse with its silver star, said to be the place of Christ's birth. Then there is the Magis' Altar were Mass is celebrated by the Latins. Ostrich eggs are suspended in the Grotto, possibly a symbol of new life and fertility. The bare walls of the cave can be touched through holes in the tapestry.

Elsewhere in the Church of the Nativity, we find altars to our Lady, altars to the Wise Men and one commemorating Christ's circumcision. The eighteenth-century iconostasis at the far end of the basilica was interesting, covered with numerous little icons. St Jerome's Cloister was also a delight to visit.

Leaving the basilica we wandered down into the Shepherds' Fields close by. Here, away from the encrustations of centuries, it is possible to visualise the shepherds and their vision of angels at the time of Christ's birth. The priest commented on how pleasant it was to be away from the hustle and bustle of Jerusalem on this Sunday afternoon. I had to agree. The heat of the day made us stop at a little shop set amid the fields for rest and refreshments. A few other buildings stood adjacent to the shop, plus a mosque. The priest then asked some Arab children why they weren't at their prayers. As for the shopkeeper, he was courteous and pleasant to us all.

I looked out over the sunlit fields. Was it here that Ruth gleaned her corn and met her beloved Boaz? King David was Bethlehem-born, like Jesus. Both Ruth and King David are linked by lineage to Christ himself. Soon, I told myself, the town would be thronged by Christians of many denominations for the seasonal Christmas celebrations. An ancient landmark that broods on the horizon during the approach to Bethlehem and over the town itself is the Frank Mountain and Herodian fortress where the tyrant lies buried. The view from the top looking out over Bethlehem is spectacular, I later found. The words of the prophet Micah came to mind, written hundreds of years before Christ's birth:

> But you, Bethlehem Ephratah, you are little to be among the clans of Judah, yet out of you shall One come forth for Me Who is to be Ruler in Israel: Whose goings forth have been from old, from Ancient of days – eternity. (Amplified Bible Micah 5:2)

It is perhaps easy to see why Zealots living at the time of Christ could have interpreted the words about a ruler in Israel to mean the coming of a military Messiah, driving out the Romans with rushing whirlwinds and chariots of war. Jesus certainly had other ideas.

Close by the basilica lies the Milk Grotto where the Virgin Mary supposedly spilt a drop of her milk whilst feeding the Christ child. Also close at hand is an old ruin that is traditionally of the house were Joseph lived and the angels appeared to him. The village of Bet Sahur, not far from Bethlehem, is thought to be the place where the shepherds lived and the visitor can see the Grotto of the Shepherds. Well, it goes back to the time of the Crusaders at least. Beyond that who can say? Many of the old artefacts to be found here – paving stones, column shafts, etc. – date only from medieval times. It is to be expected that the area is littered with sites associated with the Christmas story.

Not far away from Bet Sahur stands the Greek Convent of St Theodosius, the site of a dwelling where the Magi spent a night during their visit. A slingshot away lies the Valley of Elah where David slew Goliath, and Zora where Samson was born. The history of Bethlehem thus provides the town with a crowded stage.

Archaeology has flourished in Israel since World War II. Yigael Yadin, formerly the Israeli Chief of Staff, retired from soldiering in 1952 and devoted himself to the fascinating task of unearthing Israel's past. Notable excavations in which he was involved are Hazor, the ancient Canaanite city in north Galilee, and Megiddo, that famous chariot city of Solomon, and Ahab, straddling the later Roman Via Maris where it crosses the Plain of Jezreel. The latter was the scene of many wars and Armageddon where, we are told, the final battle between good and evil will be fought. Both of these places I visited but on later trips.

One of the most fascinating sites that Yigael Yadin excavated was visited by me on this present trip – the Herodian fortress of Masada. From Jerusalem I journeyed for hours across the parched barren landscape of the wilderness of

Judea. Far down the shore of the Dead Sea I saw the shape of the huge plateau of Masada looming ahead. From the fortress that once stood atop the plateau, Herod commanded a magnificent view of the surrounding landscape during his periods of winter residence there. Today visitors usually make the ascent by cable car, which is precisely what I did along with a number of American visitors, mostly Jewish as far as I could see. They were staying at the King David Hotel in Jerusalem. The short cable car journey carried us to the top of the plateau in next to no time. A guide soon appeared and showed us storehouses, deep cisterns very much as they were in Herod's day, likewise hypocaust baths and the ruins of the Palace itself.

Work was still going on at the time of my visit, and may be continuing still. Thick black lines on walls separated genuine ancient stonework from modern additions, indicating which was which. The authorities are planning to restore it sufficiently for the visitor to gain an impression of what it looked like in Roman times. Modern stairs enabled us to traverse the entire complex. As I was descending one staircase, there was a loud swishing sound as a bird dived down from the clear blue sky above, missing me by inches, then diving down the side of the plateau and vanishing. In order to please the Americans I had to pose with a number of them, as they were taking photographs of each other in groups. I was wearing a blue keffieh and one American who asked me to pose with his family yelled, 'Will ya look this way a moment Lawrence?' Click – and my friend had another study for his album, complete with 'Lawrence' in the group.

Masada was Herod's fortress and the place he fled to in 42 BC but the most dramatic episode in Masada's history was surely the heroic and ill-fated stand which the Jewish Zealots made against the Roman Tenth Legion. I listened to our guide's telling of the story with growing admiration for this last defiant stand against the Romans. From the top of the plateau I could plainly see the Roman wall that ran all round the base of it, built to try and hemm in the Zealots. Also I noted the great ramps of earth and stones still present that the Romans had built against the side of the plateau to assist them in gaining access to the Palace. The destruction of Jerusalem that Jesus had predicted had already happened in AD 70. Jews had been sold into slavery in their millions. The vast increase of Roman legions that had poured into the Holy Land like a river of red leather and metal meant that all Jewish resistance had been put down, except for this relatively small number who had barricaded themselves at Masada. This final part of the insurrection lasted for three years before the Romans finally smashed their way into the fortress. Then they were shocked to find that the inhabitants were all dead. It was heartrending but the last survivors of the insurrection felt that this suicide killing of themselves and their families was the only thing to do. When the outer defences were penetrated, the Jews under their leader Eleazer tried to hold out for a time in the Palace of Herod itself before carrying out their suicide plan.

Centuries afterwards in our own time twenty skeletons were discovered lying in a cave on Masada, and the skeletons of a young family – husband, wife and child – were discovered. The woman's plaited hair was found. Huge numbers of Roman slingshots – balls of stone rather bigger than a Jaffa orange – have come to light, stacked in a room. They were gathered as ammunition to fire back at the attacking Romans. We have touched on the subject of the cisterns already but a closer look at them proved instructive. They were very substantial. Two rows of them were carved out of the hard rock. Altogether there were twelve cisterns capable

THE SIEGE OF MASADA was one of the most terrible episodes in the history of the Holy Land, as Josephus tells us in *The Jewish War*. Here Roman soldiers are seen preparing to attack the fortress.

of holding forty thousand cubic metres of water. Water marks on the cistern wall reveal the high level of water that these cisterns could hold. After an appreciable rainfall they would be full for months, even years. The existence of the fortress stems partly from the paranoiac fear that Herod had of anyone or anything that threatened the stability of the House of Herod, as the Slaughter of the Innocents at Bethlehem reveals. Masada was looked upon by Herod as a retreat should any usurpers get their hands on power. Flavius Josephus gives us a graphic picture of the events that culminated in the siege of Masada. In his book *The Jewish War* he mentions the enemies that Herod really feared (as already mentioned) but it seems clear that Herod saw the possibility of a very substantial threat coming from Egypt:

> the danger from the Jewish masses who might push him off the throne and restore to power the Royal House that had preceded him, and the greater and more terrible danger from the Egyptian Queen Cleopatra.

In his description of Masada, Josephus gives us some interesting facts that are worth mentioning. The armoury is mentioned – weapons enough for ten thousand men, of every kind available in those days. The larder was well stocked. There were stacks of corn, enough for years, and plenty of wine, oil, pulse and dates. When Eleazer took this fort this is what he found.

I was impressed to hear our guide describe the way in which people from all walks of life – not all of them Jews – had given up weeks of their spare time to work on the excavations of Masada. Another thing that our guide mentioned, and something that I found most moving, was the special ceremony that was carried out by modern Israelis when the remains of the victims of Masada were buried with honours.

Possibly the terrible chronology of events that preceded the fall of Masada were in the minds of those Jews as they committed suicide. We have already mentioned Herod and before him Antiochus Epiphanes, but the sons of Herod were tarred with the same brush. There was Archelaus who ruled Judea and Samaria up until AD 6, showing the same cruelty as his father. Herod Antipas – whom Jesus called 'that fox' – was Tetrarch of Galilee and Perea until AD 39. He took his brother's wife and beheaded John the Baptist. Then there was Philip who governed the north-eastern territory of Galilee. The Zealots probably remembered all this and more as they awaited the end. When the Romans finally stormed the fortress they found the Zealots all dead. In one sense victory was denied to the Romans at Masada.

Luckily I was offered a lift back to Jerusalem. On the way we stopped beside the Dead Sea, where I took a swim. I discovered that it really is possible to float in the thickly saline waters. Such is the density of the water the swimmer (or rather floater) cannot sink. The sight of someone lying on their back in the water reading a newspaper is commonplace. Appropriately enough the Dead Sea means 'Sea of salt' in Hebrew. The harsh salt-caked landscape is the result of centuries of evaporation. Although the River Jordan flows into the Dead Sea, there is no outlet whatsoever. Only very minute organisms can live in these inhospitable waters. Nothing else has emerged to adapt to the harsh environment. It is the lowest spot on earth, 1,286 feet below sea level.

Regarding Sodom, God destroyed it completely and it is faintly amusing to hear of visitors who go in search of it. However a modern town of Sodom exists in the area, and it has the largest deposit of rock salt on earth. Here the manufacture of bromide is carried out. The brine provides potash for commercial exploitation also. There is a hill of salt with a salt pillar which is often pointed out as Lot's wife. As we drove back to Jerusalem I felt sticky. We had been unable to find a shower on the banks of the Dead Sea for washing off the salt. I was still feeling sticky when I got out of the car to buy some food from a little store in Jericho, and I was very relieved to take a shower at the hostel in Jerusalem. Now I could say that I had 'swum' in the Dead Sea, even if I had committed the error of turning over in the dense waters.

Later I was back on the Mount of Olives after my journeying to the surrounding places. I stopped to see the Dominus Flevit – a small rather unpretentious church set in its own enclosure. Literally translated it means 'The Lord Wept'. Although we have mentioned this earlier, there are some points of interest that we might add. It is recorded that around AD 600 many monasteries and other religious buildings stood on and around the site. As you might expect, the Mount of Olives was very much a focal point for such devotional buildings in bygone days. It is rather less crowded with them now. Inside the Dominus Flevit I peered out through the decorative ironwork of the church window.

Nearby stands the Grotto of the Lord's Prayer, known as the Paternoster. Apparently in Christ's time it stood facing the Temple in much the same way it faces the Dome of the Rock today. We know from contemporary accounts that Christ was often seen at this grotto. Most authorities agree that at least it covers the spot where Christ frequently stopped for meditation and prayer. Documents relating to the Early Church seem to support this view. It is said that the sons of Christians who had actually seen Jesus here entering the cave had written such documents. For example, there is *The Acts of John*, current around AD 130, although some regard this document as being largely apocryphal. Nevertheless the tradition appears to be well-supported, going back as it does to the time of the Apostles and the Early Church. Passageways inside the building contain slabs of stone on which the Lord's Prayer is written in thirty-one different languages.

The present structure was built by the Princesse de La Tour d'Auvergne, Comtesse de Bouillon, a relative of Napoleon III, in 1868. One Victorian traveller noted that she was still alive at the time of his visit. She had a monument erected to her memory. In this grotto, as with many places sacred or profane, a bookstall had been installed. A Carmelite nun was running the bookstall, I noticed. Inevitably trinkets and other souvenirs were on sale too.

Actually the veneration has continued more or less unabated since the first century. The Emperor Constantine placed magnificent edifices here. His mother, St Helena, also had much to do with the beautification of the site. She had a church built here. This was revealed in the writings of Eusebius (AD 265–340) who confirmed that 'according to accurate history' Christ taught his disciples the prayer that is loved throughout Christendom here and also 'revealed certain sacred mysteries' to them. Pilgrims over the centuries have had themselves buried here.

When Saladin exercised his authority in the region he was determined to make it a holy place for Islam and interest in the grotto lapsed. For centuries after this, Christian pilgrimage was barely tolerated. Desecration of the Paternoster was therefore probable. In 1342, when the site was back in Christian hands, a Franciscan friar found a single slab of stone on which was written the Lord's Prayer. However, interest was intermittent until the establishing of the Order of Carmelite Nuns there in the nineteenth century. For almost a hundred years the sisterhood has flourished on the Mount of Olives. Mother Xavier and the Princesse de la Tour d'Auvergne established the order in those times. Eventually the Princess returned to Venice where she died in 1889 at a ripe old age.

Twentieth-century excavations revealed a wealth of archaeological treasures of the time of Constantine onwards. The foundation of the Apostle's Church was found, and the apse of St Helena's basilica – forty years before the Princess de la Tour d'Auvergne came here, and established the site. As fate would have it archaeologists abandoned the place leaving it to the ravages of time, weather and any stray Arabs who happened to be partial to a chunk of this historic stonework for building purposes of their own. The entire Constantinian structure became lost. It was such a pity. Had things been conducted otherwise, we would have had a fine building from Early Christian times. As it is today, we have at best a restoration of a Carmelite church.

On the summit of the Mount of Olives I stopped at a little school with several children pushing up against the railings for a view of this stranger who had suddenly appeared. I glimpsed the Church of the Ascension where Christ left his disciples looking heavenward. This should not be confused with the Viri Galilaei, which means 'Ye men of Galilee' and lies about half a mile away. The latter church is today a Greek Patriarch's house, whilst the former is more likely to be the real place of Christ's ascension. Authenticity? I suppose that in a work of this kind it is a subject that is bound to recur.

Many visitors to Jerusalem's Arab Bus station, where lines of antiquated 1930s style buses await their passengers, notice the dramatic rock formation. This is Gordon's Calvary, one of the Holy Sites that he pointed out. The rock has eye-sockets and forms the ideal 'Place of the Skull'. Not far away is the Garden Tomb. Outside Nazareth there is the wicked-looking 'Mount of Precipitation', where Christ was nearly thrown headlong by irate Nazareth citizens. These sites look the part and there is no doubting their dramatic appearance.

I decided to spend a little time at the Garden Tomb. The tomb itself is cut into the rock and a huge circular stone, à la Sunday School illustrations, is rolled to one side of the entrance. Visitors are always peering inside. In the garden an American woman insisted on holding hands with me and saying a prayer. It was a happy atmosphere with dozens of visitors coming and going. It is a different story when we view the traditional sites within the Church of the Holy Sepulchre favoured by Catholics. Here imagination is needed to strip away the encrustations.

At the Church of the Dormition I stopped to talk with an Assumptionist priest. He expressed the view that many visitors wandered round the holy sites 'simply to pray'. He also opined that the traditional sites within the walls of the Church of the Holy Sepulchre were indeed the places where the sublime events happened. The priest pointed out that the north wall of Jerusalem was further back in Christ's day, thus placing the Church of the Holy Sepulchre's site well outside the wall in those times, as required by the known facts. Some scholars even think that the hill outside St Stephen's Gate could be the real Calvary.

Inside the Church of the Holy Sepulchre there is a pronounced slope to and from the Chapel of St Helena. Here we walk beneath silver hanging lamps and pass masses of little crosses carved on the walls by pilgrims through the centuries. At the Chapel of Calvary we can see sections of bare rock and find evidence of an earthquake that took place long ago. Sections of such rocks can also be viewed through glass panels. There is an old tradition of Adam's skull being found here – one interpretation of 'the place of the skull'.

I found myself in conversation with a visiting Cambridge

graduate. He suggested that since Joseph of Aramathea was a rich man he would have placed his tomb well clear of a place of criminal execution. However, John in his Gospel states that Jesus' place of crucifixion and burial were close together (he was placed in Joseph's tomb):

> Now there was a garden in the place where he was crucified and in the garden a new tomb, in which no one had ever (yet) been laid. (Amplified Bible, John 19:41)

Constantine's mother, St Helena, found three crosses in an old cistern where they had been thrown and disposed of before the Sabbath. One of these was supposedly the true cross of Jesus, and it became the object of much veneration. Later on it was carried by the Crusaders to the Horns of Hattin.

Whilst in the Via Dolorosa I was intrigued to note the names of the various Christian organisations within the Old City. One sign read 'The little sisters of Jesus' whilst further on another told of 'The Church of the Holy Face and Saint Veronica of the Greek Catholic Patriarchate'.

In the modern section of Jerusalem I witnessed Charismatic Christians practising glossolalia (speaking in tongues) and the laying on of hands. It was like being back in the days of the Apostles. Indeed I met Christians of every persuasion. In some ways it is a world of contrasts. For example, the sublime dignity and pageantry of the Armenian liturgy with its robed, mitred clergy. This magnificent finery, glowing silver lamps and all the rest of their colourful trappings contrasts sharply with the simplicity of the nonconformist sects. During my stay in Jerusalem I was delighted to see a Sunday morning procession of robed, hooded Armenians passing through arches to the Church of the Holy Sepulchre. Leading the procession there were a number of soberly suited gentlemen, all wearing a red fez and each carrying a long staff which they struck against the ground in unison every few seconds. Armenian priests, by the way, can always be picked out by their pointed hoods.

The eating-places of Jerusalem differ widely, I discovered. One evening I visited a little café in the Christian Quarter and was served by a subdued portly waiter wearing a red fez. He was slightly olive skinned with a thin moustache and sloping nose. I sat there in contemplative mood over my little cup of thick Turkish coffee. Above me a trelliswork of vines was all that separated me from the evening sky. On another occasion and still in the Christian Quarter I dined on stuffed pigeon. What there was of it tasted delicious. These establishments differed, of course, from those in the modern city. For one thing most of those would be Kosher!

I visited the Rockefeller Museum close by the Storks' Tower and spent an instructive half-hour or so looking at antiquities of the region in the company of the Cambridge man I had met earlier. One piece of ancient sculpture impressed itself on me. It was a small girl's head, very delicately made, from the Hellenistic period. The Knesset building I saw briefly again but I really needed to visit the Israel Museum, which houses the Dead Sea Scrolls. These scrolls were discovered in the caves of Qumran, near the Dead Sea, by a wandering shepherd in 1949. They passed through the hands of several people, including a Bethlehem cobbler, before being received by the appropriate authorities, who eventually placed them on display. They belonged to the Essene sect of Christ's time – a strict body of men who lived in monastic seclusion. About six hundred manuscripts were brought to light from eleven caves. About a third of them are Old Testament scrolls, and are contemporary with the Old Testament scrolls from which Jesus read.

Evidence suggests that the Essenes living and working in Qumran flourished from the third century BC to AD 68. Apart from the Old Testament scrolls there was a wealth of other documents that were discovered relating to liturgies and rules of conduct. Among the Old Testament scrolls a complete book of Isaiah was found. The shepherd can scarcely have realised the value of his find when he sold many of the scrolls locally for some spare money in Bethlehem by black market methods. The scrolls presently came into the hands of Jewish and Arab enthusiasts, people who usually collect such things. Then they came into the possession of the Archbishop of Jerusalem, and from him to the American School of Oriental Research, who happened to be paying a visit to St Mark's Monastery where the priceless documents were being housed at that time. The Americans were certainly very interested indeed in these scrolls, which were clearly of great age. After the publication of their paper on the subject of the scrolls, a surge of great interest was evident in the world at large. With the help of a Belgian UN representative in Jerusalem, the men from the American School of Oriental Research enlisted the aid of the Department of Antiquities in Amman. Between them they overcame the difficulties of war and territorial dispute for the sake of the scrolls' preservation and proper housing. However, by the time the American scholars entered the caves only fragments of documents were found. The scraps that had been collected from the caves were fragments of old papyrus and leather on which was writing in ancient Hebrew. Carbon-dating tests placed the age of the documents to be from the time of Christ. Fragments of the linen which had enveloped the early scroll of the Book of Isaiah were burned and the ashes placed in geiger-tubes. Those conducting the experiment concluded that the flax of the linen also came from Jesus' time. The Isaiah scroll was a thousand years older than anything that had preceded it as a basis for our present-day versions of the Bible. It was found that this very old text of Isaiah agreed perfectly with the Septuagint, which is an early Greek translation, and with the Latin Vulgate of St Jerome – the standard documents upon which today's versions rest.* All this is a tribute to the accuracy with which the Scriptures have been transmitted down the centuries to our own time. In the years that followed, both Israelis and Arabs combed the hills and their caves. The result was that masses more of these ancient scrolls saw the light of day again after centuries of being hidden away. It was just as well that the antelope skins on which many of the scrolls were written had such durable qualities, and likewise papyrus developed from the pith of reeds.

It is staggering to think of the incredible journey that the Scriptures have taken down the corridors of time, from the old Palestine scriptoria to the present. The meticulous care of the scribes and copyists, the careful storage of scrolls considered worn-out by some ancient rabbis – all these things have contributed to the survival and accurate transmission of the Scriptures that we know today. The destruction of Jerusalem at various times and the scattering of the Jews was an added spur to the preservation of the Scriptures. It was at times like this that they were even more a people of the book. The scrolls were brought back from America by the Israeli Government. All of them, as previously stated, are now mounted on permanent exhibition in the Shrine of the Book in Jerusalem.

During their survey the Israel Exploration Society and The Israel Department of Antiquities and Museums found plenty

* However Protestants believe that the most authentic scriptures are based on the Textus Receptus manuscripts and the King James version.

in the way of tangible remains from the past. This survey was carried out in 1960–61. In wild, desolate and steep areas of the Dead Sea's shores, the explorers found many caves that yielded evidence of their past inhabitants. They found what came to be called 'The Cave of Sorrows'. It contained fourteen skeletons of both adults and children – including babies. The Caves of Nahal Hever or Wadi Khabra yielded remains from the Chalcolithic, Iron Age and Roman periods.

Also in the vicinity they found the remains of a structure measuring 150 ft square (50 metres square), a fortification designed to stop Bar-Kochba's men from escaping. Iron arrowheads and a Cave of scrolls in Hebrew, Aramaic and Greek were discovered in the Cave of Arrows situated near the Caves of Nahal Seelum (the Wadi Seigal). Perhaps the most surprising of the caves were to be found in the Nahal Mishmar (the Wadi Mahras). About fifteen letters from Bar-Kochba to his soldiers came to light, along with fragments of the Scriptures and a very substantial horde of treasures. These included a beautiful ram's head stand, utensils of bronze, copper vessels and models of birds, animals and human faces. There were mainly two reasons for the preservation of these antiquities. Already mentioned was the custom of ceremonially placing used scrolls in a room known as a geniza, usually next to the synagogue. Circumstances may have forced the Essenes and others to use a less obvious geniza, namely the caves. The persecution of those times would have meant the deliberate step of hiding all valuables including scrolls, used and new alike.

Still on the subject of caves, there was one on the Mount of Olives where, it is said, the prophets lie buried. I arrived at the cave to find a young child playing with a puppy, and an Arab who beckoned me to follow him into the cave. He had no torch, but with the ingenious improvisation for which the Arabs are well-known he produced an old beer bottle with a quantity of petrol in it. It had a rag for a wick. My guide lit the wick. I followed him with the acrid flame of his crude lamp billowing in my face as he led the way. In the dancing flames of this dangerous torch I saw shapes of tombs that had been out into the walls of the cave. Isaiah is thought to be buried here along with some of the minor prophets.

My next port of call was Silwan, which lay a short distance from the Pool of Siloam. Its little flat-roofed dwellings stand haphazardly stacked against the side of the slopes there. I sat with an Arab on the verandah of his little dwelling and enjoyed the pleasant view as we drank coffee. I did visit Bethany and look into the Tomb of Lazarus but this took place on a later trip.

Amongst the olive-wood carvings, rosaries, and mother-of-pearl souvenirs from the Bethlehem workshops, the visitor will find other delights. There are wide-angled panoramic postcards of Jerusalem as seen from the Mount of Olives. Many of them are arrowed with the places of interest. Looking through an old Victorian Holy Land and book of 1885 I saw this same view which, however, differed in some respects. Between St Stephen's Gate and the Dome of the Rock there was a building that used to be a pasha's residence. This was one of the many changes that took place after the departure of the Turks and the return of the Jewish people. The general view would surely be recognised by Omar, Saladin, Richard or indeed anyone from the Crusader period. I will leave the reader to see how many views of historic sites can be seen from the slopes of Olivet. There are many of them, including most of the important buildings within the city.

One afternoon whilst I was visiting the Church of the Holy Sepulchre I had a most delightful experience. I was standing near the Katholicon area where the Greek Orthodox Church worships. Suddenly a line of chanting, singing monks filed past me. They were singing afternoon vespers and making this historic interior wonderfully musical. On my way to the main Jerusalem Bus Station I passed through the main Jewish Mea Shearim area. Here strictly Orthodox Jews live. They wear the black garments associated with their European ghettos. Ringlets are worn on the sides of their heads in accordance with ancient Jewish Law. The Mea Shearim was first created in 1877.

From the Bus Station I caught a bus for the south of the country. On the journey we must have passed Hebron, which I visited later to see the Cave of Machpelah and the fortress of Herod which houses the tombs of Abraham, Isaac, and Jacob and their wives. The visitor can see their memorials on a top level whilst the real tombs are underneath and hidden from view.

After several hours of travel through the stark, empty wastes of the Negev desert I arrived at Be'er Sheva (Beersheba). The town was modern-looking and like I expected.

CHAPTER SEVEN

SOUTH, NORTH AND WEST

I finally arrived at Be'er Sheva's bus depot. Most of it is very modern. Indeed my first glimpse of the city had been a group of high-rise blocks of flats. The ruins of the biblical city are situated in the desert wastes a few kilometres outside the modern city. In size and general layout the excavated Tell of Be'er Sheva was not unlike those of Hazor and Megiddo to look at. Many of the interesting finds from the Tell are housed in Be'er Sheva's museum. Thereby the visitor can be transported back to the Chalcolithic Age to see implements of local culture from the fourth millennium BC. As I moved through the collection of exhibits stone artefacts jostled with ivory figures and Byzantine mosaics. The museum contains an interesting and varied collection of antiques too numerous to discuss in this book. They await the visitor eager to glimpse life hereabouts in biblical times. I had chosen a Wednesday on which to travel down to Be'er Sheva quite deliberately. The famous Be'er Sheva Camel Market (something of a misnomer as things turned out) was held very early on Thursday mornings. From the desert Bedouin flocked to the market to sell their wares. Often I rise early to greet the day whilst touring. Now I had a special reason for doing so.

However, by arriving on the Wednesday I was able to focus on other points of interest. Close to the Tell the authorities have mounted a splendid exhibition showing Bedouin folklore and lifestyle. In a semi-darkened chamber there are representations of Bedouin tent interiors, and their contents. Ideally the visitor should be in a position to compare this exhibition with the real thing as I have done. Real Bedouin have naturally been recruited to work on the project. In complete contrast to this age-old way of life, the Ben Gurion University in the city undertakes modern scientific research. It tackles things like methods of creating artificial rain, the use of solar energy, and making salt water drinkable. Before retiring for the night, I decided to explore the city. I found pavement cafés illuminated in the dark. Crowds of Israelis filled shops and cafés through late evening and much of the night. Traffic, too, was busily on the move.

It was something of a coincidence that Genesis 21 mentions Abraham rising early in the morning at Be'er Sheva – as I was about to do. The next morning I was indeed up at the crack of dawn – at around 5.30 a.m. I shivered a little, since it was cold: the sun was not yet up. Before long I left the hotel and headed down dark streets towards the Camel Market. Gradually the entire eastern sky grew light. Unfortunately the modern installations tended to detract from the romantic aspect of it. I reached the market area and saw groups of Arabs huddled together over a wide area, each staking out their own piece of territory. One Arab beckoned me to sit with him by his fire. It was still cold and I was glad of the chance to warm myself. A number of these little fires stabbed out from the darkness. The dim shapes of people slowly became clearer in the growing light of day. All kinds of goods were being spread out on the ground. No fancy stalls here. Only one section of the market was devoted to livestock. Robed figures with sun-wizened faces held on to their sheep and cows – but not a single camel was to be seen anywhere. I got into conversation with the Market Vet for a while. Several hours later I was still there, now in the full light of day, closely scrutinising the various pitches.

The really interesting aspect I found was the old Arab with a fine collection of coins that he had found while scouring the desert wastes. They were all genuine antique finds, unlike many that are sold in Jerusalem. Frequently these coins were found whilst digging or farming. I bought one or two coins dating at least from Roman times. By now the sun was well up and hordes of American visitors had arrived, and I returned to the hotel for breakfast. Later I checked out.

I noticed that a fair proportion of the population were European Jews, with a number of darker Jews, probably Yemenite in origin. Many of them spoke good English. The overall population of Be'er Sheva has soared since 1948, when the Israelis resumed control. Before then Be'er Sheva was still in the days of Abraham – or almost so! In 1948 there were about two thousand people in the city. Today the population is upwards of a hundred thousand.

In one area I noticed a muddy river with an abundant growth of vegetation. Could it have grown from the grove that Abraham planted there thousands of years ago? At any rate I liked to think that Abraham's grove had flourished over the generations, and had been the ancestor of the grove that I came upon that day. Modern Israelis have taken a hint from Abraham, and found the area good for the growing of tamarisk trees. It is a splendid example of the way in which modern Israelis have used the Scriptures as a guide in building up their country, and we shall come across more examples of this later.

Close by Be'er Sheva's very modern bus station stood a typically oriental bazaar. The way in which the Bedouin conversed and generally went about their business seemed to reflect the traffickings of Old Testament times. Had it been possible to spirit away the modern blocks of concrete and modern traffic, it might have provided me with a scene straight out of Genesis.

It was here at Be'er Sheva that Abraham banished Hagar, his bondwoman, to wander the wilderness with her child. Somewhere nearby Hagar left her son to die after her food and water ran out. An angel assured Hagar that Ishmael would indeed survive and be the father to a great nation. Hagar's eyes were opened and she saw a well – possibly the very one that I was then looking at. The boy could now drink – something that is always welcome in this thirsty land as we've seen.

Abraham carried out certain vows to two Philistines and there was some dispute with them over the well. Abraham laid on a meal for his guests. Abraham gave sheep and oxen to them. Therein lies the second coincidence that I encountered at Be'er Sheva – the only animals to be seen at the market were sheep and cows! Be'er Sheva became a place of Covenant – and this is what the name means! Abraham sealed his Covenant at the well. Groups of chatting Bedouin were perhaps suggestive of those men of long ago at their deliberations! This spot in the Negev at first struck me as an unlikely place to build a city. It may never have happened but for Abraham sealing his Covenant here. It is a city built round a well. I was standing on hallowed ground, for that notable meeting of long ago might have taken place on the very spot I was occupying.

Be'er Sheva was always used Abraham-style by wandering

Bedouin from Bible times right up to the time of the Crusaders. The Turks took it up during the period of their rule. In the 1880s they used the place for trading purposes. When the Turks were defeated, the British took over Be'er Sheva. Today it is an expanding city – the capital of the entire region. Thus it is an administrative centre, and also a centre for education and industry. Then there's the Negev University and a Music Conservatory. The modern Be'er Sheva, therefore, is something very much more than a convenient stopping and watering place between Jerusalem and Eilat. Whilst I was there plans were afoot for the creation of a green belt around the city. The entire future of the building programme was based on the garden city plan.

Was it yet another coincidence that Abraham came from the other side of the Fertile Crescent, where great building programmes were carried out and the famous Hanging Gardens of Babylon were situated? Constant irrigation is taking place in Be'er Sheva, as elsewhere in Israel. Arid desert land is giving way to areas of lush greenery. Since Bible times springs of water have appeared. Many a modern Moses has struck a rock, as it were, and brought forth water. I returned briefly to the bazaar and met other European visitors who had stayed at the Desert Inn Hotel, situated somewhere in the wilds outside the city. At least they probably got some good views of the desert sunrise.

Soon I was bound for Eilat aboard another bus, and I was rumbling through the desert wastes relieved here and there by acacia trees once more. Mile after mile the bus trundled on until we stopped at a wayside café for refreshments. 'Ten minutes,' said the driver briskly and after the allotted time we all boarded the bus again and continued on our way.

When the coastline came into view I could make out Eilat with Akaba to the east of it, where these adventures began.

Eilat loomed larger and before I knew it the bus reached the town's bus depot. On alighting, I found Eilat to be a complex of modern hotels and shopping places. The beach is superb and, of course, it is an extension of the beach at Akaba. In short Eilat had become a fine resort. Doubtless the Six-Day War of 1967, which caused the Zionists to regain Old Jerusalem, gave added impetus to the development and expansion of Eilat, as in other parts of Israel.

I based myself at a hotel near the airstrip and made for the beach after booking in. The area is called the Gulf of Eilat or the Gulf of Akaba, depending which side you are on. Those dramatic hills over on the Jordan side were bathed in late afternoon sunshine. This scenario was, of course, familiar to me from my Jordanian trip with which I began this book.

The following day I visited the Eilat aquarium, some distance down the coast. On the journey down I passed areas of docks, as on the Jordanian side. On arrival I saw knots of tourists, mostly European, huddled round the aquarium. It was unlike any other aquarium that I had seen, being built into the Red Sea itself so that visitors can actually view the underwater scene in comfort. To give the complex its proper title, it is the Coral Beach Underwater Nature Reserve. Once inside, I passed the café and souvenir shop and descended into the unique underwater viewing space. Here marine life can be seen in its natural state without any artificiality at all. It was akin to being in a submarine with large windows. I watched fascinated as lovely fish of all shapes and sizes swam lazily past. They were the same species as I had encountered at Akaba – angel-fish, surgeon-fish, emperor-fish, and so on – but with greater comfort this time. It was even more of a soothing and mesmerising experience. Eventually I surfaced; this was partly due to the fact that it was getting rather crowded on the human side of the glass.

Bedouin made a point of frequenting the aquarium area with their camels. They were giving short rides to tourists – very tame ones really, which simply described small circles in the sand.

It was during the following day's activities that I met Georges Baum, a French Israeli who was the Chief Guide for Eilat. I joined a grand tour of the area under his direction. Firstly we had a trip to see King Solomon's mines and the so-called King Solomon's Pillars. The 'Pillars' are actually a natural rock formation which soars a hundred and fifty feet (or about fifty metres) above the desert floor. It is a superb example of the stunning rock formations that are to be found in the region.

We were not permitted to go near the original mines of King Solomon but had to be content with viewing the old ruined mine workings across a stretch of desert and hilly rock terrain. In the distance I could see a notice-board which marked the location of the mines. After this we visited the modern copper workings where the process of extraction was going on. This modern plant was developed when an archaeological rabbi, Bible in hand, discovered the mines of King Solomon in 1936. The development of modern Israel from 1948 onwards saw the commercial exploitation of the copper in the land. This was the first full-scale operation of this kind since King Solomon's thriving trade here thousands of years ago. This is one of the numerous ways in which the Bible is helping the Israelis build modern Israel. By carefully following the directions left by their illustrious ancestors modern Israelis are finding the best places for mining, planting, irrigation and so on. As David Ben Gurion, one of the founders of modern Israel, once said, 'The Book has lived in the hearts of Jews for centuries'. Jews, like Christians, have always had tremendous faith in the accuracy of the divinely-inspired Scriptures. The writings have proved their worth.

The story of the discovery of King Solomon's mines in recent history is truly a fascinating one. The man involved in the discovery was Rabbi Nelson Glueck, who was President of a Hebrew College in America. He was a keen archaeologist, smitten with the romantic idea of finding King Solomon's mines. Many people assumed that it was not really possible to find such mineral resources in Israel in modern times, but the rabbi was to prove them wrong. He read some words from the First Book of Kings:

> all these vessels which Hiram made for King Solomon in the house of the Lord were of burnished bronze. In the Jordan plain the King cast them in clay ground between Succoth and Zarethan. (Amplified Bible, I Kings 7:45–46)

Thus the location was suggested and the work began. The biblical 'brass' was really copper, of course. At first Glueck's explorations yielded nothing. However in 1934 he was directed by wandering Bedouin to a place south of the Dead Sea. The Bedouin explained to Glueck that it was traditionally a place known as 'a copper ruin'. Excavations revealed that it had indeed once been used in the smelting process of copper. The remains of old furnaces blackened with copper slag were found. Still more of these ancient copper plants were found as Glueck proceeded south. Pottery dating from Solomon's time was also discovered. Before long the archaeologist-rabbi had exposed the ancient mines of King Solomon at Eilat. It dawned on Glueck that this would in any case be the ideal place for Solomon's copper mining, since it would be located in a vast rift valley which encouraged a natural flow of wind along its length. Ample draught would thereby be provided to work the furnaces.

Studies were carried out in 1949 to ascertain just how valuable these workings would prove. The Chief Geologist leading the enquiry was Dr Ben Tor, one of Israel's best men for the job. The studies proved that King Solomon's mines still had an enormous potential. There was enough ore for 100,000 tons of copper, it was estimated, with 200,000 tons more of the stuff if extensions were made. A passage from the Book of Deuteronomy became something of a motto for the modern excavators: 'a land whose stones are iron, and out of whose hills you can dig copper' (Amplified Bible, Deuteronomy 8:9). They even have the text pinned up inside one of their site offices, I understand. Georges Baum eventually showed us around some of the workings. A most interesting tour it proved to be.

We were soon afterwards spirited back to Eilat, but not before Georges had proudly pointed out to us some of the nearby Kibbutzim. 'You can tell which side of the divide belongs to Israel because our side is a good deal greener,' he told us. Indeed the area to which he drew our attention was plainly green with vegetation on the Israeli side and utterly barren on the Jordanian side.

Our guide went on to explain to us Eilat's growth and development in modern times. Back in 1948 Eilat was little more than a few shacks, as in places like Be'er Sheva. In considering the pace of Eilat's development we must take in things like its cinema, concert hall, library and all the features of a fully grown holiday resort. Consider, too, the 'Forest of Eilat', where every child has a tree named after him or her. The residential buildings are beautifully designed with overhanging portions built into the houses to give shade in the hot sunny climate. We were then driven down an avenue of palm trees which is apparently Eilat's main street.

Continuing his most interesting exposition Georges

turned to the Red Sea. 'Most young Israelis would not understand what you were talking about if you called it "The Red
Sea". usually we blame it on mistranslation. It should really
be called "The Reed Sea". As regards its colour, anyone can
see that it is azure blue and certainly not red in colour.' (I did,
however, watch the sun's reflection in its waters later that
same day and I just wondered.)

We stopped to view the ruined Crusader castle on the
Coral Island a little before sundown. I showed Georges the
drawings that I had done in Jerusalem. He liked the Via
Dolorosa drawing. When we viewed my drawing of the
Jerusalem girl – My! he was as taken with her as I was! He
asked me to sell it, but I decided to keep her.

Nightfall, and I joined some young Israelis round their
camp fire. As the sparks from their fire were hurled into the
night sky they danced – and I was encouraged to join in.

Reluctantly I headed north again and watched an eagle
soar into the sky – what a splendid sight it was!

Back in Jerusalem I prepared to join in the procession
which walks the Via Dolorosa. This takes place on Fridays,
and I had returned just in time. It began at the Praetorium,
the Judgement Hall of Pilate. Today it is the Omariyeh
College. A minaret close by is called the 'Antonia Tower'. At
the second Station a little chapel stands partly over the
Lithostros. More than once I viewed the ancient courtyard
below the Convent of the Sisters of Zion. It is the only relic
along the processional way of whose authenticity we may be
sure. The pavement still bears 'the game of the King' pattern.
The pattern shows a wheel of fortune, a gaming board, an
insect symbol (could it represent a crown of thorns?) of the
Tenth Roman Legion, and a helmet shape. It was customary
to gamble for a prized object at festival time during the
Roman Feast of Saturnalia. There are fourteen Stations of

the Cross altogether. The third at which we stopped was a Polish Chapel where, it is said, Jesus fell for the first time. The fourth Station was where Jesus met his mother, and the fifth was where Simon of Cyrene was compelled to help Christ carry his cross. The sixth Station apparently marks the residence of Veronica. She is not mentioned in the Gospels, and her story rests purely on an old tradition. The story goes that the gallant woman rushed to wipe the face of Jesus, marred with wounds and blood. Later she discovered that the image of Jesus was imprinted on the cloth. The Chapel contains a portrait of Jesus, said to be the very one obtained by Veronica. The seventh Station is called The Judgment Gate, since tradition says that Christ's death notice was posted here. The eighth and ninth Stations are sited close to the Church of the Holy Sepulchre and the remainder are within it. Station thirteen is at the traditional place of the Crucifixion. At Station thirteen we find the Stabat Mater Dolorosa, a sixteenth or seventeenth-century statue of Mary in wood, which came from Lisbon in 1778. The last Station is the Holy Sepulchre. I found the procession a moving experience despite any discrepancies.

Just off Al Mujahedeen Street, near St Stephen's Gate, we find the site of the Pool of Bethesda. At least two angles of it can be made out despite all the later Byzantine ruins which cover it. The Church of St Anne stands here, considered to be the best preserved Crusader church to be found anywhere. The sheep market is still conducted very close by, as in New Testament times.

Later I headed north and arrived in Tiberias. It was a hot, sweltering November day in this town on the banks of the Sea of Galilee. So very much of Christ's life and ministry took place in this area. I ate a traditional fish meal at a lakeside restaurant. For obvious reasons it gave me a sense of occasion.

I looked out across the lake and saw Capernaum and the Mount of Beatitudes in the distance, shimmering in the midday sun. The Crusaders' Mount Beatitudes was, of course, the nearby Horns of Hattin, where they were ignominiously defeated by Saladin.

The city of Tiberias is mentioned in the Bible just once, and was raised in honour of the Roman Emperor Tiberius during Christ's lifetime. Today, though, its former glory has long since gone. Here in Herod Antipas' city wealthy pampered Roman nobles whiled away their leisure hours at the Tiberias springs.

Tiberias was saved at one point in its history from certain desolation that engulfed it by the initiative of Suleyman the Magnificent, who was also responsible for much building hereabouts. Like the earlier Herods, he had a building mania. Later rulers here gave the city over to Don Joseph Nassi, who industriously brought work to the residents and restored the community of Jewish people here. For a time the place flourished under his good offices, only to succumb to destruction again. It was restored in the eighteenth Century. It has continued to prosper more or less uninterrupted from then until the present day. As I stood there it seemed to be going through something of a fresh renaissance. I could see a whole new building programme being carried out at Tiberias.

It is the area's associations with the life and ministry of Jesus that we remember best. It was here in Galilee (Gergesa) that Christ commanded the herd of swine to receive the demons from a wild man. This lakeside is also the scene of Peter and Andrew's calling. Then we remember the calming of the storm on the lake, and the feeding of the five thousand. I came across an interesting variation of the loaves and fishes story. Close by the edge of the lake at Tiberias, someone had thrown a number of loaves into the water and swarms of fish were greedily devouring them. We also recall that Jesus famously walked on water on this lake. The prophet Isaiah had foretold the ministry of Jesus in Galilee centuries before. Isaiah wrote of judgement coming 'by the way of the sea, beyond Jordan, in Galilee' (Isaiah 9:1).

These events described so graphically in the Gospels tend to fit so easily into the scene. The topographical layout of Galilee can still mean that storms occur here. Now, however, the waters of Galilee were teeming with fish. At a time like this the disciples could hardly have toiled all night and caught nothing, as they did on that occasion long ago. The little lakeside museum at Tiberias displayed pottery and other relics from various Galilean towns. I noted such items from Chorazin belonging to a time after the Jesus period.

I journeyed on towards Cana and had a lovely view of the lake as the bus reached the top of a hill en route. Cana itself was still only a tiny hamlet, although it has grown since my first visit there. I came upon a small domed church surrounded by cypress trees. Inside the church is a painting, obviously of relatively recent times, which depicts Christ's first miracle – turning water into wine at the wedding feast. The church is hung with the usual trappings that are to be found in Holy Land churches: icons and other accretions. There are large water jars of uncertain age. We can't be certain that they are one and the same as those that supplied the wine that Jesus had prepared to save that young couple from embarrassment. Either here or somewhere nearby the ancient synagogue would have stood. Arabs in traditional dress sat around in little groups beside a café. I found the place interesting, though some might not.

Nazareth is a town linked with Christ's boyhood more than any other. After all, he was called Jesus of Nazareth rather than of Jerusalem or Bethlehem. The Bible says very little about the years in which he grew up here. It is only by inference that we catch some glimpses of those hidden years in Nazareth. He grew up here in favour with God and man. As an adult Jesus was described as the carpenter's son. Probably he worked with Joseph in his shop and learned the trade from him. We can readily picture Jesus treading in the wood-shavings on the workshop floor. He may have toiled away at a bench helping to produce chairs, tables and doors. Local farmers would have ordered yokes and ploughs – things that Christ was to use in his teachings later on. No doubt Joseph's workshop gained a reputation for sound workmanship. I think that Jesus himself produced strongly made goods that did not come apart and did the job for which they were intended. If Jesus did fire the coals and hammer an anvil as well, as was suggested, then he must have grown sturdy and strong and not at all the anaemic, pasty, palefaced Jesus that medieval painters have presented us with. I spent some minutes watching modern carpenters at work in Nazareth; one young man was busy on a lathe.

The teachings and parables of Jesus reflect the life of those times. During those formative years in Nazareth he would have observed keenly the fever of life around him: shepherds with their sheep, sowers in the fields, and so many things. In the marketplace I saw a beggar covered in sores. Jesus probably witnessed similar instances there in his day.

The traditional workshop of Joseph is situated within the Catholic church that bears the saint's name. Statues of Mary and Joseph are to be found in the grounds there, set among cypress trees. There is also a Holy Family group sculpture in a niche in a wall at St Joseph's Church. There's a fountain in Nazareth supplying water to its residents since time immemorial and it was still in use up until recent times. It seems reasonable to assume that the Holy Family used the same spring for their water supply. The spring rises inside the Greek Orthodox Church of St Gabriel. I could hear the spring rippling away. It was all that broke the silence.

Dominating the town is the thoroughly modern Basilica of the Annunciation, which contrasts markedly with the other more traditional church buildings there. It supposedly marks the spot where the Angel Gabriel appeared to the Virgin Mary. Archaeological evidence has shown the site to have been inhabited from the Middle Bronze Age to the present. Inside the basilica I felt somewhat overawed by the proliferation of modernity. Nonetheless I came to the conclusion that it worked brilliantly and the designers were right to go for a basilica of our own day and age. All its stylised design work fits into the whole in a remarkable way. Every country in the world has contributed, form such divergent places as Japan and Australia. I liked the skilful inclusion of an ancient dwelling in the crypt, a Byzantine apse plus a vast array of modern mosaic arches, carvings, and stained glass. The old Franciscan church has, needless to say, vanished completely. Originally built in 1620 and enlarge din 1877, it was demolished to make way for the wonderful structure that occupies the site now.

The interior of the upper Basilica is very grand, with massive modern pillars that support it. Stained glass windows of the presbytery depict the story of Franciscan martyrs worldwide over seven centuries of the Franciscan Order. An Italian artist, Professor Angelo Biancini, has contributed a series of ceramic reliefs in colour portraying the Way of the Cross, showing fourteen Stations as in those of Jerusalem. Seen from inside, the cupola is very attractive and soars to a height of 59.50 metres over the Grotto of the Annunciation. Another fine example of the Italian contribution is to be seen in the Franciscan Chapel, decorated with representations of the history of the Church: Pope Paul IV is seen as a pilgrim visiting the Holy Land and commemorates his visit of many years ago, and Louis IX of France is seen as a Crusader. A Spanish contribution is seen in the Blessed Sacrament Chapel, which contains frescoes by Professor Raphael Lbeda Pineiro. Martyrs and doctors of both Eastern and Western Churches are shown. There are, of course, a host of other things besides to hold the visitor's interest. The fantastic bronze doors of the basilica's facade and the Altar of the Crypt are two such extra things to see.

I returned to the centre of town and explored the numerous souvenir shops. One thing that did catch my eye was a brass coffee pot with a long handle and a curling narrow spout – very Turkish in design – and I purchased it along with some other souvenirs. The Nazareth market is of curious appearance. It is built along one narrow street with a long gutter running down the centre.

Some little distance from the town centre I found a hotel where I was able to book a room for the night. A friendly bunch of American tourists were also staying there. They were accompanied by a stout friar dressed in traditional habit, whom I silently christened Friar Tuck. He was like something from the Crusades. That evening 'Friar Tuck' treated all the hotel guests to a slide show of the Holy Land. Everybody had a very enjoyable evening following this engaging little show. The following day I continued on my travels.

Nazareth stands on the Lebanese mountain range's southern slope and this makes for a certain hilly aspect of the local topography. The town itself stands on a hill. As an adult Jesus was nearly cast down a slope by the populace, as we have seen. His claim to have fulfilled a quote by from the

Book of Isaiah was too much for them. The Convent of our Lady's Fear is supposedly the place where Mary watched in alarm as the crowd hustled her son towards that slope. Tradition places this attempted throwing of Jesus at a dramatic cliff some little distance outside the town, as I have already mentioned – the Mount of Precipitation. Close to it are the ruins of Sepphoris, the centre of Roman administration in Jesus' time. Mount Tabor, the traditional Mount of the Transfiguration, is only a few miles away.

My next port of call was the coastal Crusader stronghold of Acre. I found it a colourful coastal town – a vision of spires, domes, minarets, honeycombs of old streets, and a whole fascinating complex of underground passageways left by the Crusaders. Acre is one of those places where the old-world oriental flavour survives despite the passage of time. During a two-year siege in 1189–91 eighty thousand Crusaders were killed in the seizing of the town. From a strategic point of view Acre was an important town. This was recognised by the ancient Egyptians. Reference to Acre is found in the writings of Pharaoh Tuthmosis III over three thousand years ago. The tribe of Ashur was assigned to the town by Joshua, but when they tried to take it they were unable to. The Phoenicians proved too strong for them. At Acre, King Solomon located a base for his chariots. Solomon's deliveries of Sicilian horses were landed here. Pliny mentions the origins of glassmaking and purple dyeing. The latter seems to have evolved at several points along the Levant coastline. Undoubtedly Acre was involved at some stage of this enterprise. Alexander the Great was welcomed here and he rewarded this enthusiasm by granting the inhabitants the right to mint their own coins. When Acre fell to the Ptolemies in 280 BC it was renamed after these people. Thus in connection with Paul's journeys it was called Ptolemios.

Caesar made a visit here in 48 BC. Roman roads ran from here to Antioch and Damascus. For time Arabs held the town after the Romans withdrew. As we have already seen, the Crusaders made Acre a major port. Actually it became the Latin Kingdom's main seaport and was known as St Jean d'Acre. It was here that the Knights and Hospitallers of St John created their headquarters. The Crusader period saw merchants of Venice, Genoa, Amalfi and Marseilles doing trade here and even having homes in Acre. Alas, the Crusaders' final defeat took place here. They held on in Acre long after surrendering other places in the Holy Land in 1291. It was the Mameluke Turks who defeated the Crusaders here in the Knights' last stand.

The Citadel at Acre is a massive eighteenth-century construction. It was built by Pasha Ahmed el-Jazzar on thirteenth-century foundations. Once inside the huge building I spent some time wandering through rooms containing documentation. These documents tell of the imprisonment and execution of Jews during the days of the British Mandate. I saw many of the cells used, with mattresses on their floors. They were small and rather cramped. The impression I had was of cages for animals, as one side was completely barred: something used for animals and not human beings. The execution chamber is still there. It was a grim reminder of a bad episode in this country's recent past. Emerging from this solemn consideration, I was soon on the Citadel's open roof and saw the whole colourful panorama of Acre at a glance. Close at hand was the Mosque of Jazzar el Pasha, one of Acre's great showpieces, which I was shortly to visit. It was a chance to view the narrow streets and market place from a high elevation.

Back inside the building I stopped again at the museum dedicated to the Jewish underground resistance fighters' memory. Even their worst enemies would concede that these men fought bravely. It is rightly called the Museum of Heroism. I stopped to read some of the news cuttings, letters and other documents concerning the treatment of Jewish fighters under British rule. After this I emerged into the street once more.

In the Oriental souk I found all sorts of foodstuffs on display, as well as other kinds of merchandise. From a craft shop I could hear the clang of hammer on metal ringing out. A young craftsman was busy beating out a pattern on a copper dish. Yet another crowd of American tourists appeared. I joined them for a while. We stopped first at the ancient courtyard of a long-disused inn or caravanserai. Arches and doors faced inwards into the courtyard. After leaving the Americans I stopped for some rest and refreshments at an old quayside café, and watched boats playing on the sea. There are a number of delightful spots like this in the area.

My visit to Acre's subterranean Crusader City proved every bit as spellbinding as the rest of the town. It's the next item on the agenda for most visitors after seeing Ahmed el Pasha's Mosque, I imagine. The entrance to the underground complex is directly opposite the Mosque. So I plunged into this curious subterranean world, walking cautiously along a narrow passage which opened out into large chambers. I was impressed with how well preserved the whole structure was. Following the tunnels I encountered several divisions. There are a number of halls with a mixture of Crusader and Turkish stonework, and the remains of an old winepress. Directly under the Citadel there is a courtyard. Then I saw the Knights' Hall. There's a huge gateway here. The Turks used to hang their victims from a beam on top of it. The Knights' Hall is pure twelfth-century, having remained, as far as anyone can tell, completely unchanged since then. Today concerns are held in the third of these halls. An exit gate lies buried in a pit four metres deep – some indication of the original height of the old walls. There is a concreted area in the ceiling of one hall where the Israeli underground fighters made a bid for freedom. Next I found the old administrative centre of Crusader times, known then by the name of the 'Grand Manier'. The different style of architecture suggested to me it was of a later period than the Knights' Hall. The crypt contained the main dining room and central guest chamber. I noted that the French fleur-de-lis is found in the north east and south east corners. Which brings us, after a lengthy connecting passage to the Post (French *poste* or guard). It is a group of six halls altogether. Some scholars believe that these housed the original St John's Hospital run by the Knights of that Order. It might even have been a khan. After all it has cylindrical cross-vaulted roofs and doors that opened one way only – typical of a khan!

Finds dating from all periods of Acre's history are on display in the local Museum. It contains Hellenistic, Roman, Arab and, of course, Crusader relics. An old Crusader tombstone stands at the entrance, which visitors will notice on leaving. After this experience, enjoyable though it was, I was pleased to emerge into the sunlight once more.

I decided to take a closer look at the Mosque of Jazzar el Pasha. Up a flight of steps, through a narrow gateway and past a soaring palm tree, I encountered this beautiful building. It is white with traceries of black and other colours and is patterned inside and out. Unfortunately, I hired a strange garrulous guide who gabbled his words out in such a torrent that I learned precisely nothing from him. The sarcophagi of the Pasha and his adopted son Suleyman stand in the courtyard. The mosque is noted for its bold simple abstract designs and quotations from the Koran that are incorporated into the scheme. I could see niches and what I took to be a pulpit.

Back in the marketplace I stopped by an antique shop. It was as if the owner had crammed a substantial amount of Acre's past into his window! I saw an old cannon on the town walls, once used by Napoleon, and I also noticed a lighthouse in Acre's bay very close to the little café that I had stopped at earlier. Apart from the Jazzar el Pasha there are other mosques here, the Mosque el Ramel and the Mosque Ishan Basha. Christian churches here are St John's and St George's, resting as might be expected on Crusader foundations. Would those Knights Templars or the Teutonic Order or the Order of St Lazarus recognise Acre today? Possibly so, as it cannot have changed too much in its general layout. I turned to leave and visit another living museum down the coast.

I was heading for Caesarea but had to pass through Haifa, Israel's largest seaport. It was dark by the time I reached Haifa. It was a typical big, bustling, neon-lit city such as anyone might encounter anywhere else in the world, complete with throngs of people walking to and fro in its pavements. There were touches of Parisian elegance and 'Oxford Street' bustle after dark. I threaded my way through the crowded traffic-filled streets towards the railway station.

On the bus journey into Haifa I had observed the sweep of the bay upon which the city is built. Had I been able to stand on Mount Carmel where Elijah defeated the prophets of Baal, the view would have been even better. Both Solomon and Isaiah spoke with approval of Mount Carmel as a place of beauty, and since prehistoric times early man traversed the area. Closer to our own times it was used as a supply base during the Second World War. Haifa had a major role to play in the expansion of Israel in post-war times. Today immigrants and visitors arriving by sea have their first view of the Holy Land here at the Haifa docks. These docks are amongst the busiest in the world. Many oceangoing liners and cargo ships are continually coming and going, the symbols of Haifa's trade and commerce.

After taking directions from a middle-aged Jew I found my way to the railway station. Then I met two young American Jews and we conversed about the state of the world in general. I managed to catch a train for Caesarea and it was late when I got there. Finding a hotel proved problematic and I travelled by bus to the coastal area of Caesarea. Here, too, it was the Mary and Joseph syndrome as I wandered from one place to another looking for a place to stay. Would I have to sleep out under the stars? I wondered, for darkness had fallen. In a high-class hotel near the golf course almost nobody spoke any English, but they found someone who did. A European Jew, a fluent English speaker, appeared and we were able to sort out my overnight problem and have a discussion about the Middle East in general.

It was duly arranged for me to spend the night at the local police station. It was not because of any default on my part, but to be frank they did not know what else to do with me. I had a reasonably comfortable night and was woken up very early the next morning. Thus it was earlier than originally intended when I arrived at the ruins of ancient Caesarea; it was before sunrise. When the sun came up I watched the glowing sunrise framed in the shape of a cactus plant. For the moment I had the place to myself and enjoyed an idyllic wander in this new day's dawn. The bird-life of Israel interested me greatly. During this early morning walk at Caesarea I saw for the first time a number of hoopoes flitting among the trees and sometimes on the ground. They are lovely crested birds with long downcurved beaks and black-and-white and cinnamon-orange plumage. It was still early in the day and I continued to wander in these sun-dappled gardens with an eye for features of interest.

It was now the Roman remains that held my attention. Chunks of Classical architecture can be seen lying everywhere. Sections of columns lie horizontally, half-submerged in the ground, and a number of old Roman capitals are to be found. The resort's Roman associations are many and we can perhaps visualise those legions of old arriving here more easily than in many of the other resorts. Caesarea was founded by Herod the Great in honour of his patron Caesar Augustus. Then, as now, it was the fashionable place to be. For three hundred years the Roman procurators had their places of residence here. Pontius Pilate lived here and a stone bearing his name was found some years ago. All that I saw before me was not pure Roman, as some of it dated from Crusader times. There is, however, a predominantly Roman feel about it all. Substantial Roman remains exist. A Roman arch here was restored by Crusaders, and some Byzantine work is evident also. At the water's edge you can see Crusader wall foundations reinforced by sections of Roman columns.

Caesarea became associated with the early Christian Church. The Apostle Peter came here to meet the centurion Cornelius (Acts 10). Paul arrived here with a party of Roman soldiers. They stopped at the house of Philip, whose four daughters started to prophesy. A prophet bound his own hands and feet with Paul's girdle. Thus Paul learned of impending trouble that awaited him at Jerusalem (Acts 21). Did he, I wonder, reflect on earlier days in Jerusalem when he breathed out fire and slaughter against the new Christian sect before becoming its great trail-blazer? May he have reflected, too, upon the Council of Jerusalem of AD 49, over which he presided? And upon how this historic meeting did much to alleviate the tense Jewish– Christian wrangles of the time? Such problems were not solved entirely in Paul's lifetime, however. This story is fully told in Acts 15.

Meanwhile Paul returned to Jerusalem after the Caesarea prophecy and soon found himself on a trumped-up charge. The Apostle was later sent to face the Governor Felix in Caesarea in the company of two hundred Roman soldiers and two hundred spearmen (Acts 23:22–26). Paul's appeal to Caesar meant being taken to Rome to face the Emperor.

Caesarea has other claims to fame. These include being an important Byzantine stronghold (the last of which was captured by Moslem invaders in AD 640 and also the place where Baldwin I supposedly found the Holy Grail.

At length people began to arrive. The groundsman was first to do so. I breakfasted at the café as the sun climbed higher in the full light of day. Soon I walked north passing an old Crusader moat until I came to a surviving Roman aqueduct – imposing even in its ruined state. Its series of arches are still splendidly preserved. I was fortunate to be able to enjoy studying these artefacts. Visitors of earlier decades wouldn't have had such luck. Archaeologists in Israel have brought to light much that was thought to have vanished forever.

In the distance a horse and rider cantered across the sand. North of the ruins of St Louis' Crusader fortress stands the Roman amphitheatre, today used for concerts. That amphitheatre, by the way, had undergone a splendid restoration. As another example of the way in which modern Israel brings the past to life I will mention the discovery of the two giant headless statues there. One of them is of a dark reddish colour, the other white. They had been accidentally discovered by kibbutzniks whilst they were ploughing the land one day. The statues represented Roman emperors from the second to fourth centuries. Around the statues are found sections of ancient walls and pillars.

A party of Israeli schoolchildren arrived to swell the numbers of other visitors who had made their way here, making it a veritable hive of activity. People looked on as I sketched a gigantic stone foot from a one-time colossus. Tourists departed after a while and I would now also have to be going. I made my way back to Jerusalem.

Author's footnote: the modern state of Israel

The modern State of Israel exists today due to a peculiar chain of events that have taken place in the twentieth century and before. Much has happened during the period of the dispersal to bring about Israel's rebirth. In the 1800s millions of Jews left Russia for New York. At this time Theodor Herzl, the Zionist Viennese journalist, laid the foundations for a Zionist State. (It was a movement that gained momentum under Chaim Weismann.) In 1897 plans were formally drafted for a Jewish State in Palestine. At the time of the early Jewish Palestinian settlements Palestine was still in the hands of the Turks, who sided with Germany in World War I.

The agricultural element

One of the most significant factors in the rebirth of Israel was agriculture. Firstly there was acquisition of land by Jews about the time of World War I. Activity on the land has continued apace in recent times, reflecting that spirit of commitment which has played no small part in the continuing survival of Israel. Also at the time of World War I the Jewish National Fund provided cash for the buying up of land from landowners who were then Arab or Turkish. Once useless barren soil was made fertile. Thus in time the well-known kibbutzim were established, and with them the communal living and discipline inherent in the system. Decisions in a kibbutz are put to vote, so all members have a hand in shaping policy. Today in Israel there are more than 240 kibbutzim. Also to be found are the moshavim, likewise based on this type of collective agriculture. In 1939 the purchase of land in Palestine by Jews was severely restricted. Arab hostility towards the Jews was acute at this time. A white paper issued by the Government of the day almost stopped the immigration of Jews into Palestine altogether.

Throughout the War years Jews campaigned for the lifting of the restrictions imposed by the British – for Jews were fleeing the terrible Nazi Holocaust in Europe. As they saw it, Palestine had to be opened up. In spite of the continuing restrictions at the end of World War II, 70,000 Jewish immigrants succeeded in settling in Palestine, penetrating the British blockade. As so often happens in these situations, violence exploded. In 1947 Britain turned to the United Nations. A Committee looked into the problem and made its recommendations. The result was that the UN recommended that Palestine be divided into two states, one for the Palestinian Arabs and one for the Jews. Jerusalem was to be an international city. However, in order to understand this period of unrest in the history of Palestine more fully, we must return to the year 1917 and a series of major events that were to have far-reaching implications.

The Balfour Declaration

In 1917 three major events took place which brought Herzl's plans to fruition. Firstly, there was the Arab Legion (fully

Snake charmer, Marrakech

Roman aqueduct, Caesarea, Israel

Egyptian on Nile passenger craft

The Great Pyramid, Egypt

Water seller and visitors, Jerusalem

At Djemaa el Fna, Marrakech

Steamboat on the Bosphorus, Istanbul

Cab driver in reflective mood, Çanakkale

Turkish fishing boats, Alanya

Step Pyramid, Egypt

Our driver in Jordan

Solomon's Pillars near Eilat, Israel

Corinthian capital, Ephesus

My Bedouin friend in Jordan

Turkish fishmonger

formed 1920) – a fighting force that became allied to the British Army in Palestine at that time. Secondly the Balfour Declaration was signed, making provision for a homeland for the Jewish people in Palestine, whilst being unprejudiced towards non-Jewish communities there. Thirdly, Field Marshal Lord Allenby formally received the Turkish surrender of Jerusalem. The Sykes-Picot agreement envisaged the Arab lands split between France and Britain. This was drawn up between Britain, France and Russia. Thus political overseers saw France getting most of Syria in exchange for a Mesopotamia under the British. Palestine was to have been governed by an international body. Massive persecution of the Jews in Europe occurred, and massive immigration of Jews into Palestine followed.

A League of Nations Mandate had placed Palestine under British administration in 1920, but in 1948 a new Mandate was signed after a recommendation from the United Nations General Assembly. Israel was proclaimed an independent State, a Republic, and the British withdrew from Palestine.

David Ben Gurion became Israel's first premier. In 1949 Palestine was partitioned by Arab–Israel armistice lines. Maps of the period show a divided Jerusalem and substantial areas of no man's land were created round the Old City. The now-vanished Mandelbaum Gate allowed uneasy passage between the two sides. After the Six-Day War of 1967 all of the Old City was in Jewish hands. Israel again had to fight her Arab neighbours in the Yom Kippur War of 1973, and incidents have been legion. The taking of Old Jerusalem meant that Jews now had free access to the Wailing Wall. In the past Eastern European Jews were not assimilated – a further reason for establishing and reinforcing a Jewish homeland. The Yad Vasham War Memorial reminds us of their terrible treatment during World War II and how this gave added impetus to the creation of the Jewish homeland.

Israeli borders are always a matter of dispute: in recent years large tracts of Sinai reverted to Egypt following the Egyptian President Sadat's dramatic flight into Jerusalem. No doubt the Israelis were reminded of their advance towards Egypt at the time of the Suez crisis in the 1950s. After their withdrawal the area became a UN patrolled buffer zone. The eastern side of Sinai was settled by Israeli holiday villages, which are now in Egypt.

Author's note: the Israel–Arab situation in 2001/2

What would the founders and pioneers of modern Israel make of the contemporary scene in their beloved land? It seems not so very long ago that the media were deluged with reports of Israel's massive bombing of Lebanon. Most recently the world is still reeling from the terrible events of September 11th, 2001 and the destruction of the World Trade Center in Manhattan, USA, by terrorist action. The Intafada, or Arab uprising, in Israel has plunged the Middle East into what seems like a worse crisis than ever with massive casualties. The rest of us can only look on with apprehension as the story of Arab–Israeli relations continues to unfold.

CHAPTER EIGHT

MOROCCAN JOURNEY

Why include Morocco in a book on the Bible lands? My inclusion of this distinctive land in my story is for at least three good reasons. Firstly I was attracted to its exotic Eastern flavour – and not merely the cuisine. Secondly Morocco, along with other North African countries, has retained biblical customs long after they have been erased in the Holy Land itself (examples of these later). For centuries Morocco would have enjoyed contact with the Bible lands and cross-currents of ideas and trade would have taken place. Thirdly at least two important biblical races were firmly established in North Africa.

We think of Beau Geste and dashing Arab horsemen, couscous and camel trains and other visions created by the popular imagination. I visited the old imperial capital cities and travelled the Moroccan countryside. The glorious beaches of the country are separated from the desert by the Atlas Mountains. The mountain ranges of Morocco rise higher than any others found in Africa or the Middle East. These Atlas Mountain ranges are divided into High Atlas, five hundred miles in extent with a width of between forty and fifty miles, the Anti-Atlas, and the Middle-Atlas.

Most of the inhabitants are known as Berbers rather than Arabs, though the difference to many does not seem to be very great. We rarely suspect the diversity of origin of these people who are indigenous to North Africa. There are most probably Phoenician, Turkish and Negro elements that have contributed to the shaping of these people. Most historians, however, identify Berbers with the Libyans whose history can be traced to the times of the Pharaohs. Indeed the Libyans attempted to invade Egypt. These attacks began at the time of the Thinite Dynasties. It would appear to have been an act of enormous charity on the part of Ramses III when he gave settlement to a band of Libyans in the Nile Delta, after stopping one of their forays close to Memphis.

The coastal resort of Agadir is a truly elegant place. Accolades like 'Pearl of the North African coast' seem thoroughly justified. I loved the masses of greenery and ravishing splashes of colour seen in the tamarisks, eucalyptus and jacaranda trees. Palms lined streets. Indeed I was intoxicated by almost everything I came across in Agadir. The whirling sun, sea and sand was seemingly in greater dimensions than other beaches I had visited. At any rate it was far larger and more spacious than most. The resort stands on the Atlantic coast. This was the same Atlantic Ocean that had lapped at my feet on the west coast of Scotland, surging at my feet here. As well as being virtually North Africa's Miami Beach, a haven for all the sunworshippers for miles around, it is a perfect centre for excursions into the Atlas regions and to the Deep South of Morocco. Little wader birds twinkled along on their thin tiny legs at the water's edge. I felt absolutely carefree. After miles of walking I came upon the stranded hulk of an old ship, an out-and-out rustbucket. A number of locals were climbing over the wreck and they were apparently carrying out some work aboard her. A number of vacationing Germans and Swedes had joined me as I stopped to look at the stranded vessel.

Back in the town itself, I stopped to photograph a group of local girls. They had the most beautiful olive complexions, dark hair and sunny happy smiles. After the earthquake of 1960 a completely new town was built, very white and stylish. The souks, too, were strictly modern with no attempt to recreate any old-time styles of architecture. The effect was smart and totally pleasing. An elderly American couple, whom I had met at the airport, told me about a visit that they had just made to the docks. 'They have a bigger fish market at Billingsgate', said the man. A busy animated port was indicated by the distant row of cranes at the extremity of the bay's northern curve, very close to a hill that borders the beach to the north and soon becomes a familiar landmark to the visitor.

I met a young local, a man of about twenty years of age. There was a perpetual smile on his tanned face. As we stood on a remote stretch of beach, we tried to converse but he did not know a word of my language nor I of his. In his hand he held a cluster of small fish, which he had freshly caught. He motioned me to sit down, and made a camp fire from roots, grass and twigs which he had gathered. Once it was blazing away he placed the fish carefully on top of the little fire and allowed them to cook. Our fish were soon done to a turn on the glowing embers. We both sat cross-legged in typically Eastern fashion. Gently breaking off pieces of the well-cooked flesh, we ate our fill. When I nearly took a piece of fish that was inedible, my host gestured 'no' and indicated which parts to go for and which parts to leave. There is no topping and tailing a fish in this part of the world: the whole fish is cooked. The manner in which it was done interested me – the fish being placed directly in the glowing embers without utensils of any kind. This was 'broiling', the method used by the disciples of Christ beside the Sea of Galilee. It was my first encounter with biblical customs that have survived in North Africa. We were able to enjoy a conversation of sorts, communicating mostly by gesture and grunts. The man vanished as soon as we had finished eating. At least I was able to make a contribution to the meal by offering my host some bananas I had bought in town. I noted the lines of wooden stakes and bushes. Presumably these acted as windbreaks, preventing the shifting of the sands.

Although I was enjoying my days at Agadir, I was restless to visit other places in Morocco. What I heard about the Deep South, places like Goulimine and if possible Tan Tan. As it turned out the latter was closed to visitors. I could have joined an excursion from a hotel. In the event I decided on using local transport, arriving at the bus station in good time to catch the charabanc. Why do these buses always look so 1948-ish? I asked myself. These old buses probably ran off cheap petrol and were having luggage strapped to their roofs. My case was soon hoisted on top of the Goulimine bus and djellabah-clad figures were rapidly boarding it. Soon I took my seat and the charabanc lurched off, like some drunken man sauntering unsteadily on his way.

The landscape through which this ramshackle bus meandered was hilly and had a fair amount of vegetation growing there. Still it was a good asphalt road that twisted its way south. I noted sparse country overall, with little camel tracks here and there in the undulating ground. The route skirted the Anti-Atlas in some areas. The Anti-Atlas is a region which is good for the growth of foodstuffs – vegetables, which included tomatoes, and cereals. This range of mountains acts as a shield from the searing desert winds straight off the Sahara.

After several hours of travel in the company of my colour-ful companions our charabanc reached Tiznit, where we stopped for a while. Little clay pink houses were straddled all round and the region apparently had plenty of snakes. The little town was only founded as recently as 1882 – it is not very old as towns go, but it was a pleasant if somewhat desolate-looking place. Its founding took place during the time of the Sultan Moulay el Hassan. The town was one of the results of a brisk campaign to subdue the Sousse and Anti-Atlas region at that time. Enclosing most of the town was an impressive long wall. It is nearly three miles long alto-gether. There is much besides to interest the visitor to Tiznit. Fine craftsmen here produce authentic Berber jewellery. Their silverwork is used for the decoration of weaponry. They have a Medina and a Jewish quarter or mellah as it is called in these parts. Although many Jews left for Israel, other stayed and settled here. A mechouar can also be found here. Flourishing trade has taken place between this town and the West. The produce of the region, already referred to, proved excellent merchandise for trade.

An upstart pretender to the throne appeared in Tiznit in 1912. He was El Hiba, who made a Sultan of himself here-abouts and established a position for himself in the Sousse for some time. The French also occupied Tiznit, as might be expected in a French colony between 1917 and 1956.

After the short stopover in Tiznit we rumbled off again and kept going for what seemed an age until at last Goulimine came into view. An island in a sea of sand is how someone has described Goulimine – a description couched in the lan-guage of the Koran. The little streets were narrow and bor-dered by modern reddish-pink buildings. Disembarkation was at a bus depot situated in a tiny square alive with Berbers buying and selling. Everything felt small-scale here. I asked one youth about his religious beliefs. It transpired that he was neither Moslem nor Christian.

'So you're not a Moslem?' I asked him.

'Mohammed is dead', answered the boy drily.

I booked into the town's only substantial hotel and settled into a comfortable room. Before settling down for the night I visited the cosy but dimly lit lounge where I met two charming middle-aged couples. Soon I got into deep conversation with these new companions. There was one French couple and one French-speaking Belgian couple. Soon after I had introduced myself I had noticed and remarked on the Belgian man's excellent command of English.

'I used to live in London for a time', he explained. 'When I arrived there I could scarcely speak any English at all.'

I nodded in surprise. 'Well, you certainly managed to learn the language without too much trouble', I said. Certainly, he could speak my language far better than I could speak his.

'When you land in a strange city and need to know its language in order to survive then you hurry up and learn it, my friend', he chuckled.

The Belgian man was a stocky character, whilst the Frenchman was thin and wiry and very Gallic. They asked me my reasons for visiting the Deep South. I pointed out that I had timed my visit to coincide with the Camel Market that was to take place the next day. The Frenchman spread out a map on the table and invited me to look over his shoulder. It was a map of the region round Goulimine. 'There is one place you must not miss, Monsieur – it is the Oasis of the Blue Men.' I was very pleased to hear that, since one of the great aims of this visit was to meet some of these mysterious men of the desert. Now I was to have the chance to do so.

'Tomorrow I shall take you to the Oasis, Monsieur.'

'And how much will this cost?' I asked.

'You, Monsieur? It will cost you nothing – I should be very pleased if you would come along as our guest.'

'Delighted to accept your offer', said I.

Before the trip to the Oasis came the visit to the Camel Market and that night I opened the window of my room wide. In the street below I could make out shapes of camels in the darkness being led to the market area. In all probability these animals and their owners had crossed the vastness of the Sahara desert, possibly all the way from Timbuktu. Now here they were walking beneath my bedroom window.

The next morning arrived quickly, and I looked out of the bedroom window again as soon as it was light. Already a considerable number of camels were assembled in the market area. I dressed hurriedly as I did not wish to miss any of the fun. After a quick breakfast I dashed outside. It was a truly superb Camel Market – by far the best of its kind that I had seen. On occasions like this it was customary for the hotel manager to ride up and down outside the hotel dressed in the robes of the Blue Man. As I stood there witnessing this spectacle, my Belgian friend who was standing nearby simply shrugged and laughed. 'He is crazy – just crazy' was all he could say.

For what must have been hours, I wandered in and out of the groups of camels and robed men. These sons of the desert had emerged from that vast wilderness just a matter of hours previously. Now they chatted quietly in little groups. Some of them squatted on pieces of stone – improvised stools. Some of the camels were only young ones, probably born somewhere out on the trail between Goulimine and Timbuktu. In one section I came across a little flock of hairy black goats. As I took in and pondered the scene the sheer romance of the Blue Men caught my imagination. They belonged to the vast sea of sand that washed up to the shores

of Goulimine. Many of the Berbers present wore the characteristic indigo robes. The custom of wearing these robes and
turbans originated with a Britisher who introduced them to
North Africa at the time of the Spanish Armada. Often the
heavy blue dye used in the colouration of their robes and
turbans transfers itself to their skins. Sometimes the garments are dark indigo blue, at other times lighter in colour,
probably due to the bleaching of the sun.

Transactions continued to be carried out in the Camel
Market. At the conclusion of one deal I saw a smallish herd
of camels being trotted out of the market area at a brisk pace.
Hobbled camels were obviously awaiting buyers – and the
beasts tried to stand or move with difficulty. Having
expected everyone to be swathed in blue I was surprised to
note the variety of colours to be seen amongst the djellabah-
clad figures but, of course, not everyone involved in the
transactions was a Blue Man. Some of the Berbers had their
faces covered in their raised hoods. One very beautiful little
Berber girl wearing a rich blue head cloth proudly held up
her little black goat.

Some of the architecture surrounding the market enclosure was flat and rather box-like and seemed to blend in with
the rest of the town.

Water-sellers are a regular feature in North Africa and the
Middle East, as we saw in the section on Israel. The
Moroccan water-seller is a gaudy and colourful figure. One
such man appeared: a thin ascetic type in characteristic red
jerkin over a grey jersey. His whitish turban was topped by
a decorative brimmed hat. Copper bowls hung on his front
and his water bag behind. Again the biblical pattern was
more in evidence in Morocco. Metal containers, Turkish in
design, are found in Israel, whereas the Moroccans use
pliable containers of leather. In the main street I found a little

craft shop that sold some very Eastern tea or coffee pots with finely curved handles and finely curved spouts. Also they had items of female decoration made partly from amber beads. After leaving the little shop I came to another where a group of Berber women were doing the enigmatic guedra dance. The constant whirling movement I found intoxicating. It was something akin to the whirling dervishes, I imagine.

I had visions of the Blue Men and their families stealing away into the desert any day now. They would disappear as mysteriously as they had appeared. In biblical times it was commonplace for camel caravans to cross from one place to another over vast tracts of desert, as we have seen. The Moroccan caravan is a last survival of this mode of trading. Salt extracted from deposits in Taoudeni is carried by camels to Timbuktu in Black Africa. Camel-borne trade has flourished with such merchandise as ivory, ostrich feathers, leather goods finished or unfinished, henna, gold dust, gum and slaves! Indeed the slave-trading routes were actively engaged in slave trading up until the nineteenth century.

The French influence is still very strong and the French have explored the area for hundreds of miles round about. General Trinquet explored as far as Senegal in the 1930s and he presided over certain developments. Some of today's Berbers are French-speaking. As a language, Berber is undoubtedly the oldest in North Africa but the sub-division into localised dialects is complicated. The mountain people of the Rif, the eastern region of the Middle Atlas mountains, plus other east Moroccan tribes, and those in the Figuig area speak with a different dialect entirely from the Berber group of dialects used by nomadic people of the central part of the Middle Atlas, the eastern area of the High Atlas, the Ziz Valleys, those of the Dadès as well as areas like the Gheris, Todgha, and Sargho districts. The third group of Berber dialects are known as the Chleuh group, comprised of the settled non-nomadic people of Centraland, the western High Atlas, the areas of the Sousse, the Anti-Atlas and the Bani Oases. This great diversification of tongues can mean that Berbers from one area cannot easily comprehend Berbers from some other area. For the visiting outsider this can prove difficult indeed! Anyone with a good grasp of French can usually get by. Belgian and Spanish are also understood in some areas. Also there is Arabic, the language of the Koran. Classical Arabic is the province of the educated classes while colloquial forms, as we have seen, are spoken elsewhere in the region.

Those nomadic camel-driving Blue Men were the people that fascinated me most of all. Very soon I was going to meet one of them for tea on the Oasis of the Blue men. Monsieur and Madame Lepage were waiting beside their hired Land-Rover along with the Belgian couple. I climbed aboard with the others and we were soon underway. Ahead of us lay some rough terrain. To begin with it was relatively flat country through which we were driving. It was sandy with clusters of scrub here and there. It must be remembered that not all desert consists of sand dunes, as in films like *Lawrence of Arabia*. These are called *erg* landscapes. The flat areas which can stretch for hundreds of miles are known as *Serir*. Other areas have fantastic rock formations, sometimes nipped at their bases by wind erosion. These are *buttes*. Then there is that flat land strewn with small sharp rocks referred to as *Hammada*.

Well out in the wilds now we passed a number of dark pointed tents, belonging to nomads. On we drove until we reached a river. Here we were forced to stop. After due deliberation it was decided to ford the river without the vehicle. Even the shallowest parts of the river were too deep for driving through. So we continued on foot. Luckily we did not have far to walk as the Oasis was visible in the distance, with its palm trees and mud huts and walls. The river was very muddy indeed and it was not always easy to gauge the depth of the water. We wondered if we would sink up to our waists in it. Fortunately it only came up to our knees. We had correctly chosen the right area in which to ford the river.

Arriving on the opposite bank we carried on until we reached the Oasis. Then we were walking beneath those palm trees and down narrow lanes, walled on either side, which ran between fairly irregular clusters of huts. We could easily see over the tops of these mud walls to observe the little garden plots. It was a beautiful little oasis and I watched as a veiled woman drifted silently past down one of those mud-walled lanes. We stopped by one of the mud dwellings. Suddenly without warning the door burst open. There, framed in the doorway, was a tall robed figure – a noble desert Blue Man, who promptly flung his arms around me with a kiss of greeting. It was an experience to be greeted by a man of the desert thus. He cordially invited us all into his little home where he lived when not on the move. The chamber in which we sat was so tiny that there was barely enough room for us all to sit down cross-legged on the floor. Our genial host prepared mint tea for us. 'Bon Appétit', purred Lepage contentedly as our Blue Man poured the tea in a little glass before him. Like me, Lepage could savour such simple contentment. It is certainly a case of the *genius loci*, that elusive and, some might think, ephemeral spirit of place. Taking tea in an English café would not evoke such feeling. Lepage and our Berber host chatted together for some minutes in a mixture of French and Arabic. Their conversation was too rapid for me to follow. I asked Lepage what they were talking about. 'He is talking about the desert journey to Timbuktu, my friend, and about the amber beads that are used in trading.' Our driver had come along with us. He had a reasonable command of English, which was useful.

Back in the mud-walled lane I felt a surge of romanticism (again) about the desert and these Blue Men with their camel caravans. I thought that it would be a great idea to ride with them one day, and said so.

'You?' asked one Berber eyeing me squarely. 'The desert is hot, my friend, very wearying, and the journey is long.'

For a moment he had pricked the bubble of my romanticism. 'All the same,' I mused, 'it's a thought.' The story of these desert travellers with their camel caravans following their trade routes across the desert had always fascinated me. The various annual fairs and events that are held in Morocco most probably give added impetus to such trading. In days gone by, many grew flabby and soft on the riches that accrued from such trading.

A glaring example of this is the Tajakant, a people who established themselves very firmly in the area. They created a flourishing trade after defeating the Reguibate nomads in battle. With their fifteen thousand or so camels the Tajakant rode the desert trails, no doubt with an air of great confidence and very profitably, as we have seen. At the turn of the century, however, the Tajakant were in their turn defeated by their old enemies, the Reguibate. In time the Tajakant were disbanded as a separate people and were scattered among the other people of the region. All that easy living made them an easy prey to their enemies.

There is a great annual caravan from the Sudan which reaches Morocco's Deep South around October and November. It is known as the Azalai and it is made up of about five thousand camels. As a safeguard the caravan travels under special escort. Much of the salt for the Sudan is transported back there by this caravan. It would be a pity if these great caravans were to vanish and it is my fervent wish that they will survive and flourish despite any twenty-first century advances.

That evening we were all back in the comfortable little lounge of the hotel, enjoying a conversation about the day's events. If my speech ever got too fast for Lepage, he would gently chide me with a restraining 'Slowly, my friend', then again 'slowly'. Next morning it seemed that everyone was moving on except me. I received a warm farewell from Monsieur and Madame Lepage and I wished them bon voyage, and very soon they had gone. The jovial Belgian and his wife had likewise departed.

I asked a member of the hotel staff about the possibility of travelling another hundred of miles or so to Tan Tan. This village is so much in the desert that sand blows across its streets. It was one of those romantic and fabled places that adventurers feel the urge to visit, but the chance to do so was denied me on this occasion at least. The Hotel Assistant shook his head and told me that Tan Tan was closed. When I asked him why, all he could tell me was that there was some sort of skirmish with Algeria going on in the area. The police had set up a road block on the desert road to Tan Tan. This was clearly as far south as I could go. I returned to the hotel.

Less than twenty-four hours later I was heading back towards Agadir in a trusty old charabanc, my suitcase once more strapped to the roof of the vehicle. Once back in Agadir I briefly settled back into the hotel there but did not intend staying for very long. I booked a local flight to Marrakech – another of those places I had set my heart on seeing. The flight was scheduled for the following day.

After a longish wait at the airport I did board the plane but a little later than the appointed hour. As the aircraft rose in

the sky I looked out through the window at the long line of
Agadir's beach that I had got to know so well. I could make
out the stranded vessel also. For a few moments the whole
of Agadir was laid out before me, then the plane turned
round and nosed its way across the mountains. This was a
view of the Atlas Mountains that would be hard to beat, with
their higher reaches spangled with snow. At ground level or
from the air the Atlas Mountains were a delight. It is only a
relatively short flight from Agadir to Marrakech and the
flight was over before I knew it.

As soon as I arrived in Marrakech I was aware of the
warm glowing reddish colour of everything. It was not
unlike Petra in this respect – a Rose-Red City in its own
right! This was a city beloved of Sir Winston Churchill, to
say nothing of umpteen Moroccan sovereigns – the
Almohads, Wattasids, Alaouites and Saadians being among
those whose monarchs provided the patronage. In the red
city of Marrakech, the Berber peoples meet and mingle
perhaps more freely than elsewhere in Morocco. To them
Marrakech is a metropolis. Small wonder then that such
Moroccan cities are called imperial capitals. Others are Fez,
Rabat, and Meknes. Moroccans call them *Makhzen*.
Inevitably royal patronage would be extended to such places
in preference to lesser towns and cities in the country.

To begin with I stayed at a small hotel near the Place
Djemaa el Fna for a couple of nights, but soon moved to
another more stylish hotel. The immediate happening that
catches the attention of the visitor is the exotic open-air
theatre in the Place Djemaa el Fna. It is a totally mesmerising experience. Crowds congregate as if from nowhere to
watch the performances.

Snake-charmers play their enigmatic pipes over baskets
from which deadly snakes rear menacingly. Often I saw men

take snakes in their hands, raising them above their heads. There are storytellers who get agitated if the visitors get too close. Another showman had a small number of monkeys chained to a box. Many found them a great attraction. One of the most fascinating attractions as far as I was concerned was the team of Black drummers. Their vibrant performance was as intoxicating to the senses as the guedra dancers whom I saw in the Deep South at Goulimine. I listened to them for some time. The jugglers were no less skilful than the other performers there. The rapid rhythm of the Black Drummers, however, was building up into an ever-rising crescendo. All the performers held the audiences spellbound. It was a truly unforgettable experience. The theatre is something that is traditional but clearly an integral part of the present. Visitors are entertained, poor people are helped and the tourist organisations are certainly pleased. One visit to the open-air theatre is never enough, and I planned to revisit later in the year.

I found several little café stalls there where I could eat cheaply. The very extensive souk close to the Square is crammed with colourful merchandise, as is typical of an Eastern souk. As expected there were little sacks of spices open for the visitor to see the colour of each one. I saw distinctive local craftwork hats of leather, pottery and wood-carving. In one area I found huge skeins of dyed wool and open sunken vats of bright colour where the wool is dyed. It was another example of a biblical custom surviving in modern times in Morocco (see Ezekiel 27:7, 24; Acts 16:14).

There were some distinctive conical baskets and I paused to look at woodturning. The craftsman here produced beautifully turned bars of sweet-smelling wood. Curious to see how it was done without any kind of electric machine, I asked for a demonstration. An assistant duly clamped a piece of wood between two fixed points, then wrapped a length of string round one end of the length of wood. He then gave a vigourous tug at the cord, which sent the wood spinning whilst he applied a sharp instrument. Thus the wood was finely shaped without mechanical aids of the present day. Another survival from biblical times?

I was accompanied for some distance by an Australian girl who appeared to know every Arab youth for miles around. She had developed a soft spot for one particular urchin boy who kept following us around. When the boy made friendly or humorous gestures, the Australian girl would smile in a tolerant manner and say, 'Mohammed, you're crazy.' He kept following us for a time before vanishing into the vastness of the souk.

Practically the whole of the Old City of Marrakech is enclosed by an ancient wall, which has towers at intervals. I turned from the Place Djemaa el Fna for a while. Often I would stop to watch flights of swifts screaming past the heights of the Great Mosque, or take a cool meditative walk through the Municipal Gardens. I was not alone in these meditations. Local djellabah-clad young men were enjoying the gardens in like manner. One youth was walking beneath the shade of the tress very slowly, reading his copy of the Koran. Another sat contemplating, seated on a fallen log. The heat of the day was considerable and I had frequent recourse to the tiled swimming pool at the hotel where I had moved to. I would regularly walk between the Place Djemaa el Fna and my hotel, which was situated more towards the modern part of Marrakech. This was less colourful but retained something of the general ambience of the Old City. Mosques predominate, but a number of Christian churches flourish, as is the pattern in many Moslem countries.

Marrakech is very well supplied with hotels. Some of them

are luxurious and huge like the Mamounia, where Sir Winston Churchill used to stay and from where he made his painting forays. The Atlas Mountains in the distance were a favourite subject with him. Other plush richly oriental hotels can be found in the area. One of these I was staying in myself. Many of the visitors must have been extremely well-to-do. At night the rich step from their fine hotels to board horse-drawn carriages. Then the crack of the driver's whip would be followed by the clip-clopping of horse's hooves as the carriage carried its passengers to some nightclub or other. The merry jingle of the horse's bells, along with the clip-clopping, would fade as the carriage vanished from sight. The cost of hiring a carriage can be a matter of some haggling.

The new city already mentioned is worth visiting. This is known as Gueliz, with cleanly laid-out streets and pleasant residential areas. Any portrait of Marrakech would, I suppose, be incomplete without some remarks about its history, however incomplete.

The origins of the city appear to be obscure, but some historians place the date of origin at around 1070. The founders of Marrakech were apparently nomads from the Atlantic region called Almoravids, led by a chieftain called Abou Bekr. They were Berbers of the Lemtouma tribe, a proud race who referred to their contemporaries with utter distaste and scorn. Whilst their mouths were veiled they felt some justification in calling others 'flycatchers'. This city base was used by the Almoravids to control their rivals and enemies. They did this by blocking valley entrances and exits. This was a cunning and ruthless piece of strategy. One huge advantage was that they could obtain supplies of wheat from a nearby granary, in the Douk Kala area.

Control of the city passed into the hands of Youseff ben Tachfin, cousin of Abou Bekr. He is said to have built a vast cathedral-like mosque here, of which nothing remains. It may have resembled the present Koutoubia minaret that can be seen today. It lies close to the Tomb of Youseff. Youseff travelled to Spain, where he hired some Christian mercenaries. They were trained to be Youseff's personal bodyguard. The activities of this man and his son who succeeded him were very extensive. The son, named Ali Ben Youseff, became a valiant warrior and a man of great piety and learning. In time Ali continued to build up and reinforce Marrakech, launching fresh building programmes: important things like underground water channels and conduits.

Alas, much of Ali's splendid work was destroyed by the Almohads when they took over. The fine buildings, the splendid fountain, everything vanished in the onslaught. Like Baghdad, this city had become a centre of intellectual activity. Philosophers, doctors, learned scholars and Golden Poets all came to Marrakech during the Almoravids' era. Ali's son, Tachfin, reigned for only two years. Ichaq, the grandson of Tachfin, met his death at the hands of assassins. It was this assassination that opened up the way for the Almohads. As so often happened in history, here as elsewhere one dynasty takes over from another. Through all the years of their rule, the Almoravids had to live with the constant threat of mountain tribes of the High Atlas, the Masmouda – these people were never entirely subdued by the Almoravids. Violence in gaining religious and social reforms was sometimes advocated by fanatical preachers like the Mahdi Ibn Toumert, who was active at that time.

As time passed Marrakech grew and flourished under its various leaders, and seemed to survive such catastrophes as the plague of 1176. Many other notable leaders arose in Marrakech over the centuries, such as Abd el Mou'min who had the first Koutoubia built and Abou Yaqoub Youseff who followed after him. The latter carried out a programme of development which included the addition of a new quarter for new settlers.

Abou Yaquob Youseff lived and reigned in the twelfth century. His first son was born out of a union with a negro slave girl, and he became known as the Black Sultan. He continued the tradition of building mania in Marrakech and indeed throughout Morocco. Some splendid architectural creations are attributed to him; for example, Rabat's Hassan Mosque, which was surrounded by a huge wall. In 1185 he started building a new casbah in Marrakech. It must indeed have been a very sumptuous affair, as it contained about twelve palaces with exotic names like House of Myrtle and House of Crystal. Lake gardens and pavilions were included in this grand design. We are reminded of the eighteenth-century building sprees that took place in Europe in the Roccoco period. The Sultan had his cavalry, and drilling of the same would be carried out on a great Hippodrome Square that was part of the fantastic programme initiated by the Black Sultan. Prominent Arab physicians attended the court of the Prince. Likewise there were doctors who ran the hospitals that he built. The economy of Marrakech and most of the other aspects of its life prospered mightily under the Almohads. Some historians claim that this was its greatest period.

Commercial links with Spain were enjoying great success, and imported goods – merchandise of all kinds – were sold in the marketplace. Morocco also exported her produce, which consisted partly of leatherwork that is still a Moroccan speciality today. Later rulers failed to sustain the same cohesion and prosperity that their predecessors had created. Disputes, quarrels and instances of internal strife broke out. A palace revolution occurred and soon a new

dynasty of Berbers came to the throne. These were the
Merinids – the third Berber dynasty to rule in Marrakech.
Civil war broke out in the thirteenth century between rival
claimants to the throne. In spite of the capture of Marrakech
by the champion of the Almohads, Yahia, the throne went to
the opposing tribe, and Rachid was the successor of
Ma'moun.

Meanwhile other eyes were turned towards Marrakech.
The Ben Meri tribe, like many another, had designs on the
city. They were aware of the unrest that had bedevilled recent
administrations, and they were only waiting for the right
moment to strike, and strike they did! In 1269 they took
Marrakech. The new ruler, Abou Youseff Abd el Haqq,
moved the seat of power to Fez, which for a time became the
capital city of Morocco. Marrakech, however, remained the
south Moroccan metropolis. In the fourteenth century
Marrakech became again a capital – this time of a Merinid
kingdom which was a separate entity from Fez and the
administration that existed there. A pretender to the throne
had himself made ruler in Fez in 1374 – Abou el Abbas. He
made Abd el Rahman Ben Ali Ifallousin his Viceroy in
Marrakech. This resulted in civil war erupting all over again
and the Marinid Empire was nearly torn in half. For a whole
long decade this dreadful conflict continued.

Despite the attempts of the Portuguese to take the city,
Berbers continued to hold it. The sixteenth century saw the
rise of rulers who raised their own magnificent buildings.
There were two Saadian princes of note who made
Marrakech their capital city. It was once more a capital that
was carefully and jealously guarding the territory against the
Portuguese infiltrators. They were Achmed el-Araj and his
brother Mohammed esh-Sheik. The two brothers often quar-
relled, which sometimes made life difficult for one or the

other of them. The next sovereign to rule in Marrakech was Mohammed esh Sheik whose power extended over the entire area of the Sousse, and Fez was his seat of power before Marrakech. One ruler in particular who brought back great riches for Marrakech was El Dhebi, the Gilded One. The name would seem to betray something about the magnitude of the riches he obtained. One ruler would outdo his predecessor in the beautification of Marrakech. These buildings must have been a splendid sight, embellished as they were in Carrara marble. The El Badi Palace upon which most of the care and glory was lavished was later demolished by Moulay Ismail. At this time the Saadian Tombs and the city of Meknes were under construction.

Marrakech continued to be ruled by ambitious monarchs in the centuries that followed. Usurpers were among them. The pattern exerted itself again until the nineteenth century. The French took over early in the twentieth century. It was undoubtedly with a fair amount of relief that local inhabitants saw a detachment of French troops led by Colonel Mangin move in. The date was September 9th, 1912. The French restored order to the city and indeed to the area round about which had suffered strife for so long. This Protectorate lasted until 1956. Under its supervision the new city came into being.

This sketch of Marrakech's history is, of course, far from complete. No doubt there are many stories of rivalry and intrigue that can be further unearthed for those sufficiently interested. For the moment, though, I must return to my personal narrative.

For days I continued to absorb this intoxicating trance-like atmosphere. At night I still visited the Place Djemaa el Fna. The stalls each had a storm-lantern which picked out the position of each stall. The horse-drawn carriages were

doing plenty of trade. The little lamps on the carriages flick-
ered in the darkness, as did the storm-lanterns of the stalls.
The jingling bells and clopping hooves of the horses, as they
drew their affluent passengers around, sounded out constantly.

Before long departure day had arrived, and it would be
autumn before I returned to Morocco to continue my peri-
grinations here.

CHAPTER NINE

MOROCCAN HONEYMOON

Several weeks later I was back in Morocco, now travelling with my wife. As we approached Gibraltar our aircraft cast its shadow on the sea. The shadow flitted rapidly over boats at anchor as we came in to land on the Rock. On my previous visit I had encountered the Barbary apes, and plunged down into the cathedral-like underground caverns. Now we browsed in little shops or sat in the sun at pavement cafés. The British influence still predominates. Even the policemen appear to have arrived from London by instant teleportation. Horse-drawn carriages are for hire on Gibraltar, as in Marrakech.

The Arabs call the Rock Jebel Tariq. It was part of the Pillars of Hercules in ancient times. We are told that Hercules bestrode the gap formed by Gibraltar and Mount Acho on the African side, like some sort of mighty colossus. By some staggering feat he tore asunder the land barrier between the Mediterranean and the Atlantic. Geologists would doubtless offer a much less fanciful view. According to the old Phoenicians this was the place that marked the boundary of the world. It was the meeting place of Heaven and Earth.

Beyond these rocks lay a mysterious realm, the abode of the gods. It was hard for the Phoenicians to think otherwise, for their ships were often hurled back by rough seas. However, they passed the Pillars on their third voyage here, and founded Gades where Cadiz now stands. In southern Spain large quantities of silver were found. Cadiz is thought to be the biblical Tarshish, which may have included the northern tip of Morocco as well. The Phoenicians would have sailed back to their bases on the Levant coast or Carthage, their ships laden with silver obtained from southern Spain. The cargoes of silver were so huge that even the ships' anchors were made from silver. As the Phoenicians became more adventurous they became increasingly rich from these enterprises. Small wonder, then, that Tyre and Sidon enjoyed the wealth described by Ezekiel, who wrote:

> The ships of Tarshish were your caravans for your merchandise, and you were replenished (Tyre) and were heavily loaded and made an imposing fleet (in your location) in the heart of the seas. (Amplified Bible Ezekiel 27:25)

Silver spread into plates was brought from Tarshish and the kings of Tarshish and the isles brought presents to places like Tyre (see Jeremiah 10:9 and Psalm 72:10).

In their turn Saracens, Moors, Spaniards and others, including armies of both World Wars in the twentieth century, have found Gibraltar to be strategically valuable. Some of the caves were used for power plants and some were requisitioned for hospital accommodation. Apparently an admiral has or had a residence on Gib. Gibraltar is not quite an island, since it is linked to the Spanish mainland by an isthmus – a narrow neck of land. It is referred to as the North Fort. Ornithologists of today find the Rock interesting, too, as it lies on the main bird migration route between Europe and Africa. RAF radar screens show vast bird movements over the Straits of Gibraltar and Gib itself at night during migration times.

North Africa is famed as the land of the Moors, those conquerors who once carried Islam into Spain and Portugal. Fine examples of Moorish architecture can still be seen in places such as Cordoba, Seville and Granada. The Romans called North Africa Mauretania, and its people Mauri. Centuries later the French also called this part of North Africa for which we were heading Mauretania, and regarded the Arabs as freebooters to be kept in check.

Whoever called Tangier an out-and-out visitor rooking town was not far short of the mark. One of the first things we did was to visit the casbah with its promise of mystery and intrigue. A wizened little Arab beckoned us to follow him. Talk about 'Come with me to the Casbah'. With him in the lead we threaded our way down the narrow passageways, teeming with colourful locals in traditional robes. Continuing along the eratically busy streets we came to a very Eastern restaurant where we were entertained by male dancers. Djellabah-clad figures often stopped and sat down to drink mint tea in the Petit Socco (Little Square) to which many students and hitch-hikers gravitate. This Square is walled in by crumbling hotels and cafés, like other parts of the town. There are Spanish cafés, and the one-time Palace of the Sultans, now a museum. There is a Great Mosque dating from the seventeenth century, built by the Sultan Moulay Ismail.

After seeing the Mosque we found ourselves looking over a terrace wall and out across the harbour towards Gibraltar and Cadiz. There was still much to see – the Dar el Makhzen, the Museum of Moroccan Art, and the Museum of Antiquities – but we decided to press on to Fez, but not before taking a quick look at the Caves of Hercules, which were occupied in Prehistoric times. Neanderthal man once roamed the area. A curious legend suggests that because Tangier looks with one eye at the Atlantic and the other at the Mediterranean this gives it its fickle character. The surrounding hills, now denuded, were once very wooded and gave the Moors plenty of cover during their attacks on Spain. A palace of some importance here is the Palace el Moulay Abd el Aziz where King Hassan II came to stay for part of the year. We reached the lighthouse and our driver stopped to let us look at it. The locals call it Cap Malabata. We rested in the gardens of the Sultan's Palace Museum. Interestingly, the Atlantic and Mediterranean meet precisely at the point where the lighthouse stands.

Legend has it that Tangier was founded by a Libyan King Anteus. In those far-off times the town was referred to as Tingi or Tingis. Men of Carthage passed this way and enjoyed the salted fish or garum for which the region became well known. The Roman involvement and how it came about is an interesting story. It was the conflict between Anthony and Octavian that resulted in Tingis becoming part of the Roman Empire. The battle that Anthony and Octavian fought took place in Spain and it involved the inhabitants of Tingis. The town was ruled from Spain and came under Spanish administration. This meant that in time it became independent from Rome. The remainder of western Mauretania was firmly annexed to it by the Emperor Claudius during the years AD 40–45. In Diocletian's time, some time at the end of the third century AD, the town was known as Mauretania Tingitana, the capital of the area. Down the centuries various rivalries continued to shake the area. As a province of the Roman Empire Tingis was a port from which goods were exported to Rome: corn, which was grown near Tingis itself; oil, which was produced at Volubilis; plus, of course, the garum.

Spanish links were always there, and the masters of Spain or Vandals took over Tingis in 429. They had always regarded Tangier as one of the six parts of their country anyhow. Now they planned to subdue all of North Africa under King Genseric. To what extent they succeeded is not fully known. In 705 Mousa ibn Noceir took the town. He rapidly organised an army of Berbers to attack and conquer Spain. When the Omayyad Caliph Hisham ruled in Tangier, an uprising of Berbers from the Rif and Chaouia regions threatened the town's peace. Many fought over Tangier. In 1274 the Merinids captured it.

The fourteenth century saw Tangier as the scene of much animated commerce, as it was in Roman times. The quaysides were a lively scene as traders from Pisa, Genoa and Venice in Italy and from Marseilles in France brought in their cargoes of spices, metals, and birds of prey for hunting purposes, and sailed away with goods such as sugar, wool, skins, hides and carpets. The Portuguese attempt to take Tangier in 1437 was foiled. Surrounded by soldiers at the foot of the walls, they were forced to withdraw. It was not until a later assault that the Portuguese succeeded in their objective. On August 29th, 1471, they won and turned the Great Mosque into a cathedral.

Philip II of Spain brought Tangier under his rule when he controlled Portugal as well. In 1640 independence was restored to the Portuguese and they recaptured Tangier. The English were to take control on the marriage of Catherine of Braganza and Charles II in 1661. Despite the special charter which was drawn up for the town, trade was not very good at the time. The British troops were to withdraw, sacking much of Tangier before doing so.

Sultans ruled until the nineteenth and twentieth centuries, when the various powers of Europe hotly contested the right to Tangier and Morocco as a whole. The French were trying to prevent the Germans from gaining control and vice versa. When the Kaiser visited Tangier in 1905 he made a good impression, accompanied as he was by all the pomp and ceremony that went with such visits. With Wilhelm II's support the Sultan called a conference at Algeciras, which resulted in the signing of a treaty which gave the French and Spanish a good deal of control over Morocco. This new set-up helped to resolve ages of strife and dispute. Difficulties were further resolved in the signing of further treaties.

The Treaty of Fez, signed in 1912, pledged French protection. But the statute of 1923 meant that several countries were now allowed to have a share in the control of Tangier – France, Britain, Spain, Sweden, Portugal, Belgium and Holland among them. These were countries who had not lost in World War I, and all were countries who had signed the Treaty of Algeciras. Today we find an independent Tangier, but with a strong French flavour, and Spain's influence is still strong in Spanish territories of Morocco.

We moved on to Fez, one of the great Moroccan imperial cities. 'Whatever happens, don't miss Fez', we were told. In the foyer of our hotel we met a local guide – a Frenchman. It was by design rather than accident that we met him, even though he told us that we were very fortunate to have caught him at that precise moment. Normally he was up to his ears in guide work. Fez is arguably the most colourful of Moroccan cities. It is certainly the oldest. Even the 'new' part of the city dates from the thirteenth century. Thus something of the antiquity of Fez can be realised. After a taxi ride along a magnificent stretch of road, almost regal in its layout, we were to explore this gem of an old Moroccan city. Once inside the city walls we found ourselves threading our way through narrow tunnels. Without our guide we would have had an impossible task in finding our way about. We were truly transported back over the centuries. Nowhere else in Morocco can we find such a perfect example of a medieval Islamic city. 'Medieval' cities elsewhere tend to be a mixture of old and new – but not here. As in other parts of Morocco, robed veiled figures glided past and some vanished into tiny doorways. In other narrow doorways men sat working at their trades that had probably not changed since the Medina was first built. Overhanging windows rarely found elsewhere were in evidence here. It reminded very much of sights that I encountered in Old Jerusalem.

From its earliest days, Fez was a ferment of culture. It is still important from an educational as well as from a political and spiritual point of view. The French Protectorate saw to it that ancient parts of the city were prevented from clashing with any later developments. The ancient part of Fez is known in Arabic as Fez el Bali, whilst the new city is called Fez el Jedid. The former is the best place in all Morocco in which to meet the artisans, scholars, and wise men of the country.

The Tomb of Moulay Idriss II is a shrine to which all Moslems in the area go. We were not allowed to enter. There is a good reason for the locals to regard this as a sanctuary. It was Moulay Idriss who founded Fez in 809. Apart from founding the city, there is little to suggest that he was a particularly good or saintly character to prompt such veneration. However, it appears that he embodied the spirit of Old Morocco sufficiently for his tomb to be regarded as a national shrine.

The end of the Idrissid Dynasty and the commencement of the Merinids' reign marked a period of decline. The Merinids

Bedouin at Be'er Sheva, Israel

One of the many faces at the Temple of Karnak

Turkish war veterans at centenary celebration, Istanbul

Classical bull-head motif, Ephesus

Headless statue, Ephesus

The Temple of Hadrian, Curetiae Road, Ephesus

The Cedar grove, Lebanon

Postcard from Istanbul showing a Turkish Sultan

Cappadocian landscape, Turkey

were those who established again the zawiya*, and with the finding of the tomb of Idriss by the Wattasids in 1437 the cult of the tomb as a place of pilgrimage was rekindled. A particularly colourful souk lies close to the sanctuary of Moulay Idriss. The world's oldest university can be found at Fez, along with the famous mosque, the Kairaouine. Refugees from other Arab cities flooded into Fez during its early days. They often introduced skills and learning, making a great contribution. To begin with Fez experienced troublesome times. Two rivals, the Cordovan Omayyads and the Tunisian Aghlabids, fought over the declining Idrissid set-up.

In the eleventh century the Almoravids carried out many improvements but when the Almohads took over in the following century they pulled down many of the walls. But a programme of reconstruction was put into operation when they managed to gain control of the whole of Morocco. It is believed that much of the wall of Fez el Bali to the north is of Almohad building.

During the Merinid period Abu Yussef Yaacub proclaimed Fez his capital, and it remained so all through the Merinid era. The Sultan instigated the building of Faz el Jedid. It was formally opened on March 21st, 1276, and the consecration of the Great Mosque took place three years later. It was clearly a very ambitious programme of building involving, as it did, houses for officials, barracks, baths and a palace, to say nothing of the great walls that surround the great complex. Here in Fez we can glean something of what it must have been like in the days of the old sultans of the Amoravid, Almohad, or Merinid Dynasties.

As in many Moroccan cities, there is a Mellah or Jewish quarter. Jewish communities here, as elsewhere, have always

* zawiya a cult confraternity centre

made a valuable contribution to the life of the city in which they live. You might wonder at this stage which dynasty rules today. It is the Alaouites who are now in control. This dynasty began in 1667 when Moulay Rachid captured the city.

I was impressed with the Bab Boujeloud gateways. In the Classical pattern, there is a large central gateway flanked by two smaller ones. It was decorated in superb arabesque treatment which included magnificent glowing blue tile-work. We sat on a low wall close to the gateway and watched the constant stream of people's comings and goings. Little knots of robed figures stopped to gossip and stand at the gateway. Shouting Arabs drove pack-laden donkeys through one of the smaller gates. Following the example of other visitors and many of the locals, we sat down for coffee at an outdoor café.

Whilst we were there a funeral procession went past at a rather hurried pace – with the corpse being carried by a number of men. it was quite uncovered except for a shroud. One of the main gates leading into or out of the Old City complex was the Bab Chorfa and we stopped to look over the open-air souk. A mass of inanimate objects lay before our gaze. Spanners and pieces of worn-out machinery jostled with other items of interest. The Bab Chorfa gate is itself flanked by two huge octagonal turrets. Our guide told us that we had to watch out for flies and small boys. There seemed to be no shortage of either wherever we went.

The Moslem Sabbath always brought crowds thronging into the Old City, as I witnessed one Friday. Our guide led us into a metalworker's lair where we purchased a small brass-topped folding table. The pattern that adorned the table top was copied from a design on the 'Golden gates' of the Cherratin Medersa. These metal-faced gates may be viewed from the Rue Cherratine. The interlocking geometric

patterns of Islam on the gate contrast with the figurative realism of Christian art. A carpet shop was the next place we stopped at, and we watched carpets being woven on big looms. The excellence of the work was obvious but I did not buy. As in Marrakech there are dyeing vats here. Local boys worked at the vats, the bales of wool and the falls of running water. It was a buzz of activity. Traders of all kinds were busy in the Fez el Bali. Leatherworkers, Jewish goldsmiths, coppersmiths, and sellers of just about anything that was saleable were hard at it. The Frenchman who had guided us through the labyrinth of Old Fez for two hours or so beckoned us to join him in a little crowded café somewhere in the maze. Here we settled up with him before his djellabah-clad figure vanished from sight down a narrow passageway.

We had another trip through the labyrinth the following day on our own. A local boy invited us into his home for mint tea. Stepping through a little doorway we were surprised to find that it opened out into a fair-sized courtyard. Despite the usual male dominance of Moslem society, the women seemed to be ruling the roost when we were at this house. The men were nowhere to be seen.

Panoramic views of Fez are interesting and we decided one day to leave the hustle and bustle for while and walk up a hill overlooking the city. I noticed the river on the outskirts of Fez. It was in a most insanitary state, being a depository for much of the city's refuse. On the little winding road that led up the hill we were passed by a man and his donkey coming down. The donkey was carrying his load of logs with apparent ease. Heat and flies continued to oppress, but we soldiered on climbing to the summit of the hill. From here we could view the entire city of Fez spread out far below us.

We stayed in Fez for a few days in order to savour its 'fossilised' atmosphere more completely. Its situation must certainly have helped in the prosperity of Fez in days gone by. Fez is situated on an old-time caravan route which ran from the Sahara to the coast of Tangier. Communications were therefore good even in the fourteenth century when the fame of Fez spread far and wide across Europe, especially as a great centre of learning. It was also a seat of power then, since Fez reached its zenith of affluence and glory at the time of the Merinids. The number of mosques is about three hundred in Fez alone. Small wonder, then, that it is called 'The City of Mosques'. The Karouyyin Mosque of Fez is the biggest in the whole of North Africa. It boasts fourteen doors and a large nave which rests on two hundred and seventy pillars. Successive generations have added their own touches, like the twelfth-century bell which came from Spain. The Mosque can accommodate thousands of people – about twenty thousand in all. The University has a vast collection of manuscripts, a repository of Moslem cultural material. Outsiders are not allowed to enter the Mosque; they can nevertheless pay a visit to the Medersas – those old theological colleges, now disused, built originally to provide places for the thousands of people who came here to study. Even in the fourteenth century masses of students came to Fez. Not far from the University a fountain can be seen in the Place Nejjarine. This fountain is decorated with colourful tilework, which is another typically Islamic innovation.

It is difficult for any student of Islamic culture to tear himself away from Fez, such is its attraction. In one section of the labyrinth we came upon a carpenter's shop. A little stack of shaped wood lay just outside the wide-open doorway. Other shaped sections of wood were stacked end-on inside the door. A man wearing a dark djellabah was conversing with the carpenter, who was dressed in a white djellabah and white turban. Old-style saws hung from convenient hooks above the head of the seated carpenter. I found it irresistible to think that Joseph's workshop at Nazareth might have looked like this. Joseph would most probably have been more industrious.

Regretfully it was time for us to leave Fez and journey on to our next locale. Many regard Meknes as being of lesser interest than Fez. It was smaller than Fez for one thing, although it does have a number of very stately gateways. Here again it was Moulay Ismail who instigated the building of those monumental gateways – also the huge walls, the palaces and mosques. Ruins at Meknes are of stables where the Sultan's twelve thousand horses were stabled, massive granaries, pleasant gardens, and the Kouba el-Khiyatine where the Sultan entertained special guests. It is said that King Hassan II's bodyguard are descendants of Moulay Ismail's Black Guard. Since the present monarchy is part of Moulay Ismail's dynasty it is not unnatural to suppose that the royal servants could have kept their family line intact also in the service of this royal dynasty.

We found the Great Gate of Meknes, the Bab Mansour, very imposing. Begun in Noulay Ismail's reign, the gateway was completed by Moulay Abdullah, the son who followed in Moulay Ismail's footsteps. Areas of stonework round the gateway are, like similar areas elsewhere, decorated with fine arabesque motifs.

As the visitor probes into the city's history, amazing facts are unearthed. For example, the local reservoir was dug out by fifty-thousand slaves in olden times. One of the city's gates known as the Bab Berdaine is the entrance to the Bab Berdaine Mosque, which I suppose is logical. Architecturally speaking, the gate, mosque, and minaret all complement each other perfectly. Whilst perhaps the visitor should not expect to see the same degree of encapsulation of Islamic tradition as in Fez, the smaller imperial city of Meknes is still captivating.

The huge rectangular Place El Hedin is a place where you can sit and watch the fever of life, and Arab traders carrying on their business. Here also we saw the largest assembly of scooters that we had seen anywhere in the country. Going by scooter is a favourite way of travelling for Moroccans. Certainly they are a great deal faster than camels. That night we stayed at an unpretentious little hotel close to the bus depot – close by the ruins of Volubilis, an old Roman city, one of several to be found right across North Africa.

We decided that Casablanca would be our next destination. After a brief stopover en route to Casablanca due to a burst tyre on the charabanc, we finally disembarked. To our surprise we found that we were in Rabat! A happy accident really, since we enjoyed our visit. Thus I was pleased about our miscalculation, and impressed by the stylish shops, and air of sleek sophistication that pervades the place. Here at Rabat stands the official residence of King Hassan. Indeed sumptuous Palaces are kept going in most major Moroccan cities for the King.

The colourful souk was an absolute must for us to visit. It is something of a contradiction but it is the regular sameness of these souks that inspires my interest. What we did find depressing was seeing a number of very sick and crippled people – the wreckage of humanity that lay beside the stalls where craftwork and spices were sold. This was the Quadias Casbah, completely surrounded by a huge wall. We had entered the casbah by a twelfth-century gateway from Yacoub El Mansour's reign. Many visitors make for the famous Moorish café, but we decided to stop off at some of the others instead. Downing several tiny cups of that thick

Turkish coffee, and eating the pastries (a bit sweet for my liking), we fortified ourselves for the moment.

Clearly there is a strong Spanish element in this area, since Moslem times, since Moslems who fled from Spain centuries ago settled in the city's Medina area. It was they who built the Andalusian Wall in the seventeenth century. A prominent focal point in Rabat is the Tower of Hassan which is seen towering above the mosque ruins. The builder of this tower fully intended it to compare with Seville's Giralda. The idea of building a mosque of such dimensions was originally to accommodate the Sultan's army. Sadly work on the great building stopped and it served other purposes when the Sultan died. King Hassan II's father, Mohammed V, is interred here. It is the former King's memorial as well as being his mausoleum, which visitors will find close to the ruined mosque on the east side of the grounds. The Sunna Mosque of more recent origin is a dominant feature on the Avenue Mohammed V. It is a very imposing avenue, lined as it is with palm trees and decorative flower beds.

Once Rabat was a Roman city – and excavations carried out have unearthed the remains of Roman baths, of which the Romans had plenty in their cities. Shops of the same vintage were also discovered. It was lovely to see the orange trees and jacaranda blossoms – a feature of many places in Morocco, as we have seen. We spent much time in exploring the elegant avenues that abound in Rabat. Going through an aperture called the Ambassador's Gate, we entered the Mechouar area and found ourselves in grounds adjacent to the Royal Palace. At certain times the changing of the guard may be watched there.

There were other things that I would have liked to see, such as the scribes at work in the Bab El Had, or perhaps the interiors of Rabat's mosques, but the latter are always subject to restriction in Morocco. From Rabat we looked out across the Bou Regreg river and saw Rabat's sister town Salé. We descended the sloping sea wall and hailed a ferryman in his little boat.

One item of clothing I was carrying was a hooded cloak with a tassel on the hood that I had bought in one of the souks. This cloak is known as a bournouse, and is usually worn over the djellabah. Both these items of clothing are eminently practical. Another souvenir I purchased in Morocco was a thimble-sized jar of gunpowder. These are used by Arabs in the tatooing of their skins – a custom going back to biblical times in Eastern countries. Arabs have a veritable craze for tatooing, and it is the gunpowder that produces the familiar bluish tint. In another part of Africa Egyptians use soot from smoke mingled with milk from women, then apply a paste of clover leaves or white beet. This is undoubtedly the older of the two methods. Forehead, chin, hands, and chest may be tatooed, as I have seen many times during these travels.

Author's note

Other examples of North African Bible customs? I will include three more with this chapter.

Once I watched a native woman in Tunisia throwing grass into a blazing mud brick kiln (Matt 8 v29).

I have seen birds sold in a market in Tunisia with a boy holding starlings by their legs (Matt 10 v29).

In Tunisia's deep south women still grind at small handmills (Matt 24 v41).

CHAPTER TEN

RETURN TO MARRAKECH

Gingerly we descended the stony slope and clambered aboard the little craft. I slipped a few coins into the hand of the robed ferryman and we both took our seats beside a motley collection of swathed figures silently huddling against one another. The ferryman dipped his oars and the little ferry boat was moving across the waters of the Bou Regreg towards the little town of Salé. Within a short space of time we cruised in to land on its shore.

Salé is a little walled town, far smaller than Rabat but interesting for all the little tunnelling passageways which it contains. Certain things are different here – for one thing we encountered styles of dress hitherto unseen by us. One figure swept past us dressed in a skirt or baggy trousering of white-and-red stripes. The upper garment was white. On the person's head (I could not tell whether the person concerned was a man or woman) was a broad-rimmed hat. Then a man with dark baggy trousers, light blue flowing coat and small tight-fitting beret walked past, towing a small cart with worn rubber tyres. Continuing on our way we were sometimes walking under quaint little arches and sometimes coming out into streets that were open to the sky.

In the Middle Ages merchants from Britain and Flanders came to Salé for the purposes of trade. Refugees by the score came to Salé to escape their persecutors. We did, of course, walk through the monumental gateway – The Bab El M'Risa – which formed the harbour entrance in times past. Inside, the visitor can browse for jewellery and such like in the Sidi Marzouk Souk. It must be said that Salé can boast its fair share of craftsmen. There are carpenters and masons to be seen in the Rue Ketchachin. The Rue Haddadin has its resident metalworkers and blacksmiths. As in many Moslem towns, there is a shrine in Salé dedicated to its patron saint. Special lanterns are kept inside the shrine, and coloured wax is used for their decoration. A procession is staged carrying these lamps through the streets of Salé to the place of the Chief Coppersmith for repair. It is undertaken annually on the day before the Prophet Mohammed's birthday (called the Mouloud). Close to the Grand Mosque stands the College of Abou El Hassan from the fourteenth century.

Crossing the river back to Rabat was a little eerie with a robed figure rowing us across. It reminded me of the crossing of the Styx in Greek legend. I decided that there was time for another look round in Rabat before we travelled on to Casablanca. One section of Rabat that did interest us was the Kasbah des Oudaias. It is a fortress which overlooks the mouth of the river. The beautifully laid out gardens within the walls we thought of as being akin to a Japanese garden. The fortress lies adjacent to the Old Medina and also the Mellah Jewish quarter. Court diplomats of the eighteenth century once lived close to the fortress in the Rue des Consuls. The old Customs houses down on the quayside were converted into warehouses for Salé by one of the sultans. Our trip over to Salé had been most enjoyable. It is possible now to cross over by way of a bridge, detracting perhaps from the romance of being rowed across by the ferryman, as we had been. I later wondered whether the 'Salee Rovers' had anything to do with this place. (It will be remembered that the 'Salee Rovers' captured Robinson Crusoe.) Sla is the Arabic name for the place, derived originally from the Roman name of Sala Colonia. The Arabic scripts found on the tombs of bygone sultans are beautifully executed, like the embellishments on European tombs of the eighteenth-century Roccoco period.

Rabat is today the Sherifian Kingdom's capital city. So much has developed here under the French Protectorate. The city was scarcely in the running as Morocco's capital in recent times, as the other alternatives were considered. The French had their Moroccan capital here, and after independence it was retained as the capital, as the old unwieldy nature of Fez, Marrakech and Meknes argued against them. To centralise things at any of these cities after the ancient pattern was impractical, the authorities decided. Rabat was infinitely more modern and functional and flexible. To have an administrative centre on the Atlantic seaboard was also necessary. There are still French buildings in Rabat that will no doubt evade the nose of the bulldozer, as least for a while. Also the extensive parkland in Rabat shows its excellent sense of city planning. Apparently there was a certain rivalry between Casablanca and Rabat in terms of them both being centres of commerce and playing a vital role in modern Morocco. What would Charles Dickens have made of this 'Tale of Two Cities', I wonder? He did at any rate see the beginnings of modern society, living us he did in the midst of a great ferment of thought and development.

Morocco has plenty of pomp and ceremony, as we were to find out a few days later in Marrakech. Meanwhile a few comments on the events in Rabat. Being the capital, Rabat does have ceremonies when the King rides to the Mosque at the side of the Mechouar. Prayers are held at midday. Guards and detachments of soldiers are at their posts. The Doctors of the Law join the King at his prayers, dressed in white like the King. Afterwards the Doctors of the Law emerge to join the King in the procession back to the Palace. Even the horses were resplendent in trappings that were fitting for the occasion. Those horses are taken to the Mosque prior to the King's return. Each animal is suitably draped with a blanket of a different colour. Whilst the King rides back to the Palace on his white steed, a parasol is held over his head. A great tradition – and speaking of Rabat's old traditions the Musée des Antiquités has a display of valuable Roman bronzes from Volubilis. Somewhat reluctantly we left this splendid city as we had to press on.

Our first look at Casablanca was a little offputting as the train approached the railway station of that city. All I could see in the rapidly gathering darkness was a large number of very tall buildings that seemed to be a mixture of skyscraper and warehouse. Soon we hailed a taxi, and we had to rely on the guidance and local knowledge of the driver. Through empty shuttered streets we were driven until the driver put us off in a hotel area. Following the directions of a stranger we came to a hotel that was within our budget. Our room had full-length French windows opening out on to a little balcony that hung directly over the street below. Shortly after booking in and dumping our bags we went out again. The streets of Casablanca are very much alive at night with eating places and food stores doing what seemed to us a roaring trade. Orientation in a strange city is often a problem, but I managed to take note of landmarks in order to find our way back to the hotel.

Casablanca is Morocco's commercial centre, and an out-and-out modern city. It seemed something like New York (the latter known only by books and films to me). A little Medina down by the port is perhaps the only reminder of the city's past – and a past Casablanca does indeed have.

The recorded history of Casablanca begins in about the twelfth century when the inhabitants of those days called it Anfa. In the fifteenth century the Portuguese ransacked the then existing city, and created the name Casa-Blanca, or the White House (shades of the USA). Thus the Portuguese gave it its name. Eighteenth-century earthquakes caused havoc here, and widespread evacuation. Resettlement by the Moors occurred only two years after.

The harbour of Casablanca is the biggest in Morocco and probably one of the most substantial in the world. I could see long fingers on concrete pointing out into the sea. These elongated jetties are ingenious feats of modern engineering, creating safe harbours for shipping. I asked directions to the shore from a nearby Arab. 'La Mer?' I intoned. He pointed and gabbled in incomprehensible Arabic. It was a pleasant seascape, but spoiled by the indiscriminate dumping of rubbish at certain points. Not far from the Medina we saw an old swimming pool situated right on the coast, possibly a hangover from colonial times. Also close by we visited the city's aquarium. Marine life in abundance could be seen there. It was one of the best of its kind.

French Protectorate imprinting is still evident in the street names. Boulevard de Bordeaux, Avenue Pasteur, and Boulevard Victor Hugo are notable examples. But streets with Arabic names like Boulevard Sidi Mohammed Ben Abdulla may certainly be found as well. After getting footsore from tramping the city streets we stopped for a while in the United Nations Square, or, in French, Place des Nations Unies. Most

of Casablanca's important institutions converge here – the main central post office, the City Hall, the Municipal Theatre, and Royal Automobile Club building. There was an impersonal sensation amid the hustle and bustle, as with many large cities. We glimpsed the brilliantly white Cathedral of Sacré-Coeur but only had a brief glimpse inside. Built in 1930 it is not really old as cathedrals go, but inspiring just the same. Any connoisseur of stained glass should head for the Notre Dame de Lourdes Church, where fine examples of it can be viewed.

The hordes of people of differing races that have descended on North Africa's shores have doubtless helped to bring about Casablanca's cosmopolitan make-up. I couldn't find Rick's Café which featured in that *Casablanca* film. May be it was merely a figment of a screenwriter's imagination after all.

Soon we boarded a train again. This time it was a return visit to Marrakech. I conversed with a jovial Frenchman who happened to be sitting in our carriage and we got on famously. The countryside through which we passed was alternately flat and hilly by turns. The hills were green and grassy as opposed to them being sandy and desert-like. I knew that the real desert was to be found on the other side of the Atlas Mountains. This present landscape was of a different type entirely. I noticed many smallholdings where farmers were busy ploughing the land with their little primitive wooden ploughs. One plough was being pulled by a camel and an ass. It was surely in direct contravention of the biblical edict about the non-hitching of different animals together.

As we approached Marrakech we passed a refuse area – not the nicest way to approach so romantic a city. What did interest me, though, was the large concentration of egrets – small white storks that are indigenous to North Africa. It was the largest gathering of egrets that I had ever seen at the time.

The train arrived at Marrakech and soon we were looking for the hotel at which I had stayed a few weeks before. I had inadvertently forgotten its name and precise location. We clip-clopped through the pink streets in a horse-drawn carriage, as befits a honeymoon couple. Then I spotted the hotel and we disembarked with our luggage, and an altercation with the driver followed about the cost of the ride. We could have booked in at another hotel but I had a yen about staying at the one I used earlier. The hotel staff recognised me at once and they were pleased to see me back. It was a hotel fit for a sultan and my eye ran over its rich decoration once more.

Soon we made our way back to the Place Djemaa el Fna to see again that incredible open-air circus and its heady intoxicating atmosphere. It was an absolute Babel with everyone, it seemed to me, trying to speak at once. Every performer was vying for our attention, and every car horn was honking into the bargain. Certainly God did not make all birds eagles, or all men white. The rich variety of life finds expression here at the Place Djemaa el Fna in its performers and visitors. The balmy, heady, quasi-drunken sensation never lets up – to everyone's delight.

Men in white djellabahs and white turbans appeared. This attire indicated that they had just returned from the *Haj* – the pilgrimage to Mecca. Every able-bodied Moslem is expected to do the pilgrimage to Mecca at least once in their lifetime. From Jerusalem, the focal point soon moved to Mecca, the birthplace of the prophet Mohammed. The Great Mosque is the most venerated shrine in Mecca and in all Islam. Pilgrims enter a vast courtyard, bearing their copies of the Koran, and splash themselves with sacred water. At the centre of the courtyard stands the huge cube-like 'Kaaba', draped in black, where it is claimed Abraham built the original shrine. The pilgrims then circle the Kaaba seven times in all, chanting a catechism which runs as follows: 'Lord God from such a distant land I have come to thee. . . . Grant me shelter under thy throne.' Such, briefly, is what these white-attired men would have experienced. In one corner of the Place Djemaa el Fna charabancs were busy loading passengers and their luggage, which was strapped to the vehicles' roofs. They would be bound for destinations in the Atlas region – some of the destinations remote and sand-blown, no doubt. I was reminded of my own forays earlier in the year.

It was getting late, and towards the end of the day the sinking sun cast long streaming lines of light and shadow across the Place Djemaa el Fna. A certain amount of activity was still in evidence. One little demonstration being carried out amidst all the hubbub caught my attention and held it. There was a Berber merchant sitting in his tiny patch, surrounded by a little crowd that had gathered to watch him.

What he had to offer was very different from displays of the jugglers, acrobats and drummers. Our man had a dead crow and a living one, and a dead hedgehog and a living one. He also had at his elbow a series of little jars containing what appeared to be spices. I later asked someone at the hotel what it meant. He told me, 'It's all to do with witchcraft. He was trying to convince his audience that he could restore dead animals to life.' So that was it! Certainly Africa has a reputation for magic and superstition.

The hotel manageress, an attractive young French woman, told me about the Independence Day celebrations that were to take place the next day. 'This is one occasion you should not miss, Monsieur', she purred in her soft French accent. My visits to various places often coincide with some important celebration there. I could only wonder why.

Crowds gathered thick and fast in the streets of Marrakech the following day, forming a virtual phalanx. The crowds had started forming early on, as was to be expected. The impressive celebrations were soon under way. Soldiers in all their finery marched past with great military bearing in seemingly endless sections. They were followed by a parade of tanks. It's pomp and ceremony that owe much to the French colonial influence. The crowds became more and more pressing (we were standing directly opposite our hotel). A Berber girl standing next to me made that famous enigmatic ululating cry. I had never heard it this close to before. The cry is made by holding the mouth wide open and vibrating the tongue. Every so often these ululations were let out over the crowds, and everyone dutifully clapped as each procession went by. The bandsmen looked smart and imposing in their scarlet uniforms and peaked caps. The scarlet of the uniforms was beautifully set off by belts and sashes of white. Presently King Hassan II himself appeared, dressed in a grey uniform which contrasted with the scarlet uniforms of the bandsmen.

As the King stood facing the crowd, a soldier dressed in camouflage jacket and trousers and dark green beret marched up to the sovereign and saluted. Then something else happened amid all this splendour. A cloud of smoke billowed in the sky somewhere behind the hotel. It hung like a dreadful pall. This was followed by the wail of a police car – or was it an ambulance, or even both? One of the aircraft, a ceremonial flight, had crashed, killing the pilot outright. It was tragic but the ceremonies nevertheless carried on as though nothing had happened. A smartly dressed uniformed band struck up with the Moroccan national anthem. It all seemed to go on for hours. At the end of the day we were pleased to rest. That night I sat up late conversing with another seasoned traveller and his convalescing friend. The first man had visited North Africa numerous times. After chatting about our adventures at some length we thought about turning in. All of us finally retired to bed at about three o'clock in the morning.

The Place Djemaa el Fna is one of those places that you never tire of. I simply had to hear those pulsating drums yet again, see the storytellers and acrobats. Those drums built up into an ever-spiralling crescendo, as always. In view of all this apparent celebration of living it is somewhat of a sobering thought to realise that in the bad old days severed heads were displayed in this very Square. It seemed that when the Sultan's displeasure was incurred in some way heads rolled.

We boarded the train to Tangier. As we travelled my mind raced back over my Moroccan travels of that year. How could I ever forget the Deep South with its guedra dancing women, or the mysterious Blue Men of Tan Tan with their black date bread, amber beads and splendid camels? Where would those desert men that I had met be now? Halfway across the vast desert, I suspected, with their beasts. They would be stopping at intervals, unrolling their rugs within their tents at night. The camels would close their nostrils and eyes to any sandstorm. Sometimes the Blue Men would even eat one if necessary. Milk was taken from the animal and sometimes greenish water from its succession of stomachs. The camels were able to draw nourishment from their humps. At Tan Tan a camel is ritually sacrificed at the time of the town's great festival. Suffice it to say, the whole of our Moroccan journeyings resonated in my mind.

I tried to settle comfortably in our train compartment, as the train thundered northward through the night. The carriage was cold and totally without lighting. A man sat opposite us and we started conversing half in French and half in English. It was very strange talking to a dark outline of a human being inside a dark carriage as we sped closer and closer to Tangier. As the early morning light began to filter its way above the horizon, the man's features slowly took on definition. After several bleary-eyed hours we arrived in Tangier and boarded a flight later that day for London.

The disturbing saga of the East continued to dominate the media in the weeks that followed. Orators held forth on Eastern issues in Hyde Park on Sunday afternoons, with leaflets being handed out. North Africa remains relatively free from trouble in all of this conflict.

WESTERN TURKEY

CHAPTER ELEVEN

ISTANBUL

Several weeks elapsed. Then Anne and I turned our attention to another part of the Orient – Turkey. Although it is a Moslem country it is separate from the Arab States. In the weeks ahead we were to experience delights that were to make an indelible impression on us. There was an inebriated Turk on the plane, and his companion announced half-jokingly, 'No more dreenks for him'.

Airport formalities were soon over at Istanbul, and we were anxious to see the great city itself. Once there we made for the Sultan Ahmet Square on someone's recommendation in order to find suitable accommodation. We were soon billeted, and the Square became a convenient centre of operations for us. This was by all accounts a very off-beat part of the city, where cheap hotels nudge backgammon joints, and half the hippies on the trail to Katmandu gather. After settling in at our hotel we lunched at a tiny restaurant known to all and sundry as the Pudding Shop. Today, alas, it no longer exists – its space taken up by other activities. Then, however, it provided a meeting-place and stopover point for travelling youngsters. Those youngsters I saw were variously clad in fur-trimmed garments, typically Eastern robes more suited to Arab countries, and denim outfits from their local stores back home. The Pudding Shop had a notice board. Young Americans and Europeans who used the place a great deal had letters posted there and anxiously scanned the board for letters from home.

Later we dined at another café in the city. A conflict between two Turks erupted there and seemed to indicate warlike tendencies in the general populace. The two pugilists, firmly locked in their difference of opinion, were on collision course for the table at which we were seated, and only narrowly missed us.

Our first full day of exploration in Istanbul was wonderful with so many spellbinding sights to behold. This was the fabled one-time Constantinople. Here we were on the Golden Horn of the mighty Bosphorus river looking at the minaret-pierced skyline. You can't help stopping in your tracks many times to admire the domes and minarets of the Hagia Sophia and the Blue Mosque. Also Istanbul boasts many fantastic treasures besides, such as the Great Bazaar with its hundreds of intriguing shops which we were shortly to visit, and the exotic Topkapi Palace which we were also planning to see.

Back on the ferryboat we enjoyed the views of both banks of the Bosphorus. After the sailing we continued to savour the scene as we stood on the divide between East and West. Ferries had funnels which belched black smoke, masts that supported flags and bunting, and rows of lifeboats lining their sides. Continuing along the Bosphorus waterfront we came close to the Galata Bridge.

Here there were little fishing boats bobbing in the water, which looked dark blue from where we were standing. Fresh fish were fried aboard the boats for us as we waited – a sort of floating kitchen scenario. Once or twice we would breakfast Istanbul in this way, enjoying the freshly-cooked fish which was cooked on large circular trays over glowing embers. Once I gave a gesture of approval by making an 'O' with finger and thumb. The frier on his little boat would nod assent.

Constant streams of people crossed the Galata Bridge from one side of the Bosphorus to the other. Halfway across we stopped at a café area where several middle-aged and elderly men sat contentedly smoking narghiles or hubble-bubble water pipes. I suggested sitting with the men and enjoying their company. They were certainly a bunch of characters. First I noted an old wizened man dressed in some kind of greatcoat and peaked flat hat, something of a standard head-gear in these parts. Another of the gathering was a portly French-looking man with glasses, who wore an untidy sweater. Next to him was a Slavic or Russian type with flat hat and shabby suit. I began sketching some of the characters and attracted quite a crowd. 'Welcome to Turkey,' said the young waiter as he served us drinks. There is a definite 'wow' factor that Istanbul gives visitors – it's that kind of place.

A sail down the Bosphorus was called for. This is a water-way that connects the Mediterranean with the Black Sea. We were advised to take one of the local ferries rather than a typ-ically tourist craft. This we did and were soon sailing down the famed waters. Leaning over the boat's side I noticed swarms of jellyfish that drifted past. It was not long before we fell into conversation with a Turkish solicitor. He was a kind avuncular type who could speak English fluently. His easy pleasant disposition made him a worthwhile compan-ion for the sail. Our new-found companion was quick to come to the point about human nature.

'Watch out for crooks,' he said. 'There are crooks in every country – English crooks, French crooks, German crooks.'

'And Arab crooks?' I suggested casually.

With this he let out a whoop of laughter. To be fair, though, we concluded that crookedness was a universal problem. Our solicitor friend went on to tell us about the severe penalties incurred by drug smuggling and money changing in the streets of Turkey. I told him that this was unlikely to affect us. At one point in the sail the solicitor indicated the direction of the Black Sea – and it could just be seen. Continuing the discussion our man said, 'You must watch your wife, my friend. After all this is the Orient, you know.' I smiled at his humour. Then with a mischievous twinkle in his eye he added, 'How much is your wife worth? Mine is worth a great deal to me.' Acting as our unofficial guide, the friendly man pointed out many features of interest to us. The castle of the Sultan Mohammet, who conquered Byzantium, and the highly decorative palace of Sultan Abdul Aziz, which was seven-and-a-half centuries old, came into view.

'Just look at these old buildings that back onto the Bosphorus' was all I could say at that moment.

'Yes – and many people are able to dive straight into the water from their balconies,' the solicitor continued.

'Don't the divers mind the jellyfish stings?' I asked.

'We don't bother about a few jellyfish; their stings don't bother us,' he said as though scorning the very idea of it! I imagine that many Turks are likewise spartan in their attitudes.

Then our friend was determined to make certain that we knew how to deal with anyone who might accost us in the street for drug abuse or money changing. He passed on to us his own special recipe for such occasions.

'Make a snarling face and shout YOK (no in Turkish) at them. Come on, let's see you try!'

I duly followed his advice and produced a simulated 'YOK' but would it have done the trick?

We stopped at Yeniköy, which means New Town or New Village. When we disembarked, the solicitor came with us and ordered grapes for us from a little store. We walked along the deserted waterfront, which contrasted with Istanbul rather sharply. Yeniköy was a pleasant little village; its streets were suggestive of a French resort. At length we sailed back up the Bosphorus to Istanbul, noting the rows of empty seats at the deserted waterside cafés that stared blankly back at us. We passed beneath the massive suspension bridge as we had done on the outward journey. Back at the Galata Bridge we bade farewell to the solicitor, thanking him for his entertaining company.

Moustaches are the pride and joy of Turkish men. In the window of a photo-parlour I noted a photograph of a man with an enormous handlebar moustache. It was well clear of his face; at the ends it was waxed and curled. A luxurious growth indeed! I saw a man riding his cart in one section of the city, standing like an old charioteer, reins in hand. Two horses were pulling, as with a Roman chariot. Autumn leaves were falling in the parks of Istanbul, as they were doing in Europe. It appeared strange to see this in the Orient, but Turkey is split into climatic zones. Istanbul is situated in a temperate zone and latitude.

Our next visit was to the Sultan Ahmet Mosque, a building of sheer magnificence. A person can hardly fail to be awed by those huge domes and soaring minarets. The blue tilework is stunning. It is because of this that it also popularly called the Blue Mosque, not surprisingly. Apart from being overwhelmed by the sheer magnificance and scale of the Mosque, I found the acoustics impressive too. Romantics have listened out for the echo of their loved one's name under the central dome, which has smaller domes nestling round it. As we trod the rich carpets inside we pondered on the labour of love that all this represented. The Mosque was built in the seventeenth century by Sultan Ahmed I, the foundations being laid in 1609 with the Sultan himself in attendance. The ingenious architect was Sedefcar Mehmed Aga. Nine years in the making, it was completed in 1617. The ground plan covers an area of seventy-two by sixty-four metres. Being elevated on a hill the mosque with its six minarets is all the more prominent, especially when viewed from a distance. At this mosque the Janissary powers were abolished by Imperial Edict, which was read out from the mimbar in 1826. Close by Sultan Ahmet I's tomb stands with those of Ahmet I, Osman II, and Mother Sultana Kesem. The mother-of-pearl decorations are superb – one of the Blue Mosque's most interesting features.

Istanbul abounds in mosques that are large and impressive; for example, the New Mosque in Eminono Square, a fine example of seventeenth-century Turco-Islamic architecture. Then I would cite the Sehzade Mosque, built by Sultan Suleyman the Magnificent in memory of his well-loved son Sehzade Mehmet in the sixteenth century. Another one that we visited was the Hagia Sophia – nowadays more of a museum. The Hagia Sophia was always pointed out to me in architecture lessons as a supreme example of Byzantine building, and rightly so. It is every bit as eye-catching as the Blue Mosque and has the same feeling of towering magnificence about it.

The Hagia Sophia had its beginnings in Roman times when pagan temples stood on the site, dedicated to Artemis, Apollo and Aphrodite. Incensed by the presence of these pagan temples, the Christian Emperor Constantine ordered their destruction and a church built in their place. It was the

Church of St Irene, which was first opened in 326. The foundations of the Hagia Sophia were laid next to it. Constantine did not live to see the completion of the magnificent building.

It is doubtful whether any of the Hagia Sophia's first builders would recognise the existing structure if they came back today, since it has been sacked, destroyed and rebuilt many times. The building that visitors see today is the Church of Justinian, who fully intended his version to be one that surpassed anything that had gone before. In short he intended it to be the most stunning piece of religious architecture ever – and he was not far short of the mark. In the fabric of the Hagia Sophia there are areas of stonework from Ephesus, Baalbeck, Athens and Egypt and other places. The richness of the different coloured stones from the various locations certainly helped the Emperor Justinian in the realisation of his dream. The dark red stone is from Egypt, the green stone from Greece. The marble was brought here from the Mamara Islands and is of a beautiful pure white. It took five years to complete the building work, using a vast army of masons and artisans numbering ten thousand workers in all.

Over the Emperor's Gate in the narthex are to be found the famous Christian mosaics which show a traditional Christ, along with the Virgin Mary and some emperors of Byzantine times. The apse also contains some of these mosaics. Although Suleyman the Magnificent had these works whitewashed, they saw the light of the day again in later years. One thing that surely holds the visitor's attention is the vast central dome's interior. It is 55.60 metres in height, soaring above the gaze of those who stand there. The four massive pillars on which this decorative dome rests have been repaired a few times since Justinian first had them erected. However, to all intents and purposes they remain much as they were. Also of interest is the Gallery of Women,

Old turk with hubble-bubble pipe.

raised above ground level. It has one hundred and seven columns – sixty-seven of them being above ground level, and the other forty on ground level.

In 1935 the Government of Turkey made the Hagia Sophia a museum, recognising its outstanding merits. Often a masterpiece of religious architecture has to serve as both museum and place of worship (like St Paul's Cathedral in London).

We sat in the gardens adjacent to the Hagia Sophia and no sooner had we seated ourselves than we were accosted by a trinket seller. He had toy creatures that were made to run along the ground under the power of his thrusting hand. He tried to impress us with his knowledge of Britain.

'Man-chest-aire, Lids, Lon-den,' he intoned. 'Yes, I have a brother in Man-chest-aire. He has settled down there and is very happy'.

Returning to the Pudding shop which we did on a fairly regular basis, we rejoined those hippies, some of them just back from Katmandu. Some of them were dressed in baggy loose-fitting trousers with turbans and other head cloths. A more traditional mode of dress certainly exists in eastern Turkey but in IstanbulTurkish men wear modern clothes with natty flat caps, as we have seen.

Later we watched a man with a performing bear, this being something that had vanished from the streets of England centuries ago. The animal was made to stand on its hind legs and clutch a stick. Wandering through the little medieval-style streets that skirt the Blue Mosque, we saw women chopping wood for their stoves outside their doorways. Chivalrous to a degree, I relieved one woman of her axe and finished her chopping for her! I noted the thin chimneys of tin from their wood stoves that projected horizontally from the walls of their dwellings. When we temporarily lost our bearings a dark fierce-looking Turk with a long black drooping moustache gave us directions. Near our hotel in the Sultan Ahmet Square we noted other exotic destinations advertised, such as India, Nepal, and Katmandu, presumably used by some of the hippies. A rat ran down the street and we suspected that many such lurked in dark corners here.

The Hotel manager engaged us in conversation along with his father, father-in-law or uncle – I was not sure which. The old man was ninety-three years of age and his grizzled face was full of character. It transpired that he was a retired professor from Istanbul University. He said that he found my pronunciation difficult to follow, so I spoke more slowly.

When we tired of this hotel we moved to another – an awkward move as things turned out. At the reception desk there were four shabbily dressed men with stubbly chins. This hotel was next door to a newspaper printers which kept us awake at night with its awful racket. The following morning we breakfasted at the Pudding Shop as usual. Our waiter or was he the manager? seemed to be busier than ever. To us he looked very French with a dark moustache and a wisp of plastered down hair. Returning to the gardens near the Hagia Sophia we noticed a very striking clean-shaven man with a hawk-nose. I did a sketch of him and asked him where he came from. He said Afghanistan and I began to realise the distance some people travel in order to see Istanbul. The railway station looked particularly unkempt. As the terminus for the famous Orient Express, so fêted in fact and fiction, it was a disappointing station indeed.

The date was Saturday, October 29th, 1977 – a special date for the Turks. The *Turkish Daily News* carried as its headline 'Turkish Republic 54 years old today.' Grand ceremonies were being laid on in Istanbul and Ankara and indeed in Izmir as well. The very first ceremony of all would be held at the mausoleum of Kemal Atatürk, the founder of the modern Turkish republic. Kemal Atatürk was the country's first president as well as being its founder. Anyhow we planned to go and attend some of the celebrations later in the day.

Browsing my copy of the *Turkish Daily News*, there was an item about the kidnapping of a Dutch millionaire by a German Red Army faction. Page two carried an interesting article on the story of the formation of the Turkish Republic, devoting much space to it, as you might expect, and we shall take a brief look at how it was instigated and organised in the early years of the twentieth century. The basic precepts were hammered out in the early 1920s. It was then that Ankara was made the Turkish capital. The authorities felt that they could best conduct the affairs of state from there. At a meeting on October 13th, 1923, the Turkish Grand National Assembly accepted the resolution for the establishing of Ankara as the seat of power. A document was signed by the then Foreign Minister Ismet Pasa, along with other members of the Government. Mustafa Kemal was clearly the instigator of this new system, which he went about organising with great enthusiasm in those early years. Frequently we see portraits of Mustafa Kemal Atatürk in Turkey today, very much as Egypt displays portraits of the its President, or Britain displays portraits of the Queen. Mustafa Kemal considered that any prolonging of the Caliphate was not at all compatible with the needs of an increasingly modern world that was emerging. The abolition of the Caliphate was made effective on March 3rd, 1924, when these laws were passed. The Caliphate was abolished from that day, and all the remaining members of the Ottoman Dynasty were ordered to leave the country. Probably the influence of the caliphs would have waned anyway, even if the Caliphate had not been brought to such an abrupt end. Thus the old picturesque order is but a distant memory now.

At about midday we made our way to the far side of the city where the anniversary celebrations would take place. As is usual for such occasions, crowds several feet deep lined the route. Vendors did a roaring trade, and Swedes and Germans helped to swell the crowds. Two elderly bearded men stood close to us and looked my way. Resplendent in their uniforms, they were clearly war veterans. Possibly they fought at Gallipoli in World War I. I noted the khaki uniforms with Sam Brownes and black fur hats. Their tunics were proudly emblazoned with medals. Would they, I wondered, have remembered the days of the old Caliphate? Or known some Grand Vizier or other? Parades marched past with soldiers in immaculate blue-grey uniforms set off with white helmets, white belts, white gaiters, white lanyards and white gloves. They carried their rifles sloping on their left shoulders as they marched.

At the end of these proceedings we left for the Grand Bazaar, which is unmissable for any visitor to Istanbul. At least two hours are needed for this particular expedition. Entering the bazaar from the Çardircilar Caddesi, or Street of the Tentmakers, Portobello Road Market in London has nothing on this. It is reckoned to be the largest of its kind in the world. As we tunnelled our way through this warren-like bazaar of 4,000 shops, we relished gazing at the variety of the goods for sale. Copper shops and carpet shops were there, and huge urns of brass, and an ancient gramophone which only lacked a little white dog beside it to make it resemble those bygone adverts showing the 'His Master's Voice' emblem. I remember using similar hand-wound gramophones as a child, but nothing as grand as this, with its big cone-shaped amplifier. Apart from these little side streets where such antique objects are found, the layout of the bazaar was a good deal more modern than we had expected. But then the place had suffered several periods of destruction and rebuilding, and the last rebuilding took place in 1954. Haggling is expected here, as in most Eastern bazaars, and I haggled vigorously for a water pipe at one shop and I still have it.

Masses of monuments were to be found in far-off Byzantine times in almost every square in Constantinople, as it was then. A few monuments may still be seen today. My attention was drawn to the Egyptian Column in Sultan Ahmed Square. At one time it stood in the city's Hippodrome, but before that it occupied a place in Heliopolis in Lower Egypt. The Pharaoh Tuthmosis ordered his masons to make it complete with hieroglyphics in 1547 BC. It was transported to Istanbul by the Emperor Theodosius in the fourth century AD. Interestingly the pedestal base on which the obelisk stands relates to the time of its arrival in Istanbul. The Emperor and his family are shown in relief attending the ceremony. There are also old Latin and Greek inscriptions on the pedestal. At the top of the obelisk there is a representation of Tuthmosis offering gifts to the god Amun.

The Ormetas column, also to be seen in the Sultan Ahmet Square, was placed there by Constantine VII. It has long since been stripped completely of the bronze and brass that originally adorned it, as the metal was used for the minting of the coins during the Latin Empire period. Another interesting column is the coiled column which stood originally in the Temple of Apollo in Delphos. A section of this column is hidden from view, as it's underground. A fine golden vase once surmounted the column. It will surprise no one to know that it was stolen, probably during the sacking of old

Constantinople by the Turks. Yet another column to be seen is the Kiztazi, or the column of Marcian. A statue of Marcian once stood atop the column. This too was taken away.

Perhaps one of the most notable landmarks in Istanbul is the Galata Tower, from the seventh century, built by the Emperor Zenon. The tower has undoubtedly been much altered since the time of its inception. Indeed restoration of the tower took place as late as 1875. As its name suggests, the tower stands in the Galata quarter of Istanbul. I was surprised to learn that the tower now contains a nightclub, a restaurant and a gift shop – a far cry indeed from the days of the Emperor Zenon.

There are, of course, towers aplenty in Istanbul. They even have one out in the water at the Bosphorus entrance, called the Tower of Leandros. It is named after a man who regularly swam across the Bosphorus at this point to meet his friend, or was it his hero? Another story concerning the tower tells of it being the hiding place of a beautiful princess, and still another story about it being the storehouse of rare treasures. Was the princess killed off by a snakebite, as some relate, or did the Turkish hero Battal Ghazi make off with both the princess and the treasure? A tower of much later vintage is the Dolmabahce clocktower from 1890. The Beyazid tower first built in wood is now a fire tower.

I noticed portions of walling from the days of Constantinople still standing in places, the jagged edges of the stonework bearing witness, no doubt, to the continuous pounding of old Turkish cannons during the fall of Constantinople. These powerful cannons were capable of hurling a 600-pound ball missile. Considering the strength of those double walls, a powerful assault was needed. The Turks trained strong young boys for their army, taken from their prisoners. The army became known as the Janissaries. They became a formidable fighting force. When the walls of Constantinople fell, the Janissaries poured into the city, resulting in its sacking. There was no deliverance in spite of Constantine's Solemn Mass in St Sophia's, where the general populace barricaded themselves in. The Turks smashed their way through the doors and killed all the occupants. The Emperor Constantine was killed in the skirmish, too. Afterwards his body had to be identified by the winged sandals that he wore, so grievous were his injuries. When the visitor of today stands there in admiration at the exquisite balance of Christian domes and Moslem minarets, he should spare a thought for the bitter conflict of the past that has produced this striking union.

With the history of Turkey very much in mind, we turned our steps towards the Archaeological Museum and its interesting exhibits. In the museum grounds autumn leaves fell on the outdoor collection of antiquities. Once inside we were able to see the bust and sarcophagus of Alexander the Great. Tell-tale relief carvings on most of the sarcophagi showed the lives of those interred within them. In all twenty-six fine sarcophagi were brought to this museum from excavations in Sidon. Each of the twenty exhibition halls in the museum is named according to the exhibits – the Hall of Architectural Works, the Hall of Sarcophagi, and so on. So we spent a very worthwhile hour studying objects of archaic art. Phoenician, Roman, and Byzantine relics all fascinated us. I noticed the famed inscription from Hezekiah's tunnel in Jerusalem. I had to explain to some American visitors that it was removed from Jerusalem to Istanbul sacrilegiously at the time of the Ottoman Empire.

Further cultural treats awaited us in the following weeks as we prepared to travel round western Turkey. Our week in Istanbul had proved hugely enjoyable, and now we headed for the coach station. With the taxi-driver's help we located the right coach. The next leg of the journey was to take us to Çanakkale – a town that was reached by skirting the Sea of Mamara. At length the coach with us on board lurched out of the depot, and was soon hurtling along a very barren, unkempt stretch of road towards Çanakkale.

CHAPTER TWELVE

AN AGE-OLD BATTLEGROUND

The coach rumbled on for hours until we reached a famous spot on the north Aegean. We were journeying through the Dardanelles area, a well-known battleground of ages. It became a theatre of military operations during World War I. These straits divide the European and Asian areas; here also the Aegean and Mamara Seas divide. The scene we found was peaceful, but it exploded with the sound of war in times past.

The coach pulled in at a little village called Eceabat, where the coach broke down. The driver and his assistant must have extracted half the vehicle's innards in the process of repairing it. For what appeared to be ages, the men struggled with the job, getting themselves liberally covered in oil in the process.The passengers meanwhile passed the time walking on the waterfront, or otherwise waited until they were able to continue the journey to Çanakkale. A cold sharp wind was coming in at us from across the Straits, and we purchased a bag of hot chestnuts from a vendor. Darkness had fallen when the repairs to the charabanc were complete. Soon we were all aboard the vehicle, being carried now by ferryboat. Soon we were walking the streets of Çanakkale. If they continued to feed that old bus on cheap-grade fuel, it might not be making many more journeys, I felt.

We found a small hotel without much trouble, and were pleased to step in out of the cold night air to the warmth of a wood-stove. They're great stove people, these Turks. We continued to warm ourselves by the cheerful stove. My eye followed the long black pipe that ran up towards the wall behind it. Then I noticed that the chimney pipe projected horizontally through the wall to the street outside. At length we decided to brave the cold night air again in order to purchase yet another fish supper, and, of course, yet another plentiful supply of bottled water. Also we remembered to take our weekly malaria tablets.

Next morning in the full light of another day the complete contrast between Istanbul and Çanakkale was apparent. After a week in a big bustling city we were in a small town. Apart from that there is always the *genius loci* of a particular place – not always easy to define. Çanakkale had a quality about it that I found attractive. For one thing everything seemed much cleaner and out-in-the-open here, even if such inconveniences as waiting for the bathroom caused some consternation. Today a queue had formed into the bargain. The hotel manager, whom I took to be of German origin, and many other guests were eager to converse with us. The trouble was that we understood very little Turkish and they in turn understood very little English, but we managed to get by.

One of the most important sights to see in Çanakkale is the Kilit-bahir fortress, which sustained a huge breach during the battle of 1915. The story of that fateful conflict must be told more fully elsewhere, but we may consider it briefly here. In the First World War these straits were seen as strategically vital in supplying Russia by the Black Sea. Hence the Allied forces of Britain, France and Russia were trying to force a passage through them. We purchased a chart (now unavailable) that portrayed the Allies' battleships sailing up the straits – ships with names such as *Agamemnon*, *Irresistible*, *Charlemagne*, *Triumph*, *Vengeance*, *Inflexible*, and *Majestic* – names with a savage poetry all their own.

Minesweepers did their best, heavy fire and sometimes weather against them, but Turkish mines scuppered the Allies' ships anyhow. As in so many such conflicts the loss of life was horrendous, especially on the Gallipoli peninsula battlefields. Today guided tours of them are offered by the ANZAC House organisation in Çanakkale. ANZAC stands for Australian and New Zealand Army Corps. Their landing zone is also so named. Troops from these countries also took part in the campaign. The formidable Turkish forces were led by Lt. Col. Mustafa Kemal – later to become the founder of modern Turkey. On a Gallipoli hillside, directly across the Dardanelles from Çanakkale, and right on the narrows, you can see a huge design. The words Dur Yolcu are visible (Traveller, stop a moment) along with the symbols of a soldier and the eternal flame, clearly intended to encourage some brief and sombre thoughts. On the same side there's an ancient fortress with heart-shaped perimeter walls. Huge guns from World War I can be viewed in the town centre (and many in the open-air museum). Once they exploded with fearsome firepower. These guns have thankfully long been silent and you can now enjoy peaceful aspects of the place, as we did on that delightful 1977 visit.

In antiquity Çanakkale's waterway was, of course, the great Hellespont. The name Dardanelles derives from the founder of Troy, Dardanus. Inevitably your mind will 'stop a moment', pondering the centuries of warfare here as you stand there. On these waters the Athenian navy was wiped out by Lysander in that final battle of the Peloponnesian War. It was across these straits that the Persian King Xerxes threw his pontoon bridge of boats when going to war with the Greeks.

Mention of all this warfare reminded me of a Turk I had conversed with in a carpet shop in Istanbul, who claimed to have worked as a driver for a general during World War I. Apart from the universal habit of sitting at outdoor cafés, lingering at the water's edge is something of a pastime for these Turks at Çanakkale. At times we were likewise captivated.

The battle theme was to continue with our next stopping point – the legendary Troy, with its tales of a wooden horse and a beautiful maiden. Thanks to archaeological work of recent times Troy has seen the light of day again after centuries of oblivion. We had to hire a taxi for the journey to Troy, since I could not see a dolmush or bus anywhere. Journeying through pleasant countryside, the taxi started climbing uphill through splendid pine-forests. On the way we passed through delightfully rustic little villages where old men in shabby suits and cloth caps sat at pavement cafés (more of them) and puffed contentedly at their hubble-bubble pipes. Sunlight glinted on the little tables as we passed.

Arriving at the ruins of Troy we were confronted by the inevitable souvenir shop selling miniature wooden horses and the like. It was the full-scale replica of the original wooden horse that we climbed into from below to get some idea of what those warriors of long ago felt. For ten Turkish Lire apiece we were able to walk round the ruins whilst the driver waited for us inside the shop. The English-speaking owner of the shop was busy feeding a pigeon – a fledgling – with seeds on a little table. I looked upon the substantial portions of perfectly-preserved wall, chunks of marble columns, and Greek lettering inscribed on some of the stonework.

It is true that others came this way before the German amateur archaeologist Heinrich Schliemann found a few relics. However, it was largely due to this devoted fan of Homer that the fable city came to light. Many thought that Homer's city was mere fantasy and fabrication. Schliemann believed that Troy was a place that really existed and its stories facts of history. His persistence prevailed and he proved the scorners wrong. In the process, alas, he caused some irreparable damage by some very clumsy archaeological work. Some walling from Troy II was one part that Schliemann sacrilegiously though inadvertently destroyed whilst searching for the treasure of Priam. Likewise in a trench he dug in the south of the site he damaged Roman and Hellenistic work. Then followed his destruction of the priceless Temple of Athena.

After the death of Schliemann another phase of archaeological discovery began. This time everything was conducted on a soundly professional basis, starting in the 1890s. A number of experts in relevant disciplines came together to work on the unearthing of Troy. Experts involved included prehistorian Max Weigel, archaeologist Alfred Bruckner and architect Wilbertle. This expedition was led by an architect named Dorpfeld, who altered some of Schliemann's ideas. What Schliemann took to be Troy II was in reality Troy VI, as later discoveries showed. Whilst the original Troy was constructed on bedrock, the second Troy was naturally raised a few metres above this and it was destroyed by fire. Fire and earthquakes also brought about the untimely demise of Troys III, IV and V. The next Troy is interesting with its yields of Mycenaean pottery. Troy VI had four gates and at least three towers. Notable is the great city wall of Troy II, also ceramics of Mycenaean craftsmen discovered here, meregen houses and prehistoric remains.

The third phase of Troy's excavations was carried out by American experts who conducted their programme of archaeological excavations with typical American thoroughness. Their work began here in 1932. In the seven further seasons that followed every minutest detail was examined. Many interesting things came to light during the American excavations, including what is alleged to be the very gate through which the wooden horse was pushed into the city. Apparently the gate was too small for the purpose, and it became necessary for parts of the gateway to be dismantled. After this had taken place the horse was able to pass through the gateway. The scars of the dismantling can still be seen today. Also we may see an altar which once ran with the blood of sacrificial animals, and the remains of old temples.

The Trojan War was raging here in about 1200 BC, when the Greeks were warring with the Trojans. Paris, who was a Trojan, had kidnapped the ravishingly beautiful Helen of Troy. She had been abducted from her husband, the King of Sparta, Menelaus. This abduction and the guarding of the Dardanelles were pivotal to the conflict. Hector the Trojan slew Patroclus the Greek, thus incurring the wrath of Achilles who in turn avenged the death of Patroclus by killing Hector. As everyone knows, the only vulnerable part of Achilles' anatomy was his heel, where the waters of the Styx had not covered him when he was dipped there as an infant. Paris had fired an arrow into Achilles heel, but the death of Achilles only helped to continue the war. The Greeks had to get within the walls of Troy in order to surprise the enemy. This was done by filling the wooden horse with Greek soldiers and pushing it through one of the city gates. The fact that the occupants of Troy were engaged in a drunken orgy made it all the easier for the Greek soldiers to slay them. It was a stroke of genius on the part of

Odysseus, who gave instructions for the building of the horse.

Actually there are about nine levels of occupation that have been identified and uncovered. This indicates that it was a very substantial centre of human habitation over long periods in ancient times. By carefully following the maps given by the souvenir shop, we may pick out the various levels of civilization and their differing features: here a waterwork, there a temple or tower, or portion of city wall. Here and there we saw big mounds, presumably containing relics as yet untouched by archaeologists.

The setting appeared to me to be perfect for these stirring dramas of the Trojan War. Try as I did, it was difficult to conjure up any of these scenes of battle between the Greeks and Trojans long ago. The late autumn sun was pleasantly warm as we strolled down these ancient streets. Then we ascended a stone ramp – an incline that might even be the one on which the wooden horse was pushed into the city.

The Roman occupation of Troy was naturally a period of much rebuilding. The Temple of Athena was built by them. Typically there were numerous Roman columns and a theatre. Troy VII is associated with the war between the Greeks and Trojans, and the wooden horse episode. The site museum we found interesting with its Trojan relics. Here also we picked up the St Paul trail again, for the Apostle came here during his second missionary journey on his way to Macedonia. St Paul's Troas was part of this area, known as the Troad – the land of Troy.

As we were driven back the way we had come, I noticed the cotton-pickers at work in the fields and loading sacks of cotton onto waiting vehicles. Izmir at first presented us with an unsightly industrial blot next to the bus depot. Soon, however, we found it to be a huge attractive city. Despite the

Classical remains here (more of which presently) it was the modernity of Izmir which held my attention, belying past glories.

There's a towering Hilton Hotel at its heart. The 1926 fire has not prevented the rapid growth of Izmir up to the present day. We boarded a bus for the city centre after our arrival at the main depot. I was advised to make for Basmane Square and its adjoining Eylul Square. It was considered essential to be able to pronounce the name of Eylul Square in a Turkish accent. When I judged the bus to be in the right place I asked, 'Do-kooz-ey-lool?' At least a dozen Turks of varying ages turned and excitedly pointed out the Square to us. Once there we had no difficulty in finding fresh lodgings, for the area is peppered with hotels in abundance.

Eylul Square has a central fountain and it is here that we found the entrance to the Culture Park – or Kultur Parki. The following day we made a point of visiting the park, making straight for the archaeological museum, which has a great collection of antiques, like all the Turkish museums. Here I viewed a number of Greek statues, including the head and arm of a collossus discovered at Ephesus, seemingly searching for a body to be attached to; a statue of Artemis; and a bust of Demeter in bronze. I was refused permission to draw at this museum. The keeper on duty seemed to think the very idea was improper. That is not to say that abundant opportunities for drawing antiques in Turkey didn't await me – they did!

In a nearby restaurant fish complete with heads were served to us, as is usual in these countries. In the gardens of the Culture Park we saw a number of busts of past sultans, completely unprotected from the elements. The park seemed to be a special haunt for cats, stray or semi-domesticated.

In the souks of Izmir we bought some Turkish delight,

which I found rather too sweet for my palate. For some reason we were not allowed to visit the Roman Agora – the only area remotely connected with New Testament times. Looking through the barrier I could see over on the opposite side three statues. They were Poseidon, god of the sea; Artemis (Diana), whom we shall meet again soon; and Demeter, goddess of the corn. Workers were busy on restoration work which was why visitors were not allowed in.

On the waterfront we stopped for a while at the Konak Meydani with its cafés and Moorish-type clock tower. Dominating most of the city is the Velvet Castle, or Kadifekale, set high on top of Mount Pagus. Whilst I was aware of the dominating presence of hill and castle we didn't actually visit the castle, only walking part of the way up the incline.

The first to build the Velvet Castle was a general under Alexander the Great. Izmir is, of course, the biblical Smyrna, one of the seven churches of the Book of Revelation. In the city there was an early Christian church – a small community set against a predominantly pagan world. Thus we read in the Book of Revelation:

> And to the angel (messenger) of the assembly (church) in Smyrna write. These are the words of the First and the Last . . . I know your affliction and distress and pressing trouble and your poverty; but you are rich! and how you are abused and reviled and slandered by those who say they are Jews and are not, but are a synagogue of Satan . . . Be loyally faithful and I will give a crown of life. (Amplified Bible, Revelation 2: 8–10)

For the Christians then, it was very much a struggle in every way.

The ancient Smyrna, for the most part, lay on the other side of the bay to present-day Izmir. The area was inhabited as early as the third millennium BC. Possibly these early inhabitants were Lelges, as Strabo tells us, and as we know the Hittites featured prominently in the early history here as elsewhere in Turkey. In about 1100 BC Aeolian Greeks came to Smyrna. They were from the islands of the Aegean. One old legend of doubtful origin claims that the original inhabitants were Amazons, Smyrna supposedly being a derivative of the name Amazon. Herodotus tells us how the builders of vast civilisations in central Turkey, the Ionian Greeks, first arrived in Anatolia. Fleeing hostilities from Dorian invaders, they settled at Colophon – a mere thirty-five kilometres from Smyrna. When the refugees were cast out by the established people of Colophon, they turned their attention to Smyrna – taking over the city at festival time. Archaeological findings would seem to confirm the takeover by one tribe of Greeks from another.

After the destruction of Smyrna by Alyattes in 600 BC, decline set in until Alexander the Great restored Smyrna and brought it to its most glorious period. Shortly after Alexander came to the Macedonian throne he passed through Smyrna, having defeated the Persians in battle at Granicus near the Dardanelles. He slept on Mount Pagus next to the shrine of Nemesis. The goddess told him in a vision to move the inhabitants across the bay. Thus the pattern of present-day Izmir, at least in its rudimentary form, was established. Patterns changed, with fresh vigour and new administration enabling the city to elect its own magistrates. Smyrna, part of the Kingdom of Pergamum, was also part of the Province of Rome called Asia then as now.

There are many other notable milestones in the history of Smyrna. Marcus Aurelius commanded the rebuilding of the city after a terrible earthquake of AD 178. Hordes of invaders carried out further damage in the following centuries.

These included Turks, Byzantines, Crusaders and the rest. A Christian church flourished here, as we have seen, and Polycarp was Bishop of Smyrna between 115 and 156. It was at this time that persecution of the Christian church broke out, probably connected with the reference in the Book of Revelation already mentioned. Christians were done to death in the local stadium. Polycarp himself was burnt at the stake after refusing to deny the Christian faith. The Proconsul ordered him to be executed thus rather than having him thrown to the lions. Thus Polycarp, a vital pillar of the early Christian church, was also one of its greatest martyrs.

Visitors to Izmir often do the daytrip to nearby Pergamum, closely linked to old Smyrna, which was part of the Pergamum's territory. A visit there would have to wait for another time as we decided to press on for Ephesus. Perhaps a few remarks about Pergamum would not be out of place at this point, though. It was the location of another of the seven churches (Pergamas) of the Book of Revelation and apocalyptic judgements. Conflict was the order of the day for the Pergamenes, too, as the references in the Book of Revelation show:

> you did not deny my faith even in the days of Antipas . . .
> Nevertheless I have a few things against you: you have some
> people there who are clinging to the teaching of Baalam . . . also
> . . . the Nicolaitanes, which thing I hate (Amplified Bible,
> Revelation 2: 13–15)

From what scholars have gathered, the Nicolaitans held the dubious view that to the converted nothing was sinful. This was completely contrary to Christian teaching, and could no way be part of it.

In 388 BC Xenophon met the Spartan commander here, as

mentioned in the former's *Anabasis*. When Alexander the Great died in 323 BC one of his foremost generals took charge of Asia Minor. The rulers who followed him left behind white artefacts of marble which are still to be found there today. Most of the kings who ruled after Alexander's General Lysimachus were either called Eumenes or Attalus. One of them, Attalus III handed over control of the city to the Roman Empire. Henceforth it was called Asia. As a strictly pagan Roman capital of the region it was a cesspool for every type of evil. Hence those references in the Book of Revelation. Infiltrators in the Church attempted to spread pagan-based ideas.

Warlike Gauls caused fear by their ferocity at the time of the Attalid kings (263–133 BC). Some parts of the region submitted to paying tribute rather than take a pasting, so greatly were these Gauls feared. It was King Attalus who finally defeated them in what was undoubtedly a decisive battle. The King even wrote the words 'Victory for the King' backwards on his hand, imprinting the slogan on the liver of his oracle. The priest was then able to announce victory to the troops. By this 'sleight of hand' the King inspired his warriors to vanquish the Gauls. Today the Vatican Museum houses a well-known statue of the dying Gaul which commemorates the battle perfectly. Although Pergamum is a splendid example of a Graeco-Roman city, we were about to experience one of the very finest of classical ruins in Turkey. We were heading for Ephesus.

The railway station was a hive of activity as Anne and I purchased our tickets. The friendly clerk behind the counter thought that I was married to a Turkish lady because of Anne's dark looks. A uniformed official, probably the station master, stood watching as crowds gathered to board the train – people seemed to appear in large numbers. So many of them were swarming aboard the train that we wondered whether we were going to be able to board the train – but board it we did! Soon it pulled away from the platform. We stood for most of the way as the train thundered in the direction of Ephesus. We chatted to our travelling companions, Turks mostly in their twenties. They were of a friendly disposition. After several hours of this cramped travelling we stopped at the railway station at Selçuk – the modern part of Ephesus.

CHAPTER THIRTEEN

EXPLORING EPHESUS

The train continued on its journey, leaving us standing on the platform at Selçuk. The village itself is delightfully quaint, with all those little shops standing opposite the ruins of an old aqueduct. The two parallel streets radiating from the railway station are the Istation Caddessi and the Cengis Topel Caddessi, both suggesting post-Ottoman gentility. It was interesting to see how later buildings had been built into the arches of the aqueduct. They were not the only ones to make use of the ancient structure, as in springtime storks were in the habit of building their nests atop these old arches. However, this was clearly the wrong time of year to see the storks. Typically, there were numerous little cafés with Turks drinking coffee, talking, and smoking.

We booked in at the fashionable Aksoy Hotel and soon fell into conversation with the amiable middle-aged hotelier. 'There are some splendid views to be seen from this hotel,' he intoned. 'You can see plenty of the surrounding country-side, and from the room into which I shall place you it is possible to look directly down into the nests of the storks.' Was he anticipating a later springtime visit from us? He paused at this point and a faraway contended look came into his eyes. 'Ah, yes,' he continued, 'the storks now they will be far away in Africa and I look forward to their return.' We carried on talking about the storks and the drama of the storks raising their families. Both of us soon settled in comfortably.

The next morning we were up and about early and enjoyed breakfast in the rooftop restaurant – and enjoyed, too, those delightful views that we were promised. The early morning sun was already bathing the landscape in its radiance, as if beckoning us to venture out into it and explore it for ourselves. This was precisely what we intended to do anyway. An engaging character whom we met in Selçuk (we met others) was a chef named Moustafa. A stocky man with a small moustache set in a typically Turkish face and dressed in cook's whites – including a tall white hat – he cordially welcomed us. Moustafa presented us with two very bulky visitors' books literally overflowing with the sayings, anecdotes, and greetings from his many hundreds of visitors from all over the world. Needless to say I added my greetings and signature, together with a little sketch portrait of the chef. We frequently took our meals at Moustafa's and it was always good eating, as Moustafa was something of an experienced gourmet.

One of the main focal points in the town is the Isa Bey Mosque, and next to it is St John's Basilica, wherein lies the tomb of the Apostle John. We made a point of visiting the tomb. Legend has it that John brought Mary, the mother of Jesus, here, and we were shortly to visit the reputed house of Mary set on a nearby hill. We were determined to visit that house, and indeed did so during our stay. Meanwhile we were still exploring the ruins of John's Basilica. So far as I was concerned here was the genuine site of the Apostle's tomb. When this authenticated location became widely known, it quickly became the object of much veneration and pilgrimage. After Mary's death John settled in the place, exercising his Apostolic office. During Dormition's reign, John's banishment to Patmos occurred. There the Eagle of the early Church soared to sublime heights with his writing of the Apocalypse. After the Patmos exile, John returned to Ephesus where he wrote his famous Gospel. Of this we may be confident, for a bishop in the young church named Irenaeus, who lived a good deal at Ephesus and Asia Minor, later becoming Bishop of Lyons, records the following: 'Afterwards, John, the disciple of the Lord, who also leaned on his breast likewise published a gospel whilst he dwelt in Ephesus in Asia.' This witness is worth noting as Irenaeus was the successor to the bishopric at Lyons after Pothinus, who was martyred in the persecutions of Marcus Aurelius at ninety years of age. This being so, he must have been born before the death of the Apostle, making him more or less a contemporary of St John. So the early age of the testimony of Irenaeus may be established with a degree of certainty.

In the second century AD devotees erected a chapel beside St John's tomb, and later a massive basilica was built on the site in AD 600 by the Emperor Justinan and his wife the Empress Theodora. Although the basilica is largely in ruins now we can still discern its cruciform plan. The building must surely have been an imposing sight, with eleven domes, six of which covered the central nave and five covered the narthex. The east portion had five naves and the side portions were built with three naves each. The tomb of St John once lay under the central dome but today it is open to the skies. Nevertheless, the old walls still enclose the tomb. The immediate area was once believed to contain special healing properties.

From the famous tomb and Basilica, we headed out

towards the old city of Ephesus, which we found still retained a strong classical feel about it. The weather was hot and parched, and the walk to Ephesus was wearying. These ruins are situated two or three kilometres outside Selçuk but we soon came upon them, arriving at the same time as a coachload of tourists who had stopped off here whilst on a cruise. At the Eastern end of the complex we stopped by two souvenir stalls. There were rows of little bells which had a gentle tinkling sound. This tinkling of bells we heard on several occasions in the area, as bells are tied to the necks of goats that wander the hillsides. A huge 'armoury' of highly decorative old-fashioned pistols and rifles could be seen – including one rifle with a dragon's head handle. With the rifle's business end placed downwards, it made the handle rear at us menacingly with rows of teeth bared in a snarling grimace!

However, we wasted little time in entering the ancient City area. The air became hotter and even more parched as we commenced our exploration of this old city I had waited so long to see. I reflected on the fact that the general aspect of the town was very much as St Paul would have seen it. Most of the ancient streets were still intact with their slabs of stone still as Paul trod them. Many of the buildings were still there, albeit badly ruined by the ravages of time and earthquakes. Ruins which had tumbled to the ground during these earthquakes had been restored. Numbers of superb carvings were still there as fresh as on the days they were executed so long ago. All over the ruins we came across Ionic columns, and sometimes just the capital lying amidst the stones otherwise isolated. We wandered down these same roads that the great Apostle had once trodden, and my gaze scanned the sweep of surrounding hills, looking upon the same landscape that Paul had seen. I was able to obtain a very good idea of what the entire town and its surroundings would have looked like in those far-off times.

When Alexander the Great came this way he ordered the city to be built up again, as he found it ruined. What we can see today is largely the result of that rebuilding, and it lies between the hills of Pion and Croisus. The Romans later made certain additions. The Magnesian Gate lies close to the Roman baths built in AD 200 and the Odeon built by an affluent citizen of antiquity, Publius Vedius Antonius. Another name that was given to the Odeon was the Bouleuterion because of it being used as a public meeting hall. The remains of other public buildings still stand in Ephesus – the town hall, the Basilica, the state agora, and the girls' gymnasium, to mention some. The state agora dates from the time of Augustus and Claudius and was built at their command during the first century AD. Digging underneath the agora, archaeologists discovered sarcophagi and other ruins of an even earlier date. The site of the agora had formerly been that of the necropolis of early times.

We stopped to admire the temple of Hadrian, or rather what was left of it, on the Road of Curetiae. Here also there were rows of columns still standing, which became all the more imposing as the sun moved in the sky and the shadows deepened. The late summer heat made us pleased to avail ourselves of water from a pump that was pointed out to us behind that house of ill-repute close to the junction of the Marble Road and the Road of Curetiae. I splashed water on my face and arms and drank some of it.

The Library of Celsus, which lies at the foot of the Curetiae Road, is a truly imposing sight when viewed from higher up on the Curetiae Road. This famous library dates from the second century AD. Celsus Polemaenus began the building of the library and his son, Gaius Julius Polemaenus, concluded the work. Four statues used to stand on the facade of the building, which were most probably intended to represent the cornerstones of education. At any rate they stood for the intelligence, learning, sense, and compassion of Celsus. It was a very substantial library by any standards. It contained 20,000 scrolls. Close by is the sarcophagus of the founder, Celsus, and information about him can be found on the base parts of the statues.

Proceeding along the Marble Road we paused to admire relief sculptures of gladiators. The great theatre can accommodate 25,000 spectators. Mount Pion's western slope was clearly ideal for the siting of this vast construction. We climbed up the tiers of seating that once supported many a toga-clad rump. It gave me some idea of what it was like to be a spectator in the theatre in those far-off times. Listening in the still air and fine acoustics you can in imagination almost hear that excitable mob of 2000 years ago chanting, albeit in another tongue, 'Great is Diana of the Ephesians', when Demetrius praised the goddess after St Paul's influence threatened to curtail the trade in silver images of Diana (souvenirs even then!). Also it is possible to imagine a statue of Diana being carried in torchlight procession accompanied by dancing. Only lizards and other visitors stirred at Ephesus now. I remembered that Paul made an interesting reference to fighting wild beasts at Ephesus in I Corinthians 15. Hence those gladitorial images, I suppose.

We walked down the old Harbour Road, also called the Arcadian, towards the old jetty as Paul must have done, and saw the ruins of old Christian churches. The old jetty looks strange now, all silted up and some distance from the water. It indicates the topographical changes that have occurred here since New Testament days. I noticed a circular geometric design scratched into the paving, obviously of great age.

After Paul, Ignatius likewise came here and would have sailed from that quayside. The harbour baths are to be found here, and the double churches, known also as the Church or Basilica of Mary, said to be the first church to be dedicated in Mary's name. Pope Paul VI made a historic visit here and prayed at the site of the Basilica. A plaque erected there reads:

'Papa Altinci Paul 26 Temmuz 1976 Tarihinds burada dua etmistir Summus Pontifex Paulus Sextus in hac sacra aede preces etfudit die XXVI Jul 11 ANNI MCMLXVII.'

Presumably the Ephesus church referred to in the Apocalypse as one of the seven was the continuation of the church Paul founded:

'To the angel (messenger) of the assembly (church) in Ephesus write, These are the words of Him who holds the seven stars ... Who goes about among the seven golden lampstands ... I know your industry and activities, laborious toil and trouble and your patient endurance, and how you cannot tolerate wicked men ... But I have this one charge to make against you that you have left (abandoned) the love you had at first.' (Amplified Bible Revelation 2: 1–4).

It would appear that the Christian church at Ephesus a generation after Paul was cooling in its faith. Certainly Ephesus cannot have been an easy place for Christians to live in at a time when Roman benevolence had waned. At one time Ephesus was a capital of the Province of Asia. The intensity of pagan activities would hardly have been conducive to Christian devotion and worship. Shiploads of slaves would have sailed into the harbour – one of several signs of the decadence that prevailed.

Close by the Baths of Scholastica, a side road leading from the Street of Curetiae winds its way up the hill. A number of ancient houses are there. Many of them were under restoration whilst we were there. These homes obviously belonged to affluent residents. Frescoes are still on their interior walls, and they have fine mosaic pavings – and they had fountains in some cases! A backgammon board with the dice was discovered in one dwelling. This is a popular game still throughout the Eastern lands, as we had seen. A shadow fell on one side of the road, and it provided shade for us in the heat of the sun. Most of the frescoes are pagan, depicting scenes from Euripedes, images of Achilles and Hercules along with Eros and Apollo.

The remains of Trajan's fountain are impressive but it must have looked infinitely better in its classical days. It would have included beautiful statues. A central figure was of Trajan, a mini-colossus with one foot on the world, representing his dominion of it. Apart from the Scholastica baths Ephesus had others, like the Baths of Varius. Roman baths had a disrobing chamber, a frigidarium, tepidarium and caldarium, with upper rooms. These had resting places, a library and places of entertainment.

The gate of Mazaeus and Mitridates stands adjacent to the Library of Celsus. It was raised in honour of the Emperor Augustus in 3–4 BC by grateful slaves after receiving their liberty. It is by far one of the best-preserved monuments in Ephesus.

We did not visit Paul's prison, but it was pointed out to us.

The Temple of Diana, or the scant remains of this once-grand structure, lies some distance from the ruins of Ephesus. It used to be one of the seven wonders of the ancient world, and the only hint of the temple's former glory is no longer here. A highly decorative column drum found here is now in the British Museum. The Artemisium, as the temple was also called, surpassed its counterpart in Athens at its zenith. The temple was destroyed seven times altogether. One arsonist was an unstable person named Herostratus. The first version of the Artemisium was begun in BC 560, and several rebuildings and destructions later the Hellenistic temple was thought to be the most magnificent.

The sun sank slowly behind Mount Bulbul as it did in those far-off times! That evening I thought about some of the images I had captured with my sketchbook and camera. Amongst the things photographed was the headless statue of Scholastica and one of the objects I drew was the pedestal with a relief carving of Mercury, the winged messenger, complete with his winged sandals. The winged helmet was missing, but there was a winged staff in his left hand, whilst his right hand rested on the head of a ram.

Revisiting Moustafa's restaurant we found him entertaining more visitors. While resting in our hotel room that night, a piercing whistle shattered the darkness. It was probably a shepherd locating his sheep. We rolled off to sleep with no trouble.

The House of the Virgin Mary lies some distance from the town. Rather than hire a taxi we decided to walk. The fact that the house stands on Mount Pion a full seven kilometres from Selçuk should have made us think twice about walking. Mercifully a young Turk intervened as we struggled up the steep incline of Mount Pion. I heard this chugging sound behind us. Then a scooter pulled up and a youngster introduced himself. He was also called Moustafa, like the Chef. 'Let me give you pillion lifts on my scooter – Anne first, perhaps,' he said. I agreed and it seemed imprudent not to. Seconds later Anne and Moustafa vanished from sight up the hill. Moustafa allowed me to ride the scooter on my own for part of the way some distance further on. Alternately one of us would ride whilst the other caught up. Thus we were making steady progress in the ascent. On the last lap of the climb, Moustafa took Anne to the house and then came back for me. I was feeling parched again, but I soon quenched my thirst after flying into the house area at top speed. When I had refreshed myself at the fountain at the Virgin Mary's House I rejoined Anne. Then we began exploring and viewing the house we had come all the way up Mount Pion to see.

There are two schools of thought concerning the last years of the mother of Christ. Some scholars believe that Mary ended her days in a house in Jerusalem. On the other hand certain evidence points to the house in Ephesus as being the place of her retirement. Possibly it may be reasonable to accommodate both versions. Mary could have spent most of her later years here and spent the last phase of her life in Jerusalem.

It was a vision of a German nun Anna Katharina that started the tradition. The nun had never left her home territory but she was told in the vision of the house in Ephesus. In 1891 a body of men arrived at the Panaia Kapula, as the spot is called. The team was comprised of archaeologists and religious dignitaries. Sure enough, a Christian church of great age was unearthed. Restoration was carried out and it quickly became a shrine. From early on in the history of the Christian Church it was customary to dedicate a church to a saint associated with it. Thus this church bears the name of Mary.

Two basic facts can be ascertained with certainty. Christ committed his mother to the care of the Apostle John whilst on the cross. Secondly, it is known that in the organisation of the early Church John was allocated this part of Asia Minor. Here he worked diligently for the propagation of the gospel, and the establishing and maintenance of churches. When John came here he brought Mary with him. Archaeologists have found inscriptions here relating to the death of Mary.

The Joungers concealed the whereabouts of the house, and it was not until the dream or vision of the German nun, Anna Katharina Emmerich, that the idea was seriously considered in modern times. Research showed that pilgrims came here long before the modern revivals. Catholics make a special pilgrimage here on August 15th every year. Supposedly this coincides with Mary's ascension into Heaven. The Vatican recognises the house of Mary as a special place of pilgrimage.

I found it a sparse chapel, having an altar and a small statue of Mary. The whole area is blessed with an abundance of greenery. It was pleasant to sit beneath the trees and enjoy the coolness of the shade. We felt instinctively that this was a hallowed spot. The spring at which I drank that cool fresh water after the ascent was credited with healing properties – a natural enough assumption given its closeness to the shrine. Among the thousands of pilgrims who make their way up to the house are Moslems. The validity of Christ enters the Moslem tradition also. They accept him as a Holy Prophet.

Some obliging pilgrims gave us a lift down in their car, dropping us off by a turning that led to the Caves of the Seven Sleepers. The whirring sound of a scooter that preceded Moustafa could be heard, and moments later there he was. This time he talked us into mounting his scooter both at once – so there were three of us on one scooter once more for the ride back to Selçuk. Rows of Turks stood beside the road watching in sheer amazement as the scooter with Anne, Moustafa and myself on board chugged towards the town, like some kind of bizarre circus act.

Actually we stopped a little beforehand and Moustafa pointed to a small tumbledown hut on the opposite side of the road and a tall, gaunt, shabbily dressed man who stood beside it. Then Moustafa waved to the man. We crossed the road to join the strange figure. In his hand was a little snake. We had met the snake man of Ephesus. He had several other snakes in jars and boxes in and around his hovel. The hut interior was but a single cell containing nothing but the bare necessities. The snake man motioned us to be seated. Then he served us weak tea which we gratefully accepted, as guests of an Easterner. A number of tortoises lived with the snake man also. Some of them were only babies while others were mature adults.

Back at our hotel we got ready for a visit that we were to make that evening. A local lawyer had invited us to join him and his family at their home in St Jean Street. A very pleasant evening it turned out to be. I drew a number of portraits for them from the oldest to the youngest.

'This', said my host, 'is what you might call the rich part of Turkey. Other parts that you might visit are not quite so prosperous. Being a lawyer in these parts I am able to maintain a comfortable position.'

'I presume you mean that there's prosperity in the Aegean and Mediterranean coastal areas in the main', said I. 'For example, I don't suppose that the Turks living in the mountainous regions round, say, Ararat would be very well-off at all.'

My host nodded, then looked through the drawings that I had done of his entire family. The drawing of the lawyer's father, I thought, had character. He was an interesting subject.

Arguably the best portrait of the lot was the one I did of the young daughter. The lawyer thought so, and I think I was able to say something about the innocence and beauty of his young daughter. We continued our conversation for hours, but when it became late we rose to leave. Many times in the rest of the days that we spent in Selçuk we saw the family out walking and waved a friendly greeting.

To miss out on the museum would have been unthinkable, for most of the exhibits are marvellous. Certain pieces caught my attention. My eye came to rest on a tiny bronze figurine of a warrior from the second century AD. It was not more than a few centimetres in height. I thought that it was exquisite. Then there was a bronze of Eros astride a dolphin from the third century AD, only 16.9 cm in height and 29.3 cm in length. This is a subject that recurs in other cultures.

Then I came upon what is the Ephesus Museum's most famous exhibit – the 'many breasted' statue of the goddess Diana, a subject that I have already touched on. Are they multiple breasts on the goddess, ovaries of the sacred bee, or even testicles? One thing is certain in this connection – this cult of the mother goddess goes back at least as far as Babylon. The Hittites seem to have established the cult in Asia Minor. The Anatolian Cybele, the Greek Artemis, and the Roman Diana may be viewed as being one and the same. Widespread devotional following of the goddess was phenomenal.

I liked the old Roman lampstand on a tripod of three feet. Its design is sophisticated and not over-embellished like designs of later ages. Friezes on display were Greek. One such consisted of a somewhat jumbled design of various parts of a Greek soldier's armour – helmets, uniforms, shields of varying shapes, and strangely a tiny seated figure in the bottom right-hand corner. Most of the exhibits are priceless, of course. There's the damaged statue of the tired warrior and the fresco of Socrates which shows the philosopher in a loose-fitting toga. It used to grace the Socrates room of the Hill Palace close by the Temple of Hadrian. A head of Zeus, and various representations of Eros, and the grotesque phallic statue of the god Bes were there too. The statue of the urinating child, possibly part of a fountain, dates from about AD 200. Whilst it would be impossible for me to comment on every exhibit here, mention of a few more would be appropriate. I noted a delightful little griffon head in bronze, found at the Altar of Artemission; also a little stylised ram found there. Pottery from Mycenaean tombs from 1400–1300 BC was on display, some of it fragmentary. A statue of Diana executed in the archaistic style from the second century AD is there. I found this easier to draw than that 'many breasted' version.

After the Ephesus Museum we visited the fourteenth-century Isa Bey Mosque of the Aydinoglu Turks. Around Selçuk many artefacts left by the Audinoglu are to be found, such as baths, tombs, and other mosques – although it is true to say that the Isa Bey Mosque is without doubt the best example of any to be seen in Selçuk. Today one of the twin minarets is missing, but the two domes are still intact. An architect from Damascus named Ali built the mosque at the behest of Isa Bey, the son of the ruler Mehmet Bey. I spent a quiet reflective time wandering through the ruins of the mosque with only a few local boys for company.

It was time for us to be moving on again, for we had much still to see. Other visitors were doing a minibus tour and they were making for the Greek Isle of Samos. Our next destination was Denizli. The coach came and soon whisked us away, leaving Selçuk and Ephesus behind. I thought about the last few days. In my thoughts I wandered through the marvellous ruins of Ephesus. I heard again in my imagination the tinkling bells of those sheep and goats that wander the Ephesus hillsides. And I was still thinking about all that we had done in and around Ephesus, where the Apostle Paul had founded a church and clashed with the locals, and where the Apostle John has written about the Word becoming flesh and dwelling among us.

Artefacts from the early Christian era includes Eros on a dolphin

CHAPTER FOURTEEN

MEDITERRANEAN TURKEY

Turkey is justly famed for its strikingly beautiful landscapes. Regrettably we did not have time to savour all of them. Although we skirted Cappadocia we did not spend any time in exploration there. This was rectified in a later visit, though. Centuries of volcanic eruption have layered the area with huge deposits of volcanic stuff. Being a soft rock it has lent itself to a peculiar type of wind erosion that has produced some fantastically strange formations. Strange also are the troglodyte dwellings that earlier peoples (including Christians) carved into the soft rocks.

Now we were approaching a different kind of stark, haunting Turkish landscape. Our coach had arrived at the brooding dust-blown town of Denizli. The dust clouds were almost suffocating at times. We took lodgings close by the bus depot. After depositing our bags we took a taxi to Pamukkale, which is almost like arriving in another world. A vast calcified whiteness filled our vision. I noted the warm streams which came from thermal springs. This thermal water has famously given relief to many a rheumatic sufferer. Calcium deposited by the springs over centuries has built up

on the edge of a plateau. A series of natural circular formations have grown with rows of stalagtites fringing their edges
like petrified snow and icicles. I paddled in the large shallow
basins of water and here we met more Americans – a young
couple enjoying a leisurely vacation. A little black dog began
to follow us. Anne patted and stroked the dog, which rolled
over playfully on its back as she did so. Pamukkale literally
means 'castle of cotton' so the name is not altogether inapt.
Looking out over the Valley of Merderes and Curuksa I
found the distant view of the Kadmus mountains relaxing.

One of the most interesting sights here is Hierapolis, or
rather the scattered ruins of that Graeco-Roman city. Most
of the remains that we saw were from classical times. Yet the
city was also occupied by Byzantines and later Selçuk Turks.
The little black dog continued to follow us, and had gathered
a number of his canine friends by now. One or two standing
doorways must have given entrance to sumptuous buildings
from which there were some portions of standing walls.
Chunks of stonework lay haphazardly here and there with
carvings on them still. Terrible battles were fought here in the
years of the city's decline. The Apostle Philip spent his last
days here, and the Virgin Mary is supposed to have rested
here on her way to Ephesus.

Also in the area are the remains of the city of Laodicea.
Another of the seven churches of the Apocalypse was located
here. This church had certain judgements passed on it like
the others:

'And to the angel (messenger) of the assembly (the church) in
Laodicea write: These are words of the Amen, the trusty and
faithful and true witness . . . I know your (record of) works and
what you are doing. You are neither hot nor cold . . . So because
you are lukewarm, and neither hot nor cold, I will spew you out
of my mouth'. (Amplified Bible, Revelation 3: 14–16)

Was it merest coincidence that the thermal springs produce lukewarm water of about blood heat? A church dedicated to St Philip stood here but now only ruins are left.

In its day Hierapolis was a lively place to live in. As well as being a health centre, it had Jewish traders who were part of the bustling scene. The city lay on a caravan route between Izmir and Mesopotamia, and it existed for military purposes as well as trade. Greek was spoken as the common language, while the Romans held sway. Distinguished people aplenty passed this way – prominent philosophers, kings, religious dignitaries, and Roman senators. All these and more came to Hierapolis. A pagan temple once stood here in honour of Cybele, though nothing remains of it now. She was the goddess of wisdom, largely because of the healing waters. Chemically these waters contain several elements: hydro-carbonates, calcium, sulphates and, of course, carbon dioxide, which evaporates into the air. I mentioned sufferers of rheumatism, but people with other complaints have found relief at the springs also; for example, heart conditions, rickets, nervous ailments and debility. Remains of Roman baths, a gymnasium, a public fountain, a theatre, a triple victory gate and a main road can be made out.

Beyond the calcified areas of Pamukkale the land is very fertile and wheatfields and vineyards flourish there. I pur-chased a bottle of Turkish wine but the taste was a little too sharp for our liking. We met up with the Americans again. The girl told us about a very ancient cemetery that lay about a mile away. In a land of ancient things you cannot help but meet such at every turn. The ethereal qualities of those calcium carbonate terraces continued to linger in our minds as we were driven back towards Denizli by the Americans. The girl began talking about the grandmother she had recently lost. 'She was married to a soldier in India at the time of the Kyber rifles, and her memories of those days were still fresh and clear.' It's always fascinating to hear of first-hand memories from times past. Back in Denizli the next day we stopped at a café where one jovial Turk planted a kiss on each of Anne's cheeks after only a brief encounter. Since Hierapolis collapsed so many times due to repeated earth-quakes, the main centre of regional habitation shifted to Denizli. (The final destruction of Hierapolis came in 1354 with with earthquake of that year.)

The Turkish Mediterranean coast was no less exciting than Pamukkale. I can fully understand why Mark Anthony presented Cleopatra with a section of it as a wedding present. We were now in Antalya and the hotel we chose was a quaint one, with a fine view of the surrounding mountains. Our hotel was pure authentic 1930s, each landing being dec-orated thus, and our room was on one of the upper floors. We usually paused at each landing to admire the trappings of this veritable time-capsule. Later we chanced to meet again the Swede we had met at Ephesus.

'How long have you got here?' I asked him.

'All the time in the world,' he replied contentedly.

From the grooved minaret we descended a nearby pictu-resque path past quaint little houses to the quayside from which St Paul once sailed during his first missionary voyage. Now fishermen were busy mending their nets beside rows of fishing boats in the sunshine. We hired a rowing boat. It's funny how these boats rock unsteadily as you clamber aboard. As we headed out men were working on the quay, tinkering with their craft and scurrying about as we headed out into open water. I rowed past the moored boats and motor launches. I decided against rowing out too far from the quay. It was too much like hard work anyway. Instead I was aiming for a stretch of beach that lay to the west of the quayside beyond a massive cliff. After a protracted period of rowing, the bows of our rowing boat crunched into the pebbly beach we had aimed for. I started to walk on the beach but the large pebbles felt uncomfortable under my feet. The pebbles were hot too, baked in the sun, so we paddled in the sea. After this we cast off again and I rowed us back to the quay, narrowly missing some of the moored boats as we skimmed in to land.

At a white-walled restaurant overlooking the quay we enjoyed a meal (fish again) with all the trimmings, and met a Cypriot who had a home in North London. After all that exertion in the heat I was glad of the refreshments.

Turkish museums are always worth seeing and later we visited the local one. Inside the museum we saw displays of Turkish cultural life: objects like axes, rifles, powder flasks, bows and arrows and a brass brazier. The Turks claim that weaving originated with them and this museum had a display on the subject. In one section we saw a series of old Greek icons depicting episodes in the life of Christ – the Nativity, the circumcision, the raising of Lazarus, the Last Supper, the Crucifixion, and the Last Judgement. There were sculptures from Perge and Aspendos (second century AD). In the next room we visited I saw a small box containing the bones of St Nicholas. As a Protestant I tend to regard 'holy relics' with a certain amount of caution. The bones were all carefully mounted. On the inside of the casket lid there was a portrait of Christ.

Classical, Archaic and Hellenistic vases were on display. The last period is generally regarded by historians as the greatest flowering of culture in ancient times on the Mediterranean coast. I loved many of the designs on this antique pottery. Some were less abstract than I had seen before. One vase had a helmeted figure riding a horse. The figure on the horse was executed in black against a lighter background. The lower portion of the vase, along with the handle and the top of the neck, was also black. As a piece of design it was sheer perfection. The mounted figure was repeated all round the vase. The vases that I had seen at Ephesus were essentially abstract in design, belonging to a much earlier period, being Mycenaean tomb finds from 1400–1300 BC, whereas this vase I was admiring in Antalya was dated 4th–5th centuries BC and belonged to the classical period. It was found at Lekytou. Fine detailing on the figure was in line scraped away.

That evening when the sun had gone down, we enjoyed welcome cooling breezes as we walked the palm-lined roads. The beach that lay east of the quay we visited the next day. It was called the Lara Plaji. The beach to the west of the quay that we had rowed to the day before was the Konyaalti Plaji, we discovered. The Lara Plaji was a sandy beach unlike the other. After exploring this beach and an old stone jetty we found there we headed back to the city.

We took yet more Turkish coffee at a café in the Ataturk Cadessi close to Hadrian's Gate, raised in honour of Hadrian's visit long ago and now serving no purpose except as an interesting relic. Antalya is certainly an attractive city with its old wooden buildings in the old centre. Exotic legends came to birth in and around Antalya – legends like that of the chimera, a monster that breathed fire and was slain by Bellerophon. Today there are no fire-breathing dragons in the area that I know of, only burning gas spurting from a rock fissure or two. As with Izmir, the only feature left out from our itinerary was the fortress towering over the city. It had kept out Alexander the Great, preventing him from capturing the place, largely due to its inaccessibility.

Perge lies close to Antalya, and is remarkable for the

Roman ruins that survive there. The most outstanding of these is the theatre with its capacity for holding 15,000 spectators. I climbed up the tiers of seats then looked round the gallery above. Anne followed me but by now I think she was finding all this scampering and scrambling round ancient ruins rather exhausting. At the Antalya Museum we had noted a sarcophagus of Hercules from Perge dating from the second century AD. The Perge theatre has two lovely surviving reliefs just inside the main entrance and I stopped for several minutes to study them. One shows a lion pulling a chariot containing a seated half-draped figure. In one hand the charioteer held a staff whilst a standing figure was beating a tambourine, Salvation Army style. On the opposite wall we saw an equally fine relief which showed two toga-clad figures, one standing the other reclining. I glanced back at the other relief and noticed the figure of a god, possibly Zeus, standing behind the lion.

Outside the theatre a stallholder beckoned me to join him and accompany him into a private chamber. Warily I followed, not knowing what to expect. The man produced a small sculptured head. The fact that it was partly covered in pieces of clay did not necessarily prove its antiquity. I took the proffered head into my hands and raised it to my face for closer examination.

'Genuine marble, sir,' he said.

'How much?' I asked casually.

'Eighty pounds – go on my friend, buy it, it's worth it!'

Having decided otherwise I handed it back and quickly rejoined Anne. Then we wandered over the huge stadium which was strewn with chunks of ancient masonry, and when we reached the far side of the stadium, a young woman, I suppose in her twenties, appeared. The lines on her prematurely lined face, emaciated by years of exposure to the

sun and the elements, belied her age. She was dressed in
typical peasant clothing, in this case dark with light patterns,
and a head covering. The woman handed us a sprig of vegetation before vanishing. I recalled that St Paul had preached
at Perge – it was his very first sermon. It seemed to me that
almost the entire history of the Aegean and Mediterranean
coastal areas was written in ancient broken columns, arches,
and strewn chunks of old masonry. The well-preserved main
road at Perge, complete with chariot wheel ruts and
Hellenistic gates, is a great example of this.

Founded in Hellenistic times, Side became a centre for the
Roman slave trade. From the tumbled remains of temples
and the agora we turned to the Side museum where another
superb collection of old artefacts met our scrutiny, like the
statues and disembodied parts of the statues that were there.
Some of the finest examples of relief-decorated sarcophagi
are housed here as well. Roman sarcophagi are roofed like
miniature houses. Maybe this has to do with the housing of
the spirit, and providing housing for the hereafter. Glass
cases contained figurines and various artefacts found on the
site. Near the entrance we saw a statue of the goddess Nike
who symbolised victory. She is shown with outstretched
wings with a wreath of triumph. Other strongly symbolic
elements at the feet of the goddess are a sword, a crown, and
an eagle's head. There are partial statues of the Three
Graces with certain portions of their anatomy missing. I
admire the tremendous skill of the ancient sculptors. They
had a fine feeling for the stance of a figure, the flow of
drapery and hair, the perfection of their anatomical work.
Cherubic figures on a sarcophagus, a head of Hermes
(second century AD), a statue of Ares (third century AD) a
head of Aphrodite (third century AD) in the museum
confirm my view, if confirmation is needed. Small wonder

that masters of the Italian Renaissance found classical sculpture such a fount of inspiration.

The museum building itself was originally a Roman bath-house. After restoration it was considered a natural place to house exhibits found here. Even as broken fragments, some of the sculptures are impressive, like the naked Hermes statue in the first room (second century AD) or a headless woman in a toga statue that I saw there. Somehow, though, a sculptor was in the habit of creating the statue without a head deliberately so that clients could have their own heads added when desired.

There is a Temple of Tyche, goddess of good fortune and protection of cities. In its ancient heyday it would have had a south entrance, entered by nine steps topped by twelve Corinthian columns, which in turn supported a ceiling of huge wedge-shaped slabs. The roof was striking, being built like a pyramid, steeply rising on twelve sides. A dome was raised above the cult statue and the signs of the zodiac rendered in relief. The whole structure was finished off with a facing of marble. It's a vision long gone, and unless some measure of restoration is carried out visitors will just have to rely on their imaginations. Much of the information about the temple comes from the image on an antique coin.

Restoration work on Side began in 1947 and continued until the latter part of 1966. The enterprise was backed by the Turkish Historical Association, Istanbul University, and the General Director of Old Monuments in Turkey. The work was carried out under the direction of Professor Dr Jale Inan and Professor Dr Arif Mufid Mansel. Full-faced reliefs outside the baths looked almost as sharp as the day they were carved.

The next outstanding Roman settlement that we came to was Aspendos. It has a marvellous theatre from the second century AD, designed by Zenon, a famous architect from antiquity. Such is the excellence of this theatre's acoustics, as well as its state of preservation, that it is still graced by annual performances of classical plays. These plays are performed in May at the time of the Antalya–Aspendos Festival. Unlike the Side ruins, those of Aspendos were situated close to the sea on a peninsula. Aspendos enjoyed prosperity under the Romans in salt production from a nearby lake, especially when evaporation took place in hot weather. Wool was produced from local sheep, and there were agricultural pursuits such as corn and vine growing.

Hours later we coasted into Alanya – not to be confused with Antalya, from where we had just come. I felt that we had better make enquiries about connections for Mersin and Tarsus, where we intended going after Alanya. A boy we spoke to said, 'I know someone who talks English – come!' He led us off to the police station. I was ushered into a little office where I met an official. He was a Commissaire who could speak English with a heavy Turkish accent. When I explained the problem, and after a solemn handshake, he scribbled out a note for me to hand in to the clerk at the local bus depot. As he wrote, his swarthy face remained impassive. He handed me the note, which I carefully placed in my top pocket. I rose and took my leave of the Commissaire, thanking him for his assistance.

Alanya has a delightful beach, not at all difficult to get to. We found a beach-hut club and a young easy-going manager. Here, he told us, it was possible to see the authentic belly dance at one of their evening shows. Wives as well as husbands attended apparently – couples of many nationalities. The old city walls impressed us, looking west from the beach. We had to walk along part of this wall, built by Sultan Alaadin Keykubat in the thirteenth century, in order to reach the medieval shipyards. Alanya is, of course, the Coracesium of antiquity. The Seljuk Turks did a marvellous job of restoration on these old walls and sturdy fortifications besides. The Red Tower is a focal point for visitors. It stands close to the old shipyard. Architecturally it is considered something of a masterpiece. The ancients left about four hundred cisterns in Alanya. At the highest point of the fortification stands a Byzantine church decorated with frescoes.

Alanya is also famed for having a cave which, it is said, has properties of healing. Some observers call it 'the cave of dripping stones', otherwise called the Damlatus cave. We could have spent literally hours, or at least longer than we did, in exploring the promontory and fortifications and all the ruins of the past that are bound up within those walls. That evening we strolled along the beach and saw the clubhouse lights stabbing the darkness.

Next morning we were up dressed and packed in readiness for the next stage in our circular tour of western Turkey. After breakfast we boarded a coach for Mersin. Some of the fine views of the azure-blue expanse of the Mediterranean that we obtained from a series of cliff-top balconies at Antalya were still very much in our minds. At one stage of our journeyings, I remember, we had threaded our way along a snaking stretch of road with some very sharp bends overhung with pine trees. Anne had commented on the dangerous possibilities of these bends.

'They're certainly very dangerous to motorists', was her comment.

'Well, let's say that you wouldn't take these bends at sixty miles an hour', I replied.

So now we were heading towards Mersin on the right coach thanks to the Commissaire's note. This coastal road continues to give some splendid panoramic views and views of little coastal villages remote from the outside world. Halfway to Mersin the coach drew up at a little restaurant which seemed miles from anywhere. After a quick stop we resumed the journey. After a protracted run the coach approached Mersin. This was on the way to eastern Turkey and we were advised to be careful. I felt a closeness to Mersin when I looked out of the coach window and saw a tractor rumbling along beside us, with a boy driving it and another boy hanging on. The tractor, I noticed, had the word 'Tarsus' on it. I knew at once that we were in St Paul country. It seems possible that Paul was put to work early in life like these youngsters. Then I spotted something else in connection with the saint. Thorn bushes with enormous spikes grew beside the road, much as they would have done two thousand years ago. It reminded me that Paul complained of an affliction he called a 'thorn in the flesh', though what exactly this affliction was we do not know. For a single night we stayed in Mersin before going on to Tarsus. Oriental touches were visible here and there in Mersin, as we saw in one of the little pensions.

The journey from Mersin to Tarsus is only a short one and before long we were standing in the streets of the town where St Paul was born. We looked at a single standing archway, the only reminder of the world that Paul knew. This arch was one of those gifts that Mark Anthony gave to Cleopatra. Next to the arch there is an artificial pool. I gazed down the town's main street. It looked forlorn along with the adjacent streets. This deserted feeling was heightened by the wind hurling great dusty clouds along them.

Turning off down a side street we came upon a scene that was anything but deserted. We had stumbled upon a colourful animated market. Tarpaulins roofed over the entire souk, and the goods on sale were typical of such markets. It was

the style of dress that caught my attention. I saw sturdy
bearded old men walking with slow strides and wearing
those enormous balloon-like trousers (this is a mode of attire
that is at least 300 years old and possibly more). These were
combined with modern jackets and stylish peaked caps,
which cast strong shadows on their eyes. One ageing man
with a large nose, beard and heavily lidded eyes was almost
certainly indigenous to the area, and might have resembled
Paul himself.

A rather stocky youngster approached us and asked if we
would like to see the house of Paul.. I said yes we would, and
we were shown down a narrow passageway close to the
market. At the end of this enclosed passageway there was a
courtyard. Here there stood a well of venerable age which is
called 'St Paul's Well', the inference being that in his adoles-
cence Paul, or Saul as he was then, lived with his parents, and
this was the well that supplied their drinking water.

Traditions handed down generation after generation often have at least some truth in them. The passageway, courtyard and well all felt authentic anyway.

Back in the streets, we again studied the scene that was taking place before us. Baggy-trousered men pulled little carts, whilst others attended their street corner stalls. Street sweepers walked past with brushes carried over their shoulders. Women were wearing loose-fitting trousers also, with headcloths veiling half their faces as well, rather like yashmaks. We reached an old gate which had been constructed almost entirely from the rubble of Roman Tarsus. A horse-drawn cart came through the arch and came towards us. It was quite a lively scene with people and traffic, horse-drawn or otherwise, on the move. From behind certain buildings tall palm trees towered.

In New Testament times Tarsus was an important centre of learning and culture and was certainly more imposing than today's Tarsus. Indeed the universities and centres of learning were widely famous in the world of Bible times. It was founded in or around 1000 BC and seems to have reached its heyday in Paul's lifetime. His own references to Tarsus are illuminating:

'But Paul said, I am a man which am a Jew of Tarsus, a city in Cilicia, a citizen of no mean city.' (Acts 21: 39)

'I am verily a man which am a Jew, born in Tarsus . . . yet brought up in this city [Jerusalem] at the feet of Gamaliel. (Acts 22: 3)

'No mean city'! Paul indicated a marked affection for his home city where he spent his childhood.

I decided that this was as far east as we were going – so no trips to Ararat! Whilst looking round the souk I clashed with a Kurdish man, who had brusquely tried to order me out. A hasty exit was indicated, and help came from an unexpected source, in the form of a friendly Turk. He was about to leave for Istanbul in his little car and agreed to take us with him for a small fee. We climbed into the car and soon we were heading out into open country. This part of the trip would take us up through the Taurus Mountains to Ankara, the Turkish capital. It was very wild and beautiful country. Shortly after leaving Tarsus, peaks and rocky walls towered all round us. We were traversing the Cilician Gates, the celebrated narrow mountain pass which was created in 1000 BC. Most observers agree that it is a superb piece of engineering, cut into these Taurus Mountains by men who knew nothing of modern technology. It has surely provided a wonderful short cut for travellers from antiquity to the present day. We know that Cyrus the Younger, Alexander the Great, and the Crusader hordes all came this way. The whole of this Cilician region impressed me deeply. If Paul really was a tentmaker then he would probably have used the skins of the long-haired goats still to be found in the region.

As we were driven on through this lovely landscape I told our driver about the incident involving the Kurd in the Tarsus market. 'They're a wild bunch, these Kurds, rather like the Irish in a way', he said. 'A large percentage of the prisoners in our jails are Kurds; they always seem to get themselves into trouble.'

Ahead of us a police vehicle had stopped a lorry. 'The lorry has come over the border from Russia – probably without proper authority – and the police are sorting them out', explained our friend. Suddenly the driver pulled up to a halt. A man standing by the road had signalled for us to stop. He climbed into the back of the car with us and later we picked up a boy of about ten, who made things a little more cramped. the little car had suddenly turned into a dolmush. Several miles further on the boy climbed out with a smile and we saw him walk along a narrow track towards a tiny village. It was a very remote spot, and a village community here must have felt very isolated. The man alighted further on and called out for anyone who was looking for transportation to Istanbul to board. No one answered the call and we moved on.

'We are passing a Kurdish village and it would be better if we passed it as quickly as possible', the driver continued.

'You don't think that we would be made welcome guests and allowed to take photographs then?' I asked with a smile.

'I don't think it would be a good idea at all. They have primitive untidy houses. No, I don't think you would enjoy a visit to that village', he said shortly. We did stop at a deserted Kurdish village later, though. We skirted Cappadocia, that fabled region with the strange rock formations, and soon afterwards passed the great central salt lake, Toz Golu. The sinking sun cast its brilliant trail on its waters.

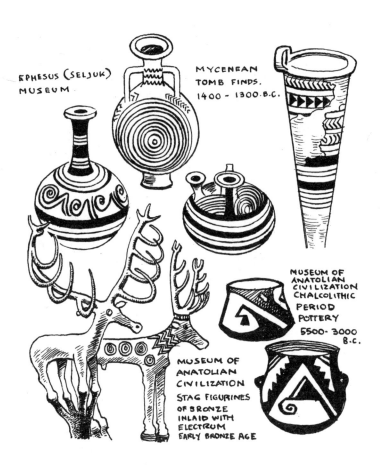

EPHESUS (SELJUK)
MUSEUM.

MYCENEAN
TOMB FINDS.
1400 - 1300.B.C.

MUSEUM OF
ANATOLIAN
CIVILIZATION
CHALCOLITHIC
PERIOD
POTTERY
5500- 3000
B.C.

MUSEUM OF
ANATOLIAN
CIVILIZATION
STAG FIGURINES
OF BRONZE
INLAID WITH
ELECTRUM
EARLY BRONZE AGE

CHAPTER FIFTEEN

OTHER TURKISH DELIGHTS

It was late when we pulled up at a wayside restaurant for supper. One wizened old man asked me to change money. I gladly obliged and he gave me a smart salute with a sharp 'Salaam'. When we returned to the car after our half-hour stop, the driver told us about him.

'Now he was a Kurd', he said reflectively.

'He seemed friendly', I replied.

Hours later we approached Ankara. I could tell by the lights glinting as we drove in. It was quite a performance finding a hotel in Ankara but we presently settled for one that was not too expensive. In a first-floor room a host of Turkish gentlemen were busily watching television. The driver stayed at the same hotel but planned to leave for Istanbul the next morning. We decided to stay in Ankara for an extra day. Our reason was that we intended to visit the Museum of Anatolian Civilizations, which is the most important museum in Turkey. First, however, we had a look round Ankara, making for the Citadel, from which splendid views of Ankara may be obtained. Ascending the flights of stone steps here can prove exhausting, but our stamina prevailed.

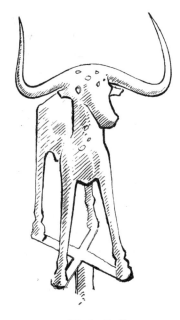

Hittite Bull

Since the 1920s Ankara has undergone vast changes. From being a small town whose main industry was in its mohair obtained from goats with fine hair, it has become a huge city. It is now the seat of Turkish Government and haunt of civil servants. Large businesses are based here, along with embassies and suchlike. The long boulevards enhance Ankara and emphasise its modernity.

We arrived later at the Museum of Anatolian Civilizations expecting something of a cultural treat. I was not disappointed. Why include museums in your book? some may ask. The answer is straightforward. They are fascinating and reveal so much about the make-up of a place and its past. I obtained the services of a proper guide, as the vastness of this museum was daunting. Besides I needed to see things in chronological order, and soon our tour de force of Turkey's past as told by this museum was under way.

We began with the Old Stone Age when Neanderthal man roamed Asia Minor (the Palaeolithic period). The section dealing with the Neolithic age of 7000–5000 BC had a reconstructed house from that age. Often I am cautious about such things, but this reconstruction was very good and deserved a mention, however contrived. There were no windows, and access was by way of the roof using wooden ladders. It is a version of a Neolithic house, the remains of which are 200 km from Ankara to the south west. Samples of pottery and polished stones from it were there. I noticed bull wall paintings. At this time horses were first used by man and agriculture had its beginnings. A clay fertility goddess and bracelets with necklaces of black volcanic stone and grey flint stone came next. Stone polished mirrors were introduced then and an example is shown. Bone sickles with stone blades, and bone buckles interested me. One grotesque statue of a fat woman is seen, feeding two babies one human, one animal.

In the Chalcolithic Age (about 5500–3000 BC) city walls, windows and doors came into general use. Pottery was improved – simple geometric designs were used with terracotta and cream. Black lava stone was widely used at this time.

The Early Bronze Age came next (3000–2000 BC). The Hittites began to flourish at this time. However, Indo-European Hittites had conducted tribal migrations to Asia Minor since earliest times. Their empires came later, and they are chiefly thought of as a second millennium BC people. The museum had a statue of a Hittite war god holding an axe, an equivalent of Mars, the Roman god of war. In time the Hittites covered much of Asia Minor. A Hittite bull in terracotta held my attention, made between 1650 and 1200 BC. Then there were isolated Hittite bull heads, short-horned, unlike others that I saw. The Hittite capital city of Boğazköy-Sungurlu (Hattuşaş) has revealed many artefacts. There was a late Hittite state in Asia Minor, and in 1650 BC the first political state was established here. I mentioned the Bronze Age Hittites and their beginnings. They were mountain folk who spread themselves out from Cappadocia. Old reliefs show them wearing short tunics suitable for scrambling in mountain country. Only when they settled in the plains did they adopt longer garments. The peak of Hittite supremacy occurred about 1650–1200 BC. I saw a slab with Hittite hieroglyphics (picture writing) and Assyrian cuneiform lettering copied by the Hittites. Much of the culture that the Hittites brought was influenced by other Eastern races.

We arrived at Assyrian trading period section (1950–1650 BC). Terracotta shoe models with pointed curl-up toes surprised me. They were like something from *Arabian Nights* and I didn't realise that the style of footwear was that old. Pots left by the Assyrians of the trading colony period had several spouts. Fifteen hundred tablets relating to the Assyrian trading period have been found with cuneiform wedge-shaped writing (invented by the Sumerians). This Assyrian trading colony period was at its peak at the time of the first Hittite movements. The Assyrian traders left when the Hittite overlords came to power in about 1700 BC.

We cannot be too rigid in our definition of 'ages' and a certain amount of overlapping must be taken into account. Thus we find Hittite bronzes. We noted an Assyrian seat in lapis lazuli and sacred wine jars in the form of animals. The wine used to be poured out through the hole in the back or through the mouth in ritual offering to the gods and goddesses. At this period crystal vases were introduced. Other Assyrian artefacts there included weights, a portable smelting unit, and a richly symbolic wedding vase. Wine was poured in through bull's head spouts on to apples placed in the centre of the jar. The apples represented stages of the wedding ceremony.

Continuing our tour of the museum we reached the Phrygian section (1200–650 BC). I noticed a host of everyday objects like ivory combs decorated with carvings, ceramics, glassware. Other things on show were a huge bronze cauldron, wine cups, and old belts, copies of which are frequently seen. Our guide stopped before a glass case where stick-like objects were laid out like spokes of a wheel. He asked me to guess what it was. Many visitors, he said, were completely baffled by it.

'It's an early form of parasol or umbrella', I ventured. Our guide laughed.

'Yes you are correct; that's exactly what it was.'

Cedar tree fragments once formed parts of doors and furniture. There were blinkers for horses, an incense burner, a cosmetic box, and what must have been the earliest type of thermos flask. The Phrygians were a seafaring people and part of the confederacy that toppled the Hittite Empire. After the last of the Hittite states fell to the Assyrians, the Phrygians established their rule from Afyon to Sivas. The Phrygian city of Gordion was where King Midas, he of the golden touch, ruled. The King committed suicide after Gordion was overcome by the nomadic Cimmerians, by drinking the blood of bulls. Hittite and Assyrian influences appear in Phrygian art. Occupying a central position in Anatolia at that time placed them in a favourable position for absorbing a wide range of influences. Doubtless they benefited by the 'silver passion' of the Hittites, who mined masses of silver from the mines they worked close to the Pass of Karabel.

The Urrartian section was where we stopped next (1000–600 BC). These people were breeders of horses, and had an agricultural economy. Their disposition was warlike and they banded together with other warlike people against foreign invaders. The eighth and ninth centuries BC represented the peak period of their civilisation. Their metalwork was of such high quality that they were able to export to places like Spain and Italy. Not only in metalwork did they excel but the museum shows their ivory carvings, precious stone cylinder seals, gold artefacts and so many other things at which they were skilled. They erected huge temples to their god Haldi and offered bloody sacrifices to him. In their tombs murals of lively design have come to light. As well as temples a column-lined reception hall was found and objects such as ivory figurines of griffon-headed winged men, and ivory lions and deer.

The Classical period began in the seventh century BC and continued until the seventh century AD. I came to a frieze of the goddess Cybele holding a pomegranate (the mother goddess again). Cybele was the goddess of the Phrygians, and identified with Rhea, 'Queen of the universe'. She was treated with awe. Priests would approach a statue of her with cries, clashing cymbals, and beating drums. To the Romans she was 'The Great Mother'. The crown of the goddess was a city wall fortification in miniature. Thus she would be referred to as *Mater Turrita*. We saw in one section the oldest forms of currency, dating from the ninth century BC and Lydian coins dating from the mid-sixth century BC. Also there were 300-year old Ottoman coins. Other things that I learned was that the word 'sukapisi' means water gate (*su* being Turkish for water and *kapisi* meaning gate), referring to a water gate at an old city on the Euphrates, and that two carved beasts were bases for statues of early Hittite kings. An early Bronze Age sewage system was demonstrated by a model. A relief showed Teshump, the Hittite weather god, being pulled in a chariot by two sacred bulls. Standing with three thunderbolts in one hand, a Hittite king poured wine with the other in another carving. Many reliefs of the late Hittite period were of basalt stone or limestone. There was a lion gate from the eleventh to ninth centuries BC. But we had to leave the museum, interesting as it had proved to be.

In Ulus Square we found all sorts of contemporary activity. All kinds of trading were taking place. We caught an overnight train back to Istanbul, arriving there all bleary-eyed in the early morning. One of the first things we did was to return to the café on the Galata Bridge where we had made such a hit nearly a month earlier. 'Welcome back', said the boy who had served us then.' I remember your visit to us weeks ago.' I smiled a greeting back. I was glad of the rest and refreshments. After the train journey we had crossed the Bosphorus on a ferry boat amid rough waters; now we took a brief rest. As we sat there in the autumnal sun we realised that our visit to this fascinating country was almost over. It was not quite over as we had time for one more visit – now to the Topkapi Palace before leaving.

The palace complex is spread out over a large area. From the restaurant the view was delightful. 'You won't find a better view of the Bosphorus than the one you are looking at, my friend', said a friendly Turk. To think that this palace was threatened with closure after the dissolution of the Sultanate. Over the 1920s the buildings here were restored. Thus today the complex exists as a museum of many sections. There are different gates and different courtyards which adhere to one homogenous whole. The Imperial Gate, or Bäb-I Hümayun, a monumental and ceremonial gate facing towards the Hagia Sophia, was built by Mehmet the Conqueror. The Middle Gate forms the main access to the Topkapi Palace Museum. At one time only the sultan was allowed to enter on horseback. The towers standing adjacent to the gate were once used for the imprisonment of court staff who fell foul of the sultan. The Gate of the White Eunuchs, also known as the Gate of Felicity, stands at the second courtyard's terminus, opposite in position to the Middle Gate or Selam Kapisi.

When we entered the first courtyard we were confronted with the Executioner's Fountain or Cellat Yeşmesi. In bygone days heads were severed on this spot, and the executioner would wash the blood from his hands and weapon of execution. The old kitchens were built by Mehmet and later restored by Suleyman the Magnificent. The domes were a still later development added by Mimar Sinan. The kitchens can be found to the right in the second courtyard. Ahmet III built his library in the third courtyard in 1719. It stands behind the audience chamber. The same ruler was also responsible for restoring the private dormitory of the Court Pages, which was first built by Sultan Ahmet I. Adjacent to it stands the bath of Selim II. The Treasury was also housed here – the Treasury of the Ambassadors. The main Treasury exists separately, next to the pantry of the Court Pages, or the Has Kiler Kogusu. The Harem is a complex structure in its own right and we were not allowed access.

When visitors speak of the Topkapi Palace Museum they are really talking about a collection of separate museums. There's the military museum, the Ataturk museum – the same building in which Atatürk lived prior to the War of Independence – the Oriental art museum which has exhibits drawn from all over the Middle East, the portrait gallery, and the municipal museum.

Let me describe some of the priceless things that I saw and pondered over in the Treasury. Here I gazed at the seventeenth-century throne of Ahmet I which is exquisitely inlaid with interlacing designs of mother-of-pearl, emerald, and precious stones like lapis lazuli. A pendant of Sultan Abdulhamid I had three huge emeralds in its design. A dagger on display had a solid emerald handle. It was a present to Mehmet IV from his mother during the consecration of a new mosque. Emeralds predominate everywhere

here. There was a pearl rosary with emeralds here, and even horses when used ceremonially had emeralds in their crests, like the crests of a sultan's turban – an example of which was there, along with a pendant of Sultan Ahmet I. Then we came upon a gold-plated cradle, also from the seventeenth century. I admired a beautiful royal pendant with wine-red rubies and many objects of jade and rock crystal. After this we saw the famous Topkapi Dagger. The film *Topkapi* was based on a plot involving it. The sheer magnificence of it all made me realise just how fabulously rich these sultans really were, like Eastern potentates since time immemorial.

Eighteenth-century objects had emeralds on them – and diamonds on enamelled gold. I saw golden censors, rose-water sprinklers, and a miniature of Mahmut II (1808–39) caught my gaze along with a caseful of medallions, one of which at least belonged to Abdul Aziz (1861–76). Then we came to a dazzling throne from the sixteenth century. A candlestick of Abdul Mecid made from solid gold (48 kg) was encrusted with 666 diamonds to represent the number of verses in the Koran. Then came some Koran satchels. I was further dazzled by the jewelled armour of Sultan Moustafa III; a jewelled statue of an elephant on a music box, the legs of which are created in the form of palm trees; a beautiful inlaid throne of Sultan Murad IV of splendid geometric design; bowls ornamented with gold filigree and jewelled craft of various kinds from Persia and Turkey. Statuettes from India were given to Sultan Abdul Aziz as presents – and many of the exhibits were from India, like the throne of Shah Ismail. A gold candlestick once belonged to Mehmet Ali Pasha, a nineteenth-century Governor of Egypt. A gold water-pipe once smoked by Moustafa Pasha was from the eighteenth century. Leaving this fabulous collection we moved off to see others.

The Chinese collection was interesting but seemed incongruous here in a sense. First we noted Early Ming Dynasty wares, blue-and-white wares of the fifteenth century, celadons of the Yuan period, a highly decorated bronze mirror-back of the Tang Dynasty and a Ming Dynasty jar of the sixteenth century. This collection, like the others, is very considerable, and much is omitted here as elsewhere in this book. I saw a reproduction of an engraving depicting a banquet in honour of a Polish ambassador by Sultan Mehmet's Grand Vizier, at which Chinese porcelain was used. I saw more animal flasks which reminded us of the Hittite artefacts that we had seen at Ankara.

Passing through the Akagular Gate to the Library of Ahmet III we saw beautiful inlaid doors. The interior was finely tiled with inlaid arches and beautiful windows. Here we saw a collection of sultans' portraits, and Shiraz period miniatures delicately coloured in blues, greens, reds, and gold. The fine collection of illustrations held my interest for some while. One of these showed a Sultan in his garden with his Courtiers, dated 1480. Then I came to a sensitive landscape with animals, birds and plants belonging to the Aq Qoyunlu (Turkish) period. I then looked at a book illustration from the Timurid period in the Herat-Bahzad style, copied for Sultan Mohammed Muhsin Bkhadir. It was a superb illustration showing four ceremonial elephants in all their finery and trappings. The scripts were written in Arabic – not often seen in Turkey nowadays. After the War of Independence the Turks changed over from Arabic to Romanised lettering. Another elephant illustration came before my gaze, and Jazarf's book of the knowledge of mechanical devices, dated 602–1250. Syrian illustration from the Seljuk period showed a David and Goliath scene. A man in splendid stance held a severed head in one hand and

a sword in the other. Lastly we visited the Apartment of the
Blessed Mantle – important for Moslems since it contained
relics of the Prophet Mohammed. Through a grille we were
able to view such things as the mantle that the Prophet wore
and three hairs from the beard of Mohammed in small circular cans. Stones impressed with his footprints were there;
his sword, his bow and his seal are among the items on
display.

Our flight time was close, so we hired a taxi to take us to
the airport. The Turkish adventure had ended, and it was to
be many years before I set foot here again.

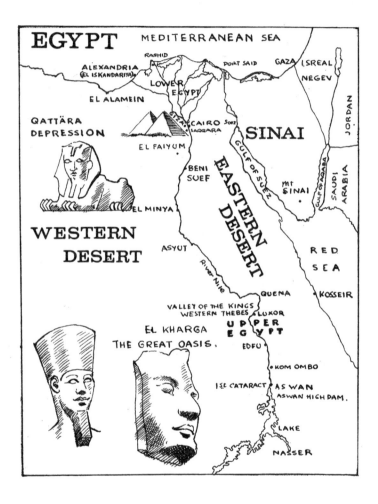

EGYPT

MEDITERRANEAN SEA

RASHID

ALEXANDRIA
(EL ISKANDARIYA)

PORT SAID

GAZA

ISREAL

NEGEV

LOWER
EGYPT

EL ALAMEIN

QATTÄRA
DEPRESSION

CAIRO

SAQQARA

SUEZ

SINAI

JORDAN

EL FAIYUM

BENI
SUEF

mt
SINAI

SAUDI
ARABIA

EL MINYA

WESTERN
DESERT

ASYUT

RED
SEA

River Nile

QUENA

KOSSEIR

VALLEY OF THE KINGS
WESTERN THEBES

LUXOR

UPPER
EGYPT

EL KHARGA
THE GREAT OASIS.

EDFU

KOM OMBO

1ST CATARACT

ASWAN

ASWAN HIGH DAM.

LAKE
NASSER

CHAPTER SIXTEEN

A VIEW OF PYRAMIDS

As a last country to visit before the completion of my story, I made certain that Egypt was to be included. So I took off for Cairo, alone this time, one autumn afternoon on a Sudan Air flight. I fell into a very interesting conversation with a Sudanese businessman who was flying to Khartoum. This was really a Khartoum flight – it was merely stopping off at Cairo.

My arrival at Cairo Airport was later than I thought it would be. It was about 4.30 a.m. Cairo time, and, rather than wait around the airport for morning light to appear, I took a taxi into Cairo. The ride from the airport takes about half an hour, and at length I was speeding past the great statue of Ramses II which stands before a pool near the main railway station. I was set down at the Windsor Hotel close by the old Cairo opera house. Even though it was about five in the morning, I was courteously shown to my room and served tea on a tray. It did not take long for the morning to get started. I could hear the loud commotion of people's comings and goings somewhere beyond the window shutters of my room, and the sky was rapidly lightening. In spite of my short sleep, I got dressed again, and descended to the breakfast room. In order to reach this room, I had to pass through the hotel lounge, which resembled a genteel club, or officers' mess, which had all the newspapers in their racks changed daily.

It transpired that I met a number of very friendly German technicians and businessmen; they were helpful in the way that they took me round many of the sights. One of the technicians invited me to ride with him as far as the Citadel on this first morning in Cairo and I gratefully accepted. From the hotel I stepped out into a very noisy and bustling scene. We climbed into the technician's car, and started threading our way through the heavy traffic. We crossed the city and suddenly the tall towering piles of the Mohammed Ali Mosque (the Alabaster Mosque) and close to it the Mosque of Sultan En Nasir reared before our eyes, and the walls of the Cairo Citadel beyond. Minutes later we drove straight up to the Citadel, baled out of the car, and commenced a walk up to the Citadel's best vantage points for a comprehensive view of the vast sprawling city of Cairo, and in the far distance on the horizon the Pyramids of Giza. I could only just make them out in this my very first glimpse of the pyramids.

The Great Pyramid is the only surviving structure from the original Seven Wonders of the World. The others were the Colossus of Rhodes, the Hanging Gardens of Babylon, the Temple of Diana at Ephesus, the Statue of Jupiter by Phidias, the Pharos or old lighthouse at Alexandria, and the Mausoleum, tomb of Mausolos. The great Pyramid, along with many other pyramids, has continued into the twenty-first century, defying the ravages of time. The dry climate in this part of the world has, of course, assisted greatly in their remarkable preservation. The Pyramids represent powerful imagery and most people would have been equally overwhelmed by the other wonders of the ancient world had they survived. Fortunately there are quantities of ancient art that are with us still for us to behold.

Arab historians tell us that much of Cairo's Citadel was constructed of stone obtained from the lesser Pyramids at Giza, which made me feel that I was standing on stones of history. Not all the Citadel begun by Saladin in 1176 remains. It is estimated that only about half to three-quarters of the north section still remains as Saladin left it. The Citadel looks out over the whole of Cairo, but still higher ground rises behind it to the south. This was effectively used by Mohammed Ali in 1805 as the major part of his strategy in forcing Kurshid Pasha, the then Turkish Governor, into surrendering the Citadel in the conflict of those days.

My German technician friend had business to attend to and excused himself. I proceeded to the Mohammed Ali Mosque, a great lofty structure almost vying with the Pyramids themselves as an attraction for visitors. The minarets were very tall and slender; some experts think they are too slender. I beg to differ, being sensitive to the gracefulness of those minarets. They do much to enhance the overall effect of the building. The mosque itself only dates from Victorian times, built on the site of an earlier structure – a palace demolished by an explosion in 1824. Any resemblance to a building in Istanbul is deliberate, for this mosque is indeed modelled on the Nuri Osmaniye Mosque of Istanbul, by Greek architect Yusuf Boshna, who resided in that city.

Inside the Mohammed Ali Mosque it is very spacious with Byzantine-style domes resting on huge columns. The domes soar high over the heads of the spectator. The overall impression is powerful, although many of the items, like the pulpit, reading desk, and niche pointing to Mecca, were little different from those in hundreds of other mosques.

Another great mosque nearby is the Mosque of Sultan En-Nasir, a fourteenth-century building which became redundant as a mosque and was requisitioned by the military forces, becoming an arsenal. The facade is plain, but shows something of the Romanesque style. There are two minarets, different in style to those on the Mohammed Ali Mosque, due to the peculiar bulb formations at their summits, possibly intended to imitate the form of pomegranates. Fine Byzantine columns were used in the building, and also some very ancient Egyptian ones, but much of the old building work has vanished now, or has fallen into a dilapidated state. Some restoration has been carried out in recent years.

A whole vast complex of buildings and a tangle of narrow streets spread out from these mosques. The streets lead to bazaars and smaller mosques, where one guide tried to charge me a pound for briefly showing me round one such place. A whole vast chaotic mass of Cairo's roof-tops and minarets spreads out before you from these two big mosques. Cairo was founded in the tenth century, which is not really old in Egyptian terms. Close by the Mosque of Sultan En-Nasir we find Joseph's Well, supposedly used by the Holy Family during their sojourn here. It seems, though, that the well is of later origin, even though it is still referred to as Bir Yusef. At one time oxen used to draw its waters to the surface by means of a *saqiya*. This is a familiar Egyptian device where animals are harnessed to a central pivot. Their turning raises containers of water to the surface, and the platform on which the beasts walked was about fifty metres below the surface.

Soon I teamed up with others who were staying at the Windsor Hotel. Together we negotiated the narrow passages leading into the souks. Sometimes these passageways would be shaded by awning and sometimes not. The day was rather overcast and at first I thought it might continue to be so, due to the fact that wintertime was approaching. I needn't have worried – plenty of sunny days lay ahead of me. We stopped off at little mosques. Very close to the Citadel area lies the Mosque of Suleyman Pasha, which was the first of the mosques to be designed in the Istanbul mosque style in 1528. The builder was Suleyman, a Mameluke of Sultan Selim.

Cairo is the most densely populated city on earth, and it felt as though a sizeable segment of the population had converged on these market areas that afternoon. Livestock there included sheep and poultry. Two fine specimens of water buffalo were being led by their noses just ahead of me. They were led off down a nearby passageway. Many of the sheep were marked with reddish dye on their fleece. The convention of grouping together people of the same trade more or less applies to this market area of Cairo. One of the group, a tall American, stopped to haggle for a djellabah. After much effort he found one that suited him.

Entering another small mosque, we were able to climb to its roof, then to the top of its tower. Once again I looked out over the greyish vastness of Cairo's roof-tops. I noticed the Mohammed Ali Mosque in the distance, now looking tiny and far less imposing. It made me quite sick to look down into the tiny street below, on to the heads of passers-by.

Later in the day back at the Windsor Hotel I rested. This was the first of several forays into Cairo and its environs. My late night arrival and consequent lack of sleep had forced me to limit my first day's activities. Even so I congratulated myself on getting round to the number of things that I did.

That evening I got into conversation with two Germans, Wilfred and his son George, who were business partners out in Cairo. Wilfred told me that he had served as a prisoner of war out in Egypt. They invited me to join them for a trip to the Pyramids the following day. I gratefully accepted.

The next morning Wilfred, George and myself were heading out to Giza in their car. The sand of the desert encroaches to the very edge of Cairo, and I was struck by the overall vision of yellows and ochres as the Pyramids loom into view. The shape of the Great Pyramid grew larger, then we were dwarfed by it. Camel owners were everywhere looking for trade and the area was crawling with many tourists of umpteen nationalities.

We alighted for a stroll on the sands. Immediately a camel owner approached me. 'Just say to him Hookrah! Hookrah! which means come back tomorrow', advised Wilfred. 'Sometimes it's better not to even look in their direction, let alone speak to them', he went on. 'They will judge your nationality and name their camel accordingly. For example, if you are British they will tell you that the name of the camel is 'Churchill'. They will try anything to get business.' The Sudanese businessman with whom I had flown out here had warned me that the Egyptians were cheeky.

Back in the car, we drove along little roadways that ran beside the canals which were part of the irrigation system. I spotted more water buffaloes. These animals, found plentifully in Egypt, are large bony handsome things with down-curved horns. 'You can sometimes see them submerged in the water with only their heads above the surface', said Wilfred. Local peasant women were busily washing their dirty linen in the irrigation channel. Further along we were to encounter time-honoured sights typical of the region that I had not seen before. First there was a boy operating an Archimedean screw to raise water from one level to a higher level. Then we saw a *saqiya* in action – two bulls were turning wheels to draw water.

We reached Saqqara, location of that well-known Step Pyramid, and sephulchres from most periods of ancient Egyptian history. The Step Pyramid itself was the tomb of Pharaoh Zoser of the Third Dynasty, sometimes known as King Djoser. It is sited inside a complex which includes many other ancient structures. The entire Necropolis has down through the ages been looted of any treasures that were lodged there. Imhotep was the architect who designed and built the Step Pyramid. The use of dressed stone originated with him. Wilfred and myself descended into a very lengthy chamber which was flanked by huge sarcophagi. Obviously this chamber was of very much later period than the Step Pyramid – which is reckoned to be the oldest pyramid there.

When we finally emerged from this long sephulchral tunnel we turned to the *mastabas* of the Old Kingdom period, where we saw wall reliefs in colour which are the finest of their kind in Egypt. There are three *mastabas* – the Mastaba of Ti (2560 BC) the Mastaba of Ptah-Hotep (2500 BC) and the Mastaba of Mereruka (2420 BC). The Old Kingdom period lasted from 2700 BC to 2200 BC, which corresponds roughly to the first Dynasty of Ur in Mesopotamia (2800–2400 BC). The tunneling inside the Step Pyramid is not as its first builders left it but has become considerably modified through treasure hunters, and also by people carrying out restoration work. As we walked through various ancient passages Wilfred would point out a cartouche of a pharaoh here or there, whilst I drew his attention to other items of interest. Scenes from everyday life in ancient Egypt were depicted in that stylised art so familiar to visitors even before they set foot in Egypt. Scenes portrayed were of butchers at work, farmers fattening geese and cranes, sailings on the Nile, reaping, winnowing, shipbuilding – all these activities of millennia ago were seen with amazing clarity.

Many ancient murals have survived almost intact whilst others have suffered damage from mutilation and the breath of masses of visitors.

The Unas Pyramid, also at Saqqara, (2450 BC) is important as the tomb of Pharaoh Unis, or Onnos as he was otherwise known. Proper scientific exploration of these sites was begun with experts like William Flinders Petrie and Belzoni in the 1880s. Sir Gaston Maspero in 1881 first opened the Step Pyramid. Flinders Petrie continued with his passion for archaeology until he was ninety years old. He took the Pyramids of Giza as his starting point, and developed many theories with other experts about the alignment of these ancient structures, and their purpose. One theory was that the arrangement of the pyramids represented a calendar or horoscope.

Deep inside the Unas Pyramid are hieroglyphics relating to the hereafter, incised in stone, and they are the oldest Egyptian writings of a religious nature in existence. The complicated system of chambers in the pyramids was created to confuse would-be grave robbers. It was part of ancient Egyptian belief that provision had to be made for the life to come by placing everyday objects within the burial chamber. Near the Unas Pyramid are shaft tombs dating from the Persian period. There are three of them and, as their name suggests, they are constructed mostly in the form of shafts and tunnels.

The tomb of Mereruka is worthy of mention. It is situated just north-west of the Pyramid of Teti. As we wandered through this early 6th Dynasty complex we saw how Mereruka was buried in one room, his wife Hertwatetkhet in a second chamber and their son Meriteti in a third. Altogether the complex contains no less than thirty-one rooms and tunnels. The walls of the tomb are decorated with murals depicting aspects of the King's life and times: Mereruka seated at an easel painting, Mereruka spearing fish, his men hunting hippopotami, various artisans at work – goldsmiths, woodworkers, butchers and so on.

The archaeologist who was directing operations at Saqqara for many years leading up to 1971 was Professor Emery. Whilst exploring the tombs of courtiers of ancient times, he discovered tunnels that bisected the tomb shafts. These tunnels were filled with animal and bird mummies. In one group of tunnels the space was filled with mummified ibises, another group mummified falcons. Baboons and cows were preserved in like manner. The purpose of all this mummification would be obscure if we did not know that the ancient Egyptians treated these animals as especially sacred. Animals often represented gods. The falcon form was the god Horus. The god Hath was represented by the ibis and the baboon. All the baboons found by Professor Emery were placed against their own personal stone slab, on which all the details of each beast were written. The bull represented the god Apis, and many bulls were found mummified here also. The bull was important to the Hittites, as we have seen, and here we have an example of cross-currents of culture and thinking. When Strabo visited Saqqara during the time of Christ he recorded amongst other things that a sacred bull was led out from the temple for the Egyptians to worship.

The list of Egyptian gods is lengthy, and we can only find space for a small number of them. The cat was also deified. It represented Bastet, the goddess of Bubastis – a deity of joy. Mut, the wife of Amun, chief of the gods, took the vulture as her sacred bird. Many deities were local rather than universal. It was their task to attend to the passage of the dead into the hereafter. It must be pointed out that much of the significance of these deities is lost to us today. Often the

Egyptians lacked a coherent homogenous system of religious belief and appeared to accept all sorts of inconsistencies. In early times territories were established. To begin with, the country was divided into Upper and Lower Egypt and the tendency was for deities to be localised, like a patron saint. For example, the god Horus was a deity of Behdet, and the god Ptah belonged to Memphis. Gods could be connected with fetishes in human or tree forms. As many Egyptians saw it, a god would enter an animal manifesting him or herself to the populace.

Bulls were kept in temples while they lived. They were of different colours. Apis was black with white spots, with a white triangle placed on his forehead, a crescent on his flank. A light-coloured bull was deified at Heliopolis. After the animal had died salt was used to treat the bodies along with palm wine, oils, resins, frankincense and myrrh. After the preservatives were used, the bodies were then bound with lengths of bandage.

At a later stage in their history the Egyptians introduced animal-headed human forms into their worship. Anthropologists who are concerned with the whole study of man readily recognise a term used to encapsulate this era in Egyptian history – Anthropomorphism, *anthropos* being Greek for man, and *morphe* Greek for form. Thus to anthropomorphise means to attribute human characteristics to an animal or bird. The human forms that the Egyptians now gave to their gods were clothed in everyday dress. Universal gods, as opposed to the localised ones, were often connected with the basic elements. Geb was the god of the Earth, Nut the goddess of the sky, Shuw was the god of the air, Re was the god of the sun and Tefnut the goddess of the dew. The religious system of Egypt certainly evolved as time went on, but remained polytheistic. The falcon-headed god Montu

was a god of war, corresponding with Mars the Roman god
of war. The god of fertility was Min, and like St Christopher
was a patron saint of travellers. To the Greeks this god was
identified with their god Pan, the goat-footed god who
played his merry pipes. Each craft had its own protector and
artisans appeared to hold to them dearly. There were lesser
deities who helped or hindered things like childbirth. These
gods frequently had to be appeased by the inhabitants of a
village or, they feared, reprisals might result.

After our very hot and dusty tour of the archaeological
sites of Saqqara, we sat down in a restaurant marque within
a short distance from the Step Pyramid. We sat there enjoying large drinks of orange, and discussed our explorations
like a group of seasoned Egyptologists. A cameraman with
an Etonian accent rushed out to film the Step Pyramid,
yelling at his girlfriend who was wearing a long Victorian
dress and large floppy hat to follow him. As we sat enjoying
our refreshments, a number of jackals wandered into the
marquee with a number of playful puppies. A mother jackal
begged me for food. Every so often the waiter would come
along to chase them away, whilst I tried to get rid of flies. I
remembered someone telling me about his friend's visit to the
Pyramids late at night. The jackals that wander wild in the
area all set themselves on him. Understandably he was star-
tled out of his wits to find these snarling creatures of the
night at his heels.

We drove on to Memphis. I felt grateful that there were
plenty of trees offering shade here. Many historic buildings
once graced this site. Little now remains except for a few
crumbling ruins. Literally the biggest thing to be seen in
Memphis is the huge Colossus of Ramses II lying on its back
and covered by a new observation building. Visitors may walk
all round the recumbent colossus on a four-sided platform,

viewing from above. As one guide was heard to say, 'We offered the statue to the British but it proved too heavy and difficult to move, so we decided to keep it ourselves. Today it is a huge attraction for tourists.'

Herodotus, the old Greek historian, relates how King Mena (after whom Memphis is named) was responsible for uniting both Upper and Lower Egypt in 3200 BC. King Mena showed shrewdness and foresight in erecting the city on the Nile's west bank. In its day Memphis would have been a fine city to behold, as ancient references suggest. Old hieroglyphics speak of Mennefer, or the beautiful dwelling, and also Anebhet, or the white-walled city. The name Memphis is of Greek origin, although derived from earlier sources. The most splendid flowering of Memphis occurred during the third to fifth dynasties. Once there stood a Temple of Ptah on the site, which had much care lavished on it. The stones of this once-graceful building have long since gone, used by builders of later times. Beside the giant statue of Ramses II there is a sphynx of modest size belonging to the New Empire period. Apart from these two main attractions, there are a number of other features, including a place where the sacred Apis bulls were once embalmed.

As we drove back to Cairo Wilfred told me about the vast technology that was booming in modern-day Cairo, as we were passing through an industrial area. 'You will find all sorts of people making a contribution', said Wilfred. 'Look at those Fiat cars from Italy and the buses which were made in Iran.' Fellucas tied up on the Nile were loaded with cement – something of a concession to modernity perhaps. I also learned that the Germans had contributed lorries and buses to Egypt.

Technicians staying at the Windsor Hotel were engaged in tracking research. All in all the number of technicians from the West working in Egypt is considerable. Even a conservative estimate of their numbers would be difficult to gauge.

The following day I returned to Giza and hired a camel. The trouble was that the camel owner insisted on jumping into the saddle with me. The creature then was made to bolt at top speed round all four sides of the Great Pyramid with me holding on for dear life. Every part of me was jolted as the camel galloped over the uneven ground that surrounded this monument of Cheops. Being close to this last surviving wonder of the ancient world is powerful. I could not help marvelling at the sheer immensity of it all, very much as Herodotus must have done when he came here in 450 BC. According to Herodotus it took 100,000 labourers twenty years to build, working for three months of every year of the time it took to complete. Most of the elaborate facing that Herodotus described has now gone, but in essence the structure is hugely impressive still. Sir William Flinders Petrie had much to say about the Great Pyramid. He maintained that the three months of the year in which the labour on the Pyramid was carried out came at times when harvesting was at a standstill, so leaving the men free to work on the Pyramid.

The mention of harvesting in Egypt reminded me of the story of Joseph. People came to him from far and wide to obtain corn from his granaries in the time of famine. Genesis tells the fascinating story of how Joseph found favour with the Pharaoh, who placed his own ring on Joseph's hand, dressed him in fine garments and gave him one of his best chariots.

'And Joseph gathered grain as the sand of the sea, very much, until he stopped counting, for it could not be measured . . . But when all the land of Egypt was weakened by hunger the people

(there) cried to Pharaoh for food, and Pharaoh said to (them) all, Go to Joseph, and what he says to you, do. When the famine was over all the land, Joseph opened all the storehouses, and sold to the Egyptians, for the famine grew extremely distressing in the land of Egypt. And all countries came to Egypt to Joseph to buy grain, because the famine was severe over all (the known) earth.'
(Amplified Bible, Genesis 41: 49, 55–57)

This tale of great resourcefulness by one very far-sighted individual relates to the Middle Empire period of 2150–1580 BC. The Pharaoh mentioned was probably from the Hyksos Dynasty which began when those people changed from being a nomadic tribe to a ruling power. It was the dissolution of this Dynasty that led to the takeover by Ramses II. The harsh ruthless administration that he introduced marked the beginning of bad times in Egypt – especially for the Jews in captivity here. Then came the Exodus under Moses.

The Nile had, of course, sustained this otherwise dry land and the rich silt washed down over thousands of years has produced rich soil. The successful irrigation of the land from these Nile waters had literally been a godsend.

After my rather boisterous camel ride I spent some time tramping round the Pyramids on foot and viewed the inscrutable Sphinx at close quarters. As far as I could see it looked worse for wear, although still very clearly the guardian of the second Pyramid's sacred enclosure. The Sphinx body is that of a great squatting lion whilst the head is that of a pharaoh in his official royal headgear. The royal serpent emblem is included in the headgear. For thousands of years this enigmatic figure has crouched there and awed all who have come this way. The creation of the Sphinx came about almost by accident. It is located in what was once a quarry for Cheops.

After much quarrying had taken place a huge mound of rock – a chunk of old limestone – was left that was apparently no use to anybody. Then Pharaoh Kephren and his aides noticed that it had possibilities! (This was the administration that followed Cheops.)

Back in Cairo the next day I wandered back into the souk, and found it every bit as lively as before. Cars were honking furiously, trying to negotiate the narrow passageways. Blacksmiths were busy shoeing horses on a pavement. Welders were also busy working cheerfully without masks as sparks flew in all directions. Beautiful doe-eyed Egyptian girls glided by, their eyes looking searchingly into mine. Men were clapping and shouting in small mosques to show off the acoustics to me. A waggon with massive wheels rumbled by. Flies swarmed over a tray full of camels' trotters on one stall I passed. Enormous pieces of meat hung in the butchers' stalls. Cartloads of goods stood everywhere with crowds of felaheen weaving their way backwards and forwards through the myriad of lanes. I passed the usual stalls of copperware and carpentry which lay close to the stacks of galvanised buckets.

Back out in the main streets I noticed a bus impossibly overloaded with its human cargo trundling past, a common sight here in this sprawling city. I stopped at a small Greek Orthodox church – and there are many Christian churches in Cairo.

The church that I was now entering was the church of St Nicholas. Later I turned my attention to the church associated with the Holy Family, the one I really wanted to see. Amongst a cluster of buildings and adjacent to a monorail station stands the Abu Serga, a Coptic church which has undergone medieval reconstruction (during the Fatimid period) but was of much earlier origin. Tradition assigns to

this church the honour of being the sanctuary where Mary,
Joseph and the boy Jesus took refuge after the flight from
Egypt. I reached the church after leaving the road I was on,
and walking down a narrow passageway to enter the building. Inside it was dark, gloomy and peaceful – something
akin to a sublime etching. If indeed this was the refuge for
the Holy Family then I was standing on a hallowed spot. I
sat there for several minutes, enjoying the peace and tranquillity away from the hustle of the Cairo souk. The marble
columns blended well with the dark wooden church furniture. The old entrances to the church are now blocked, and
screening divides the interior. It was customary for the priest
to wash the feet of the congregation during Epiphany, in
imitation of Christ's washing of the disciples' feet. The
atmosphere was heavy with the devotion and sanctity of
ages.

The churches in the area are huddled very close together,
and nearby is the Church of the Blessed Virgin. It was built
in the latter part of the fourth century or early in the fifth.
Unlike other churches in the area this one is completely
without domes. Timber vaulting was used in the roof construction. The gables are supported on pillars that used to
grace Roman temples. They are all of fine white marble
except for an odd-one-out basalt pillar. The pillars are seen
to stand in three rows.

This place of worship is also called the Moallakah Church.
In Arabic 'Moallakah' means suspended – so named because
of it being raised above the Roman fort of Babylon. The use
of the name 'Babylon' derived from the fact that Jeremiah,
the weeping prophet, came here in about 701 BC, bringing
with him the name of the place he had fled from on the other
horn of the Fertile Crescent. Thus the name of Babylon
struck, and seems to have been used for the area ever since.

A very old lintel from the Moallakah church depicts the entry of Christ into Jerusalem on that first Palm Sunday. The lintel was removed, however, and now resides in the Coptic Museum. In style the carving is typically fourth or fifth century, and gives added confirmation of the venerable age of this building. The church doors were made of cedar wood after the biblical pattern when the church was first built. Later, when new doors were made to replace the old ones, they were interlaced with suitably Christian designs involving crosses, fish, and vine leaves – all done in ivory and ebony.

As I was silently walking round the church an old priest appeared and I got into conversation with him. He commented on the division of the sexes in the church: 'The men sit on the right-hand side, whilst the women have to sit on the left – and do you know what this old custom is based on? Well, it is maintained because Eve was created from a rib from Adam's left side.'

Dividing the church there is an old arabesque screen, and much of the decoration is arabesque in style, as can be seen in the walls and doorways. One hundred and ten marvellous old icons also decorate the walls. The earliest icon here goes back as far as the tenth century. The dating of the icons is based on the Coptic calendar, which is different from ours in that it is taken, not from the approximate time of Christ's birth, but from AD 284, which was a terrible time of persecution for Christians in Egypt, worse than at any other time. There were icons depicting Mary with the Christ child, as you might expect, and some showing the Assumption of Mary. Others showed Christian saints of post-biblical times: St George, St Juliana, St Catherine. In the icon of Mary and the Christ child it is claimed that the eyes follow the spectator round, probably caused by cunningly placed highlights in the eye by the artist. Six columns frame the icon – three on each side. The columns are decorated, like most parts of the church.

One interesting icon recalls the persecution of Christians under Diocletian – the icon showing Lady Dimiana as one of the victims, along with the forty virgins from the Manscora convent. Lady Dimiana became canonised as a saint. Many were converted to Christianity by her courageous example. Today the church stands on the site of the old convent, a rebuilt version of the first church of St Dimiana, which was destroyed in AD 760. Pilgrims visit the church annually on May 12th–20th in remembrance of the martyrdom of St Dimiana.

Other terrible sufferings inflicted on the Church in the first centuries of its existence are reflected in the icon of St James, whose death came about by dismembering. Also in the collection there was an icon which showed a mother and her five children being martyred. The mother holds a crucifix in her right hand and clutches the hand of her youngest child tenderly with the other. The two eldest children also clutch crucifixes, while the younger children are still clutching at plates and spoons.

Many biblical characters are here and biblical scenes. Joseph the husband of Mary appears, so do Zachariah and Salome with evangelists Luke and Matthew and St Peter among others. Various scenes from the life of Christ are seen: his birth, baptism, appropriately the flight into Egypt, and the crucifixion.

Outside I could hear the twittering of swallows mingled with the Moslem call to prayer. For ages the Coptic church had used the ancient Egyptian language in its worship. Scholars seem to have overlooked this when attempting to interpret the inscriptions in dozens of temples and on numerous obelisks in the nineteenth century. In the event, the Victorians relied on the Rosetta stone in order to make any sense of the old hieroglyphics. All that decoration in the church in ivory and marble enhances the dignity and sanctity of the place – details like the marble pulpit with its rich symbolism and all the other features described.

I visited the Coptic Museum where Christian art seemed to mix freely with pagan. I saw illustration of Christ rising in a fiery chariot like Elijah, and Christ in benediction. Then there were scenes of the god Pan chasing a maiden. The museum building once belonged to a caliph. Immediately behind the museum there are old Roman ruins, which I was taken to see.

That church of the Abu Sàrga, or Church of St Sergius, where the Holy Family are said to have taken refuge, has behind it an old eighth-century synagogue which contains a rare Old Testament manuscript. Joseph is supposed to have worked at the Roman fortress whilst Mary and the Christ child rested at the place now occupied by the Church of St Sergius. Close at hand are the homes of Egyptian Christians marked with crosses on the doors. Other churches I visited in the area included the Church of St Barbara – pleasant to visit but lacking the interest of the others, in my view.

After a few days in Cairo I decided that it was time to move up the Nile to Luxor. A cruise up the Nile is one of the most popular trips to be had in Egypt. Unfortunately it was necessary to book well in advance for it. The alternatives were flying or going by train. I packed again for the next part of my Egyptian tour. I decided to fly and duly booked a seat on a plane to Luxor.

CHAPTER SEVENTEEN

THE TREASURES OF LUXOR

As the tiny aircraft rose in the sky, I looked out of the window to see the ochre desert rolling beneath me. Sometimes low-flying clouds obscured part of the surface, casting bluish shadows on the sand as they did so. Odd patches that represented settlements or greenery occasionally appeared, otherwise the view was fairly bleak. The flight lasted about an hour and we were very soon wheeling into land.

Once we landed, a mishap nearly occurred. Searching through the mass of luggage I quickly realised that my case was missing. I then wasted no time in racing back across the tarmac to the plane before it took off again. I prevailed upon the airport officials to open up the belly of the aircraft and search through the remaining cases thoroughly. The passengers still inside the plane were probably getting very upset because of the delay. At last it was found, my little green suitcase, and the plane was able to take off for Aswan. I knew it would be a few days before I continued on there myself. As I passed a group of Americans from the plane who had travelled down from Cairo with me, they asked me about the case.

308

'It was still aboard the plane', I told them tersely.

'You're kidding', drawled one American woman, but I wasn't.

Soon afterwards a taxi had deposited me outside the tiny hotel that was to be my home for the next few days. Luxor is a pleasant little town nestling beside the Nile, where every Arab in sight is after your money. The word *baksheesh* was rarely out of my ears. A whole vast complex was formed by the two towns of Luxor and Karnak, plus the Valleys of the Kings, Queens, and Nobles on the other side of the river.

The first ancient monument to catch the eye of the visitor to Luxor is the main Luxor Temple itself. It is within easy walking distance from any place in the town. During my stay there was always a cluster of American, French, or German visitors walking through the ruins. Many Egyptian pharaohs had a hand in the development of the temple in ancient times. The still imposing remains point back to the time when Amenophis III first built the temple in far-off times so removed from our own. The dedication of the temple was made to Amun-re, chief of the gods, and Mut his wife, also their son Khons, the god of the moon. The whole thing was a very elaborate affair indeed with sanctuaries for the various gods, and their related rooms and related vestibules. The huge double colonnade, which opens into a peristyle court, impresses the visitor with a sense of architectural grandeur. A chapel was built directly opposite the temple by Tuthmosis III.

At a later date religious reformations were enforced by another Egyptian king, Amenophis IV, and all reference to Amun, who had been regarded as chief god in the same way as the Greeks regarded Zeus, were promptly obliterated. Then after this erasure, he erected a sun sanctuary close to the temple, to Aton, and soon moved to a fresh capital, Tell el-Amarna. What a heretic he must have appeared in the eyes of at least some of his contemporaries! The boy king Tutan-khamun ordered the completion of the colonnaded hall and temple, and had the temple walls decorated. The sun sanctu-ary of the heretic Akhnaten was then wrecked. Sethos I made sure that the statue of Amun was restored. Ramses II, who was one of the those prodigious builders of Old Testament times, added hundreds of metres to the length of the Temple.

If the Temple at Luxor is imposing in its ruined state, the Temple at Karnak, half-an-hour's walk away, is even more so, I thought. Approaching the Karnak Temple from the north-west as visitors do today, I was immediately struck by the sight of these fantastic ruins. Passing down the Avenue of Rams, which is flanked on either side by squatting ram sculp-tures as the name suggests, I entered the Great Court, with the Temple of Sethos II to my left and the Temple of Ramses III to my right. I stopped suddenly before a huge statue of a pharaoh. After all these long centuries the finely chiselled features had lost nothing of their sharpness, and still bore the look of arrogance and firm authority that the monarch in all probability wore during his lifetime. Doubtless his subordi-nates cowered!

I entered the Great Hypostyle Hall with its maze of thick squat papyrus-reed columns, and wandered between those columns for some time, looking at the hieroglyphics and basking in the strong sunlight as it filtered through those close-set columns. This strong shadow effect was created deliberately by the designers and builders. These effects were still exerting themselves on modern spectators. Each main section is entered by a thick screen of walling known as a pylon.

Leaving the Hypostyle Hall by the third pylon I came to the central court or the great Temple of Amun. No mere mortal was allowed to wander at will through these sacred portals in those far-off days when the priests of the pharaohs carried out their mysterious rituals. Only members of the religious hierarchy could enter, or the pharaoh himself. Many pharaohs had a hand in the evolution of this Temple of Amun. Thus it cannot be said to have been based on any kind of plan and yet it all works brilliantly as a unified whole. The pharaohs of the 12th Dynasty were the ones that laid the foundations (about 2000–1788 BC). Tuthmosis I made sweeping new changes after he declared Thebes the New Empire capital. In the main, it appears that he built the structure as we know it today. The Temple of Amun especially was developed out of all recognition from what it was previously. Monarchs like Hatshepsut and Tuthmosis III were to add further modifications, and these also have helped to form today's Karnak.

Perhaps the greatest period of the temple's glory came during the 19th Dynasty. It was during this period that the huge Hypostyle Hall was built. Ramses I, Sethos I, and the giant among pharaos, Ramses II, were the three monarchs responsible for building this amazing structure. Many scholars think that Ramses II was the pharaoh of the Exodus, others dispute this. Not only did Ramses II have gigantic architectural concepts on a grand scale, but he was prodigious in other directions. He fathered a hundred and six girls, plus ninety-two boys. He married three queens, the third of whom was a Hittite princess before her marriage to Ramses II. As if all these were not sufficient, he married four of his own daughters. Clearly, the ancients could not abide half-measures.

A magnificent intensity of history, art and devotion finds a focus here at Karnak. The prominent French archaeologist Champillion praised the temple at every turn and rightly so! He considered Karnak the ultimate triumph of architecture.

It takes the visitor some time to adjust and get used to the overwhelming complex of temples, pylons, sphynxes, sacred lakes and sanctuaries. The services of a reliable guide are usually essential if the visitor is to obtain a good understanding of Karnak.

The passage of time has eroded many things here. All the finery and decoration has long gone. It is said that the obelisks gleamed in the sun in such a way that they could be picked out in the distance. In the central court, I stopped to admire the delightful soaring obelisk of Tuthmosis III. Four obelisks originally stood here but three have been obliterated. The small hall has two obelisks: one still stands but the other lies broken on the ground.

When I reached the Temple sanctuary, I noted the murals in relief with much of the colouring still there. Some of the early reliefs were mutilated, especially those of Hatshepsut after her death. The royal barque or sailing ship was always kept in the sanctuary and one of the reliefs depicts the sailing of the sacred ship. Tuthmosis III vandalised the murals of Hatshepsut, but refrained from any vandalism when he reached the two great obelisks of Amun, lest the chief of the gods showed his displeasure. At the far end of the huge rectangle which forms most of the Temple of Amun lies the great Festival Hall, the work of Tuthmosis III. The columns here are rather special, being of strange design with bell-like capitals. The rooms surrounding the main Festival Hall have superb reliefs, in which Alexander the Great is shown doing homage to Amun.

In the Temple complex outside the main rectangular area there is a sacred lake and a further group of pylons and other structures left by the Ptolemies. Here we find the seventh, eighth, ninth, and tenth pylons. The seventh pylon has a number of royal statues flanking it. The eighth has six statues

– the only well-preserved one being a seated Amenophis I. The pylon was raised by Hatshepsut. When we reach the ninth pylon we find it turned on its axis somewhat in a northerly direction. It was raised by Pharaoh Haremhab. After the tenth pylon we find ourselves walking along another avenue of sphynxes. At the end of it lies the Temple of Mut. This complex is also surrounded by a girdle wall, and has a crescent-shaped sacred lake.

I wandered round the ruins at least three times and stopped at least once by the reliefs of the exterior walls of the great Hypostyle Hall. In these reliefs two great pharaohs have left on record details of their armies' victories over other races of the Middle East. Hebrews, Hittites and Syrians are seen in defeat, and prisoners are shown with arms tied above their heads. Ramses II and Set I were of course, the two pharaohs whose victories are shown.

The Temple of Khonsu, which I passed by the Western Avenue of Sphynxes, was built in dedication to Khonsu as the name reveals. The basic design more or less conforms to that of the rest of the Theban Triad complex. I met a group of visitors whom I had met at the Windsor Hotel in Cairo and walked with them part of the way round one more time.

One evening I attended the Karnak son et lumière, the area's sound-and-light spectacular. The temple lends itself particularly well to this. Areas of the ages-old ruins were illuminated very dramatically and even the palm trees were lit up and used to dramatic effect. A huge crowd of visitors turned up for the show – most of them Americans. With all the other spectators, I had to follow the disembodied voice across several stages. Finally we sat down before the Sacred Lake for the concluding part of the proceedings. After attending this son et lumière, and listening to the flow of words, the visitor may be forgiven for feeling that places such as this will forever hold mysteries that defy the comprehension of modern man.

I could not see any pseudo-ancient stonework in these ruins anywhere. Everything I saw was the genuine article. If any recent patching was there it was completely unobtrusive. Hazards suffered by travellers not indigenous to these parts include frequent internal troubles and mosquito bites. I was experiencing these things at the time. On top of this there was the constant harassment by souvenir sellers. Nubian traders were always ready to pounce on the unwary. One teak-skinned white-robed vendor thrust a pair of mock-antique lamps at me.

Walks along the banks of the Nile were always pleasurable. Fellucas with their very tall masts and distinctive sails glided silently past, robed sailors at their tillers. It was uncanny to see these craft glide so smoothly through the water, even when the wind was practically non-existent. It was as though an invisible force was driving them along. Overhead buzzards described big circles in the sky, soaring on broad wings. These scavengers are plentiful in Egypt. The odd naked male bather splashed in the shallows, clearly oblivious of anything or anybody. I loved the fine glowing sunsets. Dark silhouettes of moored craft speared each reddish glow.

At a waterside restaurant I met a charming pair of French ladies. They were mother and daughter. It was their last evening in Luxor and madame was trying out Egyptian lobster. In the same restaurant a few days later I tried out the Red Sea lobster myself. Spicy foods were available, as expected, and bony fish. Visitors seemed to grow in volume daily – Americans, French and Germans among them. Little chance of solitude here now, I told myself. Indeed it was becoming a perfect bear garden.

After Karnak I turned to other archaeological treasures – those of Thebes. Soon I was making enquiries as to the best way of visiting the famed Valley of the Kings on the opposite bank of the Nile. My friends from the Windsor Hotel in Cairo suggested that it was best to hire a bike rather than go by donkey or taxi. I decided to follow their advice. After a search I discovered a tiny hotel, at the end of a dusty track away from the town, that hired the bikes. There are a number of ferries that operate between the banks of the river and I had no trouble in reaching the other bank with the hired bicycle. This ritual ticket buying that must precede the visiting of important sites can be a little irksome at times. So before anything else was done I had to travel along the El Fadlya canal to the village of Kurna – really nothing more than a cluster of mud huts – where the tickets are obtained. After buying my ticket I returned to the place where the ferry crossed.

Soon I found myself riding a tarmac road that brought me to the Colossi of Memnon. These colossi were very badly weathered at the time of my visit. The statues must have suffered erosion during the heavy rainstorms of July 1914, which drenched the hills round Karnak in which the royal tombs lie. The rains washed away loose debris to reveal hitherto hidden caves; it was this very deluge that unearthed great archaeological treasure. On either side of the road dense clusters of reeds occupied some areas. The rest was agricultural land. I noticed felaheen ploughing, using wooden ploughs which take us back to the days of the pharaohs themselves. The ploughman stood on a wooden beam to weigh the plough down as the animals pulled it over the soil.

The first prominent ancient monument I stopped at after seeing the Colossi of Memnon was the terrace temple or Mortuary Temple of Queen Hatshepsut. Rising ramps and long terraces are strongly backdropped by a stark and towering curtain of rock. This temple is known in Arabic as the Deir el-Bahari, built in honour of Amun. Other gods remembered here are Hathor and Anubis. Halls are sited at the ends of all the terraces. Two in particular are prominent. The Punt Hall murals depict the incense trade with Somalia, whilst the Birth Hall, as its name implies, deals with the birth of Queen Hatshepsut. Only on one level are the halls in good condition – the others being in a poor state of repair at the time of my visit. All of this was unfinished at the end of Hatshepsut's long reign.

What conflicts raged between her and her rivals! Tuthmosis II desecrated the statues of Hatshepsut and her inscriptions, as did Tuthmosis III, who often replaced the name of Hatshepsut with his own. It's a glaring example of family discord from antiquity. It is surprising that Ramses II was lax about the quality of the restoration work here, considering the grandiose breadth of his projects. It is clear that this terraced temple did not mean as much to him as some of his other projects.

In the centuries that followed there were very few additions or alterations, but a fellowship of monks in Christian times made their monastery here. This is where the Arabic name Deir el Bahari comes in. It literally means the northern monastery. Ancient pagan chambers were turned into Christian shrines. Vigorous deformation of old murals again took place. Much of the old Egyptian sculpture has vanished, including the avenue of sphynxes that led up to the temple.

It is perhaps a little strange to think that a queen like Hatshepsut should be formally shown with ceremonial beard – this being a particularly male feature. The beard and apron were the official signs of the sovereign and male or female sovereigns wore them.

In places we may still discern scenes from everyday life, despite the mutilations and ravages of time. In the North Colonnade, for instance, there are scenes of wildfowling that can still be made out.

By now I had been joined by two men from the hotel. Together we continued on our way to the Valley of the Kings. The barren ochre rocks and sand closed in upon us as we approached the famed valley. We stopped at a native house by the wayside, and here received a cordial welcome. Their little dwelling was made of mud reinforced with straw, which called to mind the labour of captive Israelites of long ago. Mud and straw are widely used in the building of felaheen dwellings in the area. At the owner's invitation we entered and soon found ourselves in a central courtyard, where pigeons were nesting in holes in the walls, and little goats wandered. The felaheen are fond of their pigeons and one of the family placed his hand in a nest-hole (or pigeon hole) and pulled out a baby pigeon for us to see. I indicated to the little girl of the family that she should hold up her little goat for me to photograph. She understood at once, and snatched up one of the animals, clutching it to her front. One of the boys gave us a demonstration of how he hollowed out alabaster with a brace and bit. So friendly were these felaheen that it was difficult to leave them, but we had to press on to the Valley of the Kings.

After following the tarmac road between rock faces for a while we reached the tombs themselves. Here at Biban-el-Muluk, the Valley of the Kings, we were allowed to see three of the tombs. The rest were closed for some reason. Most of the tombs that have come to light conform to a pattern, as with so much else in Egyptian culture. In the main chamber of each tomb stood the sarcophagus of the monarch concerned. The tomb of Amenhotep II was perhaps the most striking. A cleverly constructed first section meant a sudden 'terminal effect' was produced after only a short penetration. The passageways were profusely lined with murals relating to the hereafter. This was considered as necessary as the embalming and the inclusion of the pharaoh's possessions. Grave robbers nearly always took care of the latter.

A concept prevalent at that time was that the monarch sailed on a boat at night on his journey to the hereafter. It corresponded to the Greeks' belief about crossing the Styx for the same reason. The river of death occurs also in the Judaeo-Christian tradition, namely the Jordan. In the Egyptian system the pharaoh sailed as the sun god's companion. In their three books on the subject of death and the afterlife, the Egyptians sought to map out the route. The best known of these books is *The Book of the Dead*, or *The Book of that which is in the Underworld*, which teaches that the underworld has twelve distinct portions or regions which reflect the twelve hours that make up the night. Thus the book is comprised of twelve chapters, each dealing with a portion of the afterlife. A host of creatures haunt the banks of the river whilst the boat and its passengers ride through to their destination. In the other book, entitled *The Book of Portals*, huge gates are guarded by writhing serpents. Like the gateways or pylons at Karnak, these were intended to divide region from region. Every snake has a name known at first only to the sun god, and the monarch travelling with his companion on that journey had to acquire that knowledge. The sun god is greeted by other gods and fiery serpents. The last of the books describes what happens after the arrival in the underworld. Strange denizens of the underworld are addressed by the sun god.

The Tomb of Amenhotep II, which we were now exploring, reflected these beliefs very vividly indeed. The ceiling of the burial chamber was decorated to resemble a sky. The deep-blue background is decorated with constellations of stars. It shows the night of the journey to the underworld. The whole chamber is richly embellished and is the most striking example of tomb art in existence.

The next tomb we visited was very much smaller, if infinitely more famous. It was the Tomb of Tutankhamun, the boy king. This is the only tomb to be discovered intact in the twentieth century. The hoard of treasure found here now resides in the Cairo Museum. I well remember the Tutankhamun exhibition that was shown in London some years before. Now at the king's tomb we prepared to enter. A short passageway leads to the antechamber from where the visitor can look directly into the king's burial chamber. Everything except the sarcophagus that enclosed the mummy has gone to the museum in Cairo. Apart from this only the exquisite murals are still there.

The discovery of the tomb by archaeologist Howard Carter was one of the biggest news stories of the 1920s. After years of exploration in the area Carter discovered objects bearing the seal or cartouche of the boy king, and rightly concluded that the Tomb of Tutankhamun lay somewhere close by. The fifth Earl of Caernarfon was with Carter when the exciting entry was made into the tomb. Others were keenly interested and the Metropolitan Museum of New York offered facilities for organising and preserving the newly discovered treasures. As for the discoverers, Howard Carter and Lord Caernarfon, they died soon afterwards. According to some scholars this was the wrath of the boy king reaching across the centuries to avenge the desecration of his resting place, which he had expressly ordered to be left alone. Tutankhamun had pronounced judgement on anyone who interfered with the tomb.

We then visited the tomb of Seti I. The reliefs and murals are in a fine state of preservation. The King's sarcophagus, made from alabaster, now resides in the British Museum. Here also the night sky is represented, again complete with constellations. This is considered to be the best of the sky representations to be found in these tombs.

After these explorations we stood looking out over the desolate rocks of the Valley of the Kings. Like many visitors we sensed a strange solemnity about the scene which must have echoed to the sound of many royal funeral processions long ago. As I looked across the eerie landscape the shadows were deepening, and I set off on my own to do the return bicycle ride to Luxor, leaving the others to join some Arabs for a drink of tea.

My efforts to reach the Tombs of the Queens the next day were hampered when the tyre of my hired bike exploded. Local Nubian boys produced a pump from nowhere and tried to rectify matters but to no avail. The day after I set out determined to reach the Tombs of the Queens. This time I succeeded in getting there, overtaking a visitor who was riding on a donkey. The ancients used to call this area 'The place of beauty', no doubt referring to the loveliness that these women had in life. Here again we found ourselves seeing only a representative few of the many tombs of Queens, Princesses and Princes that are situated here.

I often wondered how the ancient Egyptians used to illuminate those tomb interiors when painting murals. If they had used lighted torches, surely carbon deposits would have adhered to the ceilings and the artists would surely have felt uncomfortable working in all that smoke. A Nubian guide who was present showed us how in all probability it was done. He held up a mirror and faced the entrance of a tomb which consisted of a series of long sloping passageways.

Alignment of the mirror was important, and our guide was able to catch the sun's reflection and send a long powerful beam down all the passageways of this tomb until it reached the burial chamber at the end of the structure. In addition this beam could be projected onto almost any part of the walls by a second guide with a mirror. This method would have been more practical by far.

Leonard Cottrell, in his book *Egypt*, considers the Tomb of Queen Nefertari the most interesting of all in the Valley of the Queens. I am inclined to agree. An interesting feature of this tomb is the tiny foetus of the Queen, still there after thousands of years, albeit in a very parchment-like condition, enclosed in a glass case beside the sarcophagus. In her lifetime Queen Nefertari must have been one of the loveliest of women, for she is so portrayed in the murals that adorn the walls of the tomb and its passageways. She is revealed as elegant and lithe, a woman of great sophistication. Little wonder, then, that the giant among pharaohs, Ramses II, took her for his wife. Amongst other tombs of queens worthy of interest is that of Queen Titi. This along with the tomb of Nefertari comprises the best of the tombs in this valley. Not all of the queens were buried here, but most of them were. A number of queens were paradoxically buried in the Valley of the Kings.

The Tombs of the Nobles were a little more difficult to find, so one hotelier told me. It would be necessary for me to stop at a little group of huts and seek out a guide, as the tombs were in scattered locations between houses. As things turned out plenty of guides were available, as robed children fought over me. There were three young Italians who were my companions in exploration now.

I was impressed with the finesse and delicacy of the paintings of the Nobles' tombs and they show scenes from the lives of these people, presumably to allow these dignitaries to reflect on their lives as they journeyed on to the next world. Undoubtedly the best and most interesting of the three Nobles' Tombs was that of Nakht. I had purchased a reproduction of a well-known painting from this tomb – the one that shows three barely dressed girls in diaphanous dresses playing their musical instruments. The first girl plays her flute, the middle one plays a guitar-like stringed instrument, whilst the third plucks at a harp which is as big as she is. The girl in the middle looks as if she is dancing while she plays her instrument, and it is rather splendid the way the artist has turned her head backwards, looking towards the first girl. I was surprised to find that the originals were only small – a matter of inches in height. The mural of which these figures form a part reveals scenes of feasting. The eighteenth Dynasty was certainly a time of great affluence and luxury if these murals are anything to go by – and we have no reason to think otherwise.

As we progressed through the tombs we found other less luxurious scenes of people at work harvesting the corn and other labours. After this we headed back to Luxor. I felt that this landscape was among the most sterile and barren-looking in the world. On the tarmac road close to the Colossi of Memnon, I saw a distraught child being carried by a water buffalo, whilst another child chased after it. A camel loaded with huge pieces of wood was led past, and a felaheen farmer trotted by on his donkey, which was loaded with sugar cane. After crossing the Nile by ferry I dined with the Italians. Then I considered the last stage of my Egyptian journey.

CHAPTER EIGHTEEN

JOURNEY'S END

I left behind the Theban necropolis with its ghostly memories of mumbling chanting priests of old and splendid pharaohs in all their finery. Then there was that great Mortuary Temple of Ramses III close to the south end of the necropolis of Thebes with its almost frightening scale and size. Often the ghaffirs appointed by the Department of Antiquities did not allow me to see everything.

Now the train was carrying me to Aswan, at length shunting into the railway station of that town at Egypt's southern extremity. There was much to see here in Aswan, too! Not least among the features of interest was the Abu Simbel Temple, now raised above the waters of Lake Nasser. This was all further on, though. There were a number of engaging things to see in Aswan itself first.

When I asked for a hotel the driver of the horse-drawn cab pulled up outside one of the most expensive hotels in town. I stayed there for a single night before moving on to a cheaper and, in my view, better hotel. The manager at this second hotel was of a friendly and benevolent disposition, and the service was very good indeed. This smaller, friendlier hotel suited me admirably. I did not even mind the early morning call to prayer from the mosque directly opposite. After all I was a seasoned Middle East traveller now, and well used to this enigmatic call to prayer rising from hundreds of mosques in these countries. Indeed, I consider it a beautiful sound.

By day many visitors ply the waters of the Nile in a hired *felluca*. Here again, for this I had to haggle to obtain a good price. I spent many happy hours gliding along the Nile in a *felluca*, often in the company of other visitors who would share the cost of the boat with me. One day I took a horse and buggy ride for a couple of hours to explore the locality with the driver as my guide. We clip-copped along at a steady pace, although the poor horse looked decidedly tired, under-nourished and overworked. Every so often the driver would give the horse a little crack across the rump with his whip in order to coax a little more speed from the creature.

As we moved away from the main street we had been traversing, the driver pointed to a number of modest constructions to our left. 'These are the Fatamin tombs', he said. 'They are many centuries old.' He pulled in at the little group of tomb constructions, and we alighted. Somewhere in the middle was the tomb of a local holy man, on top of which lay his turban. There was a similar group of artefacts further on and we stopped briefly at this second place.

After that we came to the granite quarries of Aswan. At the time of the pharaohs' obelisks and statues, material for building was quarried here. The excellent durable stone from these quarries could be cut in grey, black and red. The first thing that is pointed out to visitors here is the Unfinished Obelisk. I walked along its length – it was like an enormous ramp. The cutting of this obelisk was never finished because the stone cracked, rendering it useless for any purpose.

Interestingly, it provides modern man with an example showing exactly how it was done. But for finds like this we may never have known. Part of the technique involved splitting the stone by cutting slots into which soaked wooden pegs were jammed. When the wooden pegs began to swell, the force of the swelling wood did much of the splitting. The ancients displayed amazing know-how in so many areas.

We climbed back into the buggy and soon continued round the outskirts of the town. My companion pointed out the tall gleaming white building and minarets of the Nasser Mosque. It was built in thanks to Allah after the completion of the Aswan dam. After an hour or so of riding round the tree-shaded outskirts of the town I was returned to the market area and the horse urinated violently – maybe in protest at having to work on little food and in too much heat.

If many Moslems I saw that day appeared to be of a retiring disposition I was soon to understand why. It was due in all probability to El Abra – the Feast of Abraham, which all good Moslems observe at this time of the year. During this period feasting takes place and hundreds of sheep are sacrificed, reminding us of the Jewish sacrifices of Old Testament times. A few people I spoke to had visited Nubian villages and watched these rituals and ceremonies being conducted. The Nubians themselves are a handsome people with bronzed teak-coloured skins, and they are of a cheerful disposition. There is, perhaps, a denser concentration of them in this part of Egypt than in the northern regions. I met plenty of Nubians whilst I was in Aswan, but only viewed one of their villages from the back of a camel, and that from a distance.

When I expressed a desire to visit Elephantine Island, the friendly hotelier immediately laid on such an outing for me. 'Tomorrow my two sons, Ali and Ramadan, will take you

across on a local ferry', he promised. 'Just leave it to them.'
I smiled, warming to the genuine kindness of this man. If the
name Ramadan seems strange to Western ears, it is because
Westerners do not normally name their children according to
a religious event as Arabs sometimes do.

The next day arrived quickly and the two boys took me to
a little quayside where we caught a felluca to Elephantine
Island. From here we walked down little mud-walled lanes
until we came out into a small bay. Here we caught a tiny
ferry boat to Kitchener's Island, which seemed to be one huge
Garden of Eden.

Kitchener's Island was named after Earl Kitchener of
Khartoum. His associations with Egypt are well known. He
joined the Egyptian army when he was thirty-two, becoming
its Commander-in-Chief in 1892. He was a British agent in
Egypt in 1914, but he is perhaps best known for his connections with Khartoum, where he created the street planning in
the shape of the Union Jack. Everywhere we went on the
island the guide whom we met held up sweet-smelling
grasses and leaves for me to sniff – and they grew in abundance here. The well-wooded area gave welcome shade from
the oppressive sun. Then we ran into a local policeman who
promptly rebuked the boys for bringing me over to
Kitchener's Island without an official guide. When I tried to
explain the situation to the irate policeman he would not
listen, but continued to chide Ramadan and Ali. 'Does this
mean trouble for you, Ali?' I asked, after the policeman had
gone. He nodded. Despite the annoyance of this incident, I
returned to sniffing the sweet-smelling grasses and leaves.
This could have become addictive. I noted the names of some
of the trees – mango, apricot, oil-palm, matchwood, kanel
and carcadia, to name but some of them. I also noticed an
ebony tree.

Then it was time to hail the ferryman again. For part of the time we hired a boat on our own and I took the oars, much to the amusement of Ali and Ramadan. They laughed and pointed me in the right direction when I appeared to have taken the wrong course.

We landed on Elephantine Island again. After all the heady experiences across Egypt that I had thus far enjoyed, I spent a little time at the temple ruins, near which is a Nilometer. Old Greek measurements may be seen on a well close by. We re-crossed Elephantine Island, threading our way through those narrow mud-walled lanes. Ramadan signalled for me to follow him into a tiny dwelling there where his sister lived. We were welcomed by a young woman whom I took to be the sister of the two boys. She motioned us to be seated whilst she served tea. The boys produced a pack of cards and the three of us sat playing a game for half-an-hour or so before leaving Yebu this one-time frontier town of Egypt, and sailing back to Aswan town itself.

One of the really dominant landmarks in Aswan is the pile of the Oberoi Hotel on Elephantine Island, Aswan It is easily the plushest, most luxurious hotel in the area. It is very pleasant to sit at the outdoor café, as I did during my stay, if only for a cup of coffee. The hotel has its own ferryboat, a replica of the craft that plied these waters in the times of the pharaohs. Ramadan and Ali had to go straight back to work after the excursion. I rested after the exertions. One of the boys had even worn his black tuxedo and bow tie in readiness for returning to work in his father's restaurant.

The seventh-century St Simeon's Monastery is situated on the left bank of the Nile. It is a fine example of Coptic monastic architecture. In the course of time it proved to be too remote and isolated, with fresh water supplies being difficult to obtain, amongst other things. The monks were obliged to abandon the monastery in the thirteenth century. One day I hired a camel to ride there. It was unnecessary really, as it is within walking distance. A local boy led the camel, which was made to crouch after we had reached the monastery ruins. A guide showed us where the cooking was done, where the dormitories were situated, and where other activities were carried out. Other visitors were present as indicated, but I soon left them to it and remounted the camel. The boy led me off over a stretch of desert.

It was then that I saw the Nubian village. I was thankful that I was now riding over sand. Earlier, when going to the monastery ruins, my camel had walked over patches of stony sloping ground, jarring me all over. The boy suddenly jumped up in the saddle with me, and stayed there until we stopped and dismounted by the Old Kingdom tombs cut into the rock and overlooking the Nile. I was shown round some of these tombs of nobles and dignitaries and heard a dreadful squawking sound. When I asked my guide what it was, he told me it was bats. I remembered that a species of bat lived in Egyptian tombs. It made some people with vivid imaginations think of the bats as spirits of long-dead kings and courtiers that come out to dance after sunset, and I always thought that it was bird-life that inspired the paintings of winged souls. A Canadian woman whom I had met at the travel agents recoiled when a guide suggested that she should look at an ancient Egyptian body that lay in the back of one tomb. I was not too keen on the idea myself.

Back in town I booked a flight to Abu Simbel, and the following morning I arrived on time outside Egypt Air offices. At the airport there was some waiting. All technical hitches over I took off for Abu Simbel, along with other visitors. This half-hour domestic flight soon brought the famous ancient monument. UNESCO action had saved it from being irrevocably drowned in the waters of Lake Nasser. I remember the sun glinting on the vast man-made lake as the plane wheeled round for a landing, and of course I could see the Temple from the air just before we landed. A small coach took us to the site. Here we had to pay for the privilege of seeing the Temple itself. The Temple with those three Colossi of Ramses II that are still intact, plus a statue that was badly damaged, were now before my gaze. The only thing missing was the strong sunlight that would have shown the huge colossi to best effect. The delays at Aswan and the airport may have been to blame for this.

The amazing reconstruction and raising of these priceless statues was one of the greatest engineering feats of modern times. The construction of a huge semi-circular bowl to keep out the waters of Lake Nasser was considered at one stage. It might have worked except for one important consideration! The rising sun would never again have greeted the huge seated figures, or cast their rays deep inside the Temple. Coupled to this there was always the chance of water seepage destroying the Temple after the monumental effort to construct the bowl. Wisely, we must assume, this scheme was rejected in favour of cutting the huge images of Ramses II into sections, and raising the Temple high above to the new levels above that of the water.

President Nasser at that time saw the building of the new High Dam as being symbolic of his country's determination to forge ahead in terms of modernisation. The ever-exploding population of Egypt demanded such considerations anyway. Technological developments along with agricultural advancements were thus seen to be of paramount importance. In this climate of thought, the raising of the Temple went ahead. It was a very costly business, and funds poured in from all over the world to finance the massive operation. What a fever of activity it must have been as armies of workers scurried over the area, dismantling the statues and moving them from positions they had occupied for millennia, using modern technology. Those cranes must have seemed incongruous in view of the Temple's age.

I looked up at the giant figures, and also at the row of baboons above them on the Temple's facade. Today the Temple's axis is placed so that the King's images face east, so facing the sun as it rises, the same axis as it had in days of old. Flanking either side of the entrance, we find slabs which show captive Asians on one side and Negroes on the other. Inside the visitor may gaze still at the superb relief carvings which show the King fighting his Hittite foes. There are prancing horses pulling chariots and many other strong powerful images. These may be found in the pillared halls and the smaller side rooms. After the visit to this main Temple, I went through to the nearby Hathor Temple. This, like the first Temple, was built by Ramses II. All of a sudden the sun shone brightly. The Hathor Temple's fine features were enhanced brilliantly. By the time we reached the main Abu Simbel Temple again the sun had gone in.

I was accompanied for most of the way round these monuments by a middle-aged couple from London. The husband was an engineer working in Egypt. His wife had flown out to join him. As we stood and marvelled at the great monument I could not help but be intrigued by the tiny figures of Ramses' womenfolk, which stood between the shins of the massive figures of Ramses II. They represented mother, wife and daughters. This is seen at other Egyptian temples, as, for example, in the Temple of Karnak where the queen stands between the shins of a standing monarch. The gods, of course, enter the picture, as the main Temple was raised in honour of the sun-god Ra, whilst in the Hall of Pillars all

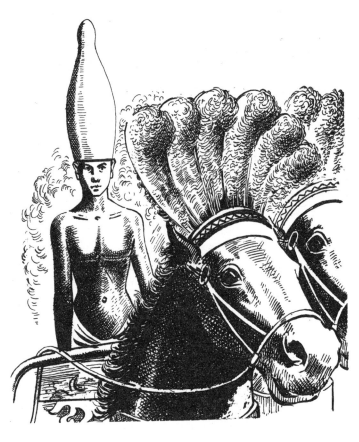

*King Senvorat I riding his chariot wearing
the white crown of Upper Egypt*

eight pillars represent Ramses as Osiris. As we have seen the smaller temple, built for Nefertari, was dedicated to Hathor. I took one last lingering look at the noble colossi with their double crowns and ceremonial beards before boarding the plane again for the flight back to Aswan.

I thought about the vastness of this scheme, involving the raising of the Temple and the creation of Lake Nasser and its dam. The High Dam is colossal. Its vast curve is 3,600 metres long and 40 metres wide. One hundred and forty metres down there is a rock and silt curtain which is made up of rocks estimated at being seventeen times the amount used for the Giza Pyramids. The dam has six turbines, each 280 metres in length, for passing water; 175 kilowats are obtained from each turbine.

From earliest times the controlling of the Nile waters was always recognised as being important. Flooding was always a possibility. On the positive side harnessing the water for irrigation was vital for growing that corn. Even back in 3600 BC gauges were used to determine water levels of the Nile, and such marks on the rocks were found at Aswan, Edfu, Semna, Philae and Esna. We have already seen that such a Nilometer exists on Elephantine Island and one was found at Roda Island, Cairo. In olden times human sacrifice was made to Hapi, god of the Nile, to appease his wrath and ensure continuation of the life-giving waters. A virgin girl was sacrificed from the sacred barge. The barbarity of this custom appears not to have been appreciated until more enlightened times during the Old Kingdom period.

Today the possibilities of increases in acreage are vast indeed. Such a cultivation area is increased by one third. In Aswan itself a New Cataract Hotel has gone up – the Nile cataracts are very close to the dams and have a close association with them. The Blue Nile, flowing down from the heights of Ethiopia, and the White Nile, flowing from Lake Victoria, still join at Khartoum and send their waters down into Egypt. I suspect, however, that the sight of the waters flowing from their sources is nowadays not nearly as majestic as it once was. A huge monument commemorating friendship between the Soviet Union and Egypt stands close to the new High Dam. Sadat, the then President of Egypt, ordered all Russians out of Egypt, but the monument to Russian–Egyptian friendship still stands.

Between the old dam and the new, half standing out of the water, we may glimpse the Temple of Philae, which stands close to the island of that name. The island has on it a number of temples of importance. The island's largest temple was dedicated to Isis. The High Dam caused other upheavals in addition to those already mentioned. The shifting of the Temple of Kalabsha was a case in point. It had to be moved from its former site and re-erected close to the High Dam. Also standing close to the High Dam is the Temple of Beit el-Wali, carved from the rock and dating from the time of Ramses II. Closer to our own times it was used by the Coptic Church as a place of Christian worship. So some monuments were saved – but how many, we wonder, were forever drowned in the flooding that created Lake Nasser.

A few days later I bade farewell to the hotelier and his boys. I headed for the railway station, passing through the souk area where I had spent a few happy evenings. One evening I had been entertained by a family of Coptic Christians, who had presented me with a photograph of their priest. Now, however, I boarded the train and sorted out my sleeping compartment. This turned out to be something of a misnomer. The two Arabs in the bunk below mine kept up a stream of incessant chattering all night long as the train sped towards Cairo. So difficult did it become to concentrate on sleep that at one stage I clambered down from my bunk. Then I had a spell in the corridor. This had its enjoyable moments, certainly. We sped past Arab villages which had little hanging lamps, then the odd camp fire stabbed out of the darkness. Arabs rise very early before sunrise in order to warm themselves. Nights here can be cold.

At about ten o'clock in the morning the train reached Cairo. I was very tired and stumbled out into Ramses Square, and made for the nearest hotel. This happened to be within throwing distance of the Ramses statue. I booked in and was soon installed in a comfortable room where I could rest undisturbed. Once I had rested I set out for the Cairo Museum, which lay close to the Nile Hilton. One visitor I fell into conversation with assured me that the London collection in the British Museum did not come anywhere near the Cairo Museum's own collection. When I went to see the Cairo Museum for myself I soon realised the truth of this. I made two visits to the museum. My first visit was more in the nature of a general exploration, whereas the second dealt almost exclusively with the treasures of Tutankhamun.

To highlight some of the antiquities that caught my eye on the first visit. There were large numbers of statues, like the statue of a noble that I saw made from hard wood. The inlaid eyes of the statue were opaque and yet had a transparent quality. Set in a copper border and once painted, the statue belonged to the Fifth Dynasty. Many of the statues were life-size, like the one of Mari the scribe holding a papyrus scroll with both hands. The figure is somewhat mutilated now, alas! It was discovered in 1926 by Frith while he was digging in a corner of the Step Pyramid of Zoser, which also belonged to the Fifth Dynasty. Less than life-size there was a statuette of King Senusert I wearing the white crown of Upper Egypt. A smaller statuette showing a king wearing the red crown of Lower Egypt now resides in New York's main museum. The statuettes belong to the Twelfth Dynasty. Both these pieces are finely painted. I then came to four grey granite sphynxes with kings' heads. They bear (on different parts of each sculpture) the names of the kings they portray. First is Ramses II (on the round base), then Merneptah (on the shoulder) and Psusernnes (on the chest). The fourth statue had its name long since obliterated. A broken but still impressive statuette of a scribe made in limestone (painted) came next. It came from Saqqara and belonged to the Sixth Dynasty.

Some of the exhibits I sketched, and I found that a young American boy was doing the same. His mother was an Egyptologist and soon we were introduced. I shook hands with all the family: father, mother and young boy. They were about to travel up the Nile to the places that I had just come from. The young lady Egyptologist, Lynne Negus, was as excited as I had been to see Aswan and Abu Simbel. I sketched the statue of another king with his tall hat and solemn expression, ceremonial beard and hands clasped across his chest. Then I drew the limestone statue of Ty found at Saqqara. Presently my tiredness got the better of me and I decided to retire to my hotel where I flaked out until the following day.

I returned to the Cairo Museum for my second visit and I met up with the Neguses again. They were still spending a great deal of time at the museum studying its fascinating artefacts.

I had already seen many of the superb Tutankhamun treasures in the London exhibition, but such treasures could be viewed many times, such is their beauty. The treasures fill many galleries. Since they all came from a small tomb of a relatively minor king, it is argued that the treasures of the

Egyptian Archers

Egyptian Soldiers Marching

Brick Making

High Priests,
Clothed in
Leopard Skin

Different Costumes of the
Egyptian Priesthood

A Priestess

Snaring Birds – Prov. I. 17.

*Facsimile drawings based on Egyptian wall paintings
showing scenes from everyday life in Ancient Egypt*

major pharaohs' tombs must have been extensive indeed. These treasures of Tutankhamun were fantastic by any standards, though. The boy king's solid gold coffin was heavy enough to require four strong men to lift it. Altogether there are three coffins involved. One of these I saw still lying in the tomb at Thebes. The king's throne is also of gold, inlaid with lapis lazuli. Inside enormous glass cases are the gilded shrines, four in number, which once encased the inner gold coffins. I remember seeing on at least one gold canopy beautiful little figures facing inwards with hands spread open. The figures wear tight-fitting garments for the most part, and have heavily (mascara) painted eyes.

How can any visitor ever forget the delightful gold statue of the boy king harpooning fish? Or the other gold statuette of him standing on an animal's back? Everywhere you look in this section of the museum there is gold! I saw a life-size statue of Tutankhamun in dark wood, and gilded with gold. Chariots that once carried the king stood motionless inside thick glass cases. You can see that they were once used because the wheel rims show signs of wear and tear. I thought that the young king's throne was intricate with its finely decorated back on which was a portrayal of the king and his young wife. Even more intricacy is seen in a magnificent wooden chest which is also included in these treasures. The decoration involves battle scenes with the king in his chariot.

I returned to the statuette of the king spearing the fish, and reflected on how perfectly the artist had caught that part of the action as the king has raised his harpoon just before making the thrust. The now famous funerary mask of Tutankhamun was there with its lovely design and lines of inlaid lapis lazuli. The royal serpent is on the front of his striped headgear. The eyes, though stylised, seem to stare at the visitor. The mask also has a thin ceremonial beard on the chin. These coffins are shaped to fit the king's body and are decorated with the king's face, headgear and folded arms. The solid gold coffin is in the form of the god Osiris. The winged motifs with which the coffin is decorated will undoubtedly refer to the king's soul passing into the under-world. The folded hands are holding ceremonial crooks and whips. There are some lovely alabaster heads of the king, and jars for the king's viscera. Beds of gold were made in the form of animals.

I could truly have spent longer than I did viewing these magnificent relics of Tutankhamun but decided at length to go off into one or two of the side rooms to see some of the other treasures on display. To mention a few objects at random that caught my interest. There was the gold head of a mummified hawk. In order to create the eyes of this hawk mask the artist had put an obsidian rod through the mask head and polished both ends smooth. The body used to be covered with sheet copper and the central core was made of wood. The head is topped by a peculiar crown or crest. It belongs to the Sixth Dynasty.

Not far away I saw a gold cup, lotus-shaped, with swept-back wings and head, neck and front legs of a griffon. Numerous other objects like bracelets, beads, jewels, vulture amulets, gold vases and jugs of silver kept company with soul-birds and queens' jewels and daggers. And Twelfth Dynasty gold lions kept company with a Twelfth Dynasty gold falcon and a gold chain supporting an attractive scarab – the image of the dung beetle. I imagine that the objects described as being overlaid with gold in the Bible must have looked very similar to many that were here.

The models in the round depicting everyday life in ancient Egypt were very intriguing. One such showed soldiers of

Mesehti, a Prince of Asyut, complete with spears and decorative shields. It was interesting to compare these figure sets with the flat two-dimensional imagery so familiar to the traveller in Egypt.

The parchment-like mummy of the once-proud Pharaoh Ramses II may be viewed here too. Was this face indeed the one that stared so defiantly into the face of Moses? Hawklike features of the Pharaoh are revealed and a few tufts of hair on the head. There are other unwrapped mummies to be viewed, like the mummy of King Merenptah which lies with the arms folded across the chest as in the images on the sarcophagi. In reality the list of royal mummies housed within the museum is lengthy. It is as though some god had ordered them all to be gathered thus under one roof. There are at least twenty-seven royal mummies within the museum from various dynasties.

A second model in the round of ancient Egyptians reviewing cattle: the Old Testament story of Joseph and his interpretation of Pharaoh's dream concerning the seven fat cows and the seven thin cows. Before leaving this vast collection of valuable things behind, I stopped to look over the museum's bookshop, which has a fine array of books, cards and models on sale to the public.

In the museum grounds I sat close to a sphynx, and the wail of a police vehicle filled the air. An expensive-looking car drew up to the museum entrance, followed by police on motorbikes. I wondered who the important visitor could be. I thought at first it was the president, but other bystanders said not.

I wandered through the streets of Cairo and found myself back at the Windsor Hotel, where I had stayed first after my arrival in Egypt nearly a month before. In a little side street a man was busy entertaining passers-by with a snake. He was working hard at it but few seemed to stop for him. Directly opposite the Windsor Hotel, sitting outside a coffee shop, I saw Abdul, a young Nubian whom I knew from my stay at the Windsor. I greeted him. He was smoking a hubble-bubble pipe, but it was not the usual tobacco block he was using, but a different substance altogether. When I asked him what it was exactly, he said it was definitely not hashish that he was smoking, simply a mixture of sugar, tobacco and oil produced in India and exported to Saudi Arabia, where apparently it was much in demand. I left Abdul later and returned to my hotel, and afterwards spent some time wandering through the old-style street that lie adjacent to Ramses Square. Here there were numerous little shops and coffee houses.

For my evening meal I was back at the hotel, where the restaurant overlooked the city from a high vantage point. I enjoyed being waited upon, and relaxing after all my activity. The sun sank in the west, bringing to a close this last day in Egypt, at least for the time being. On a nearby roof-top children were walking about and they even had hens up there with them. Below the hustle and bustle of traffic was evident as it weaved its way round the statue of Ramses II. In the far distance I could make out the slender minarets of the Mohammed Ali Mosque, one of the first places that I visited here. There is plenty to see and do in this vast city of a thousand minarets and here, as in other places visited in my book, it was impossible to do justice to it. You have only to look at a map of Cairo to gain an impression of its vastness.

I talked to a group who told me that they were off to Alexandria to stay in a flat there which some benefactor had loaned them. Alas, I missed out the Nile Delta area in my trip, and missed out on Alexandria. The rich fertile delta

became more and more fertile as silt from Ethiopia continued to be deposited here. This was always regarded as Lower
Egypt, and the Nile itself has determined these two distinct
parts of the country. Beyond these fertile regions there is
nothing, by and large, but desert and empty wasteland. I
would like to have seen Port Said, where the Suez Canal
starts, and Alexandria of course. Both these coastal towns
stand at either side of the delta, where it empties out into the
sea. The Pharos, one of the Seven Wonders of the ancient
World, used to stand at Alexandria. It was a Roman lighthouse and we can only conjecture at its appearance long ago.

Egypt teems with history. Even closer to our own time
there are famous names and battles associated with Egypt.
Napoleon Bonaparte came here in 1798, complete with his
army. The French, as well as the British, had tried to obtain
a hold on the country. Napoleon was cut off after his defeat
by Lord Nelson at the Battle of the Nile, returning to Egypt
in 1799. Both Britain and France saw Egypt as being strategically important. Napoleon tried to wreck British trading in
the Middle East and India, and he saw control of Egypt as
being pivotal in the realisation of this. The influence of both
nations has lasted in one form or another ever since.

In 1881 something of a revolution exploded in Cairo.
Egyptians were rebelling against outsiders having any kind of
say in their affairs. They were fighting for emancipation from
Europe. The British influence in particular continued, as we
have seen. Sir Evelyn Baring was appointed Consul General
and British Diplomatic Agent in Egypt. He was prominent in
the formation of modern Egypt but the Egyptian supremacy
throughout the Nile was threatened. The Mahdi rose to
power in the Sudan and the British were involved in the fighting that ensued in the 1880s. General Gordon was sent to
Khartoum to deal with the situation. When the relief column

arrived at Khartoum on January 28th, 1885, they found that they were too late to save Gordon.

The British turned their attention to reinforcing Egyptian administration rather than attempting to win back territories from the Mahdists. The Russian and French powers tried to end the British occupation but could not. Kitchener fought in the Sudan, commencing operations in 1896 with an Anglo-Egyptian force. Omdurman was taken and the Khalifa Abdullahi was defeated. The Sudan was then placed under a British Governor.

The anti-British feelings were to grow in line with the upsurge of Egyptian nationalism. After the opening of the first Nile dam, French and British forces were to realise that this surge of Egyptian nationalism was here to stay. The British agreed to leave things as they were without undue interference. In the First World War Alexandria became an important naval base for Britain. Egypt for her part declared war on Germany (today it is rather different, as German technicians are very important to the Egyptian economy).

On December 18th, 1914, Egypt was proclaimed a British Protectorate. In February 1915 attacks on the Suez Canal were launched by the Turks, who had declared war on the Allied forces. Thus began one of the biggest headaches that Egypt has ever had to deal with. In the late 1900s Egyptian nationalists again started an uprising. Their leader was a young lawyer with a peasant background named Sa'd Zaghlul Pasha. He prevailed upon the Commissioner to allow a delegation to be sent to London in order to be able to negotiate independence. Zaghlul Pasha must have exerted a great influence over his followers, as riots exploded in the streets when he was deported to Malta. He was later returned to Egypt on the advice of General Allenby, who also brought about an end to the British Protectorate, but the

British involvement continued, not least in the Suez crisis of the 1950s. When I discussed these matters with an Egyptian in the hotel foyer, he told me that English was still the main language spoken here after Arabic.

Today the emphasis is upon industrial activities, such as chemical, metallurgical and mining pursuits. Egyptian agriculture – foodstuffs, spinning and weaving – are on a mass-production basis. The Middle East continues to be a potential powder keg. The emergence of strong militant nationalistic forces round the world during the 1960s and 1970s has intensified its instability, often reflecting the rapaciousness of ancient warlike races. Nationalistic feeling has always been there but it has flared to the surface in recent times.

During my reverie my mind went back over so many unforgettable times across the Middle East and North Africa. I thought of all the interesting people I had met and wondered how they were faring now. Departure time arrived all too soon. With the help of one of the hotel staff I managed to flag down a taxi, not always easy in the massive build-up of traffic in early morning Cairo. The taxi put me down at the airport half-an-hour later. In the passenger lounge I amused myself by sketching other travellers waiting for their respective flights. After an interminable wait my flight was called and I boarded the aircraft.

Well, my saga is at an end. I can only hope that the places that I visited and enjoyed will likewise interest those who read my narrative. Like a migratory swallow returning to sunny climes, I was to return many times to many of these countries in the years that followed.

The aircraft remained on the runway for some time. This further delay was caused by a truck being parked in front of the aircraft. Nobody seemed to know who the owner was. It was a further hour or so before the driver of the truck was found and made to remove it. The plane then took off. As we rose in the sky, I looked out through the window beside me and watched as the desert sands slipped away beneath me.

INDEX

346